IMAGES
of America

MOVIE HOUSES OF GREATER NEWARK

On the Cover: In 1956, Loew's State, at 681 Broad Street in downtown Newark, was showing the feature *Sharkfighters*, starring Victor Mature. (Courtesy of the New Jersey Historical Society.)

IMAGES
of America

MOVIE HOUSES OF GREATER NEWARK

Philip M. Read

ARCADIA
PUBLISHING

ISBN 978-0-7385-9933-5

Published by Arcadia Publishing
Charleston, South Carolina

Printed in the United States of America

Library of Congress Control Number: 2012955525

For all general information, please contact Arcadia Publishing:
Telephone 843-853-2070
Fax 843-853-0044
E-mail sales@arcadiapublishing.com
For customer service and orders:
Toll-Free 1-888-313-2665

Visit us on the Internet at www.arcadiapublishing.com

Contents

Foreword		6
Acknowledgments		7
Introduction		9
1.	Newark	11
2.	Suburban Essex	49
3.	Paterson	57
4.	Passaic	75
5.	Suburban Passaic	83
6.	Hudson	93
7.	Bergen	101
8.	Union	105
9.	Elsewhere	111
10.	After the Matinee	121

Foreword

It was the smell of hot-buttered popcorn, the inviting taste of creamy, cold bonbons, the comfort of air-conditioning on a sweltering summer day, the friends or date you came with, and—last but not least—the movie you came to see, along with trailers, newsreels, and cartoons. It was entertainment heaven, affordable and so close to home.

The great movie houses of Newark and environs were a testament to a simpler time, when the vocal narrative was heard on the parlor radio at home, and the visual treat was seen on the "silver screen" downtown. The younger you were, the more impressive and awe-inspiring the grand cavern seemed. You were truly transported back to the Old West, the rolling sea, a battlefield, a dark and dreary street with danger around every corner, or you imagined that Humphrey Bogart's famous line "Here's looking at you, kid" was spoken to you alone.

Many times, the attraction was the live stage show, the big-band or rock concert, that brought you through the door. You were greeted by the classic Art Deco architecture, the lobby, replete with snacks and glimpses of movies to come, and the theater itself, where you would sit down and enjoy the images flickering on the huge screen.

The movie house came with the all-important newsreel, which, though highly edited and sanitized, kept the masses abreast of what was happening in the world, from war to Hollywood and all points in between. From silent to too loud, from poignant to horrific to action-packed scenes, movies targeted all ages, genders, tastes, and almost every desire, real or imagined.

In the truest sense, they were the all-important babysitter, one who enabled our collective imaginations to wander and dream about "What if?"

Then, there was the spillover effect, with small eateries, automats, coffee shops, and the ever-present newspaper stand benefiting from movie-going crowds. It was this symbiotic relationship that will forever keep the images, smells, and feeling of our local movie houses in our hearts and minds.

With thanks to Disney, Wallace, Ford, Coppola, DeMille, Spielberg, and all their brethren.

—Mark S. Auerbach
historian and former theater manager

Acknowledgments

There are certain people whose contributions made this pictorial work possible. As such, words of thanks go to George Hawley, supervising librarian, and librarians James Lewis and Tom Ankner of the Charles F. Cummings New Jersey Information Center at the Newark Public Library; Steve Tettamanti and Doug Oxenhorn of the New Jersey Historical Society; Jack De Stefano, director of the Paterson Museum, and Joe Costa, the museum's photo archivist, for their invaluable assistance; Mark Auerbach, Passaic historian, for his always appreciated assistance; Ron Merk, Newark native and filmmaker; Matt Lambros, a New York–based architectural photographer; Debbie Bock, head of reference at the Johnson Public Library in Hackensack; William T. Fischer, M.S. of the Montclair Public Library; Kelly Blithe of the State Theatre; Tom Wulff of the Elizabeth Public Library; and Allen F. Hauss, an educator who penned *South Jersey Movie Houses* and a projectionist who once juggled the 13 reels needed to show 1939's *Gone with the Wind* on the silver screen.

INTRODUCTION

They defined the America of its day. The silver screens were magnets for a population always on the lookout for an escape or diversion from the workaday world. Nowhere was that more evident than in New Jersey's largest city, Newark, as well as such nearby urban centers as Paterson and the suburbs dotting the northern half of the nation's most densely populated state.

The Branford. The Paramount. The Adams. The Tivoli. Loew's State. They were but a few of the palaces where flickering images of Clark Gable and Vivian Leigh in *Gone with the Wind* pulled in crowds on the chilly morning of January 15, 1940. "Long Line Shivers While Waiting for Movie Classic" read the newspaper headline. In the "seven-week siege" that followed, 270,000 patrons passed through the theater turnstile.

The movie houses, often architectural works of art in their own right, at times switched the entertainment to everything from racy burlesque shows to rock concerts. The Rolling Stones took the stage at the Mosque Theatre, just as singer Bing Crosby did before them. In 1964, more than 1,000 screaming teenagers arrived at the Branford to see The Dave Clark Five, whose 1964 hit "Glad All Over" bested the Beatles's "I Want to Hold Your Hand" on the British pop charts.

The theaters, where thousands came not just for the movie but for the experience, were the stuff of seemingly endless newspaper headlines. "Dailey's venture hits excise snag," read one. It turns out Frank Dailey, whose Cedar Grove roadhouse, the Meadowbrook, was out of reach to many during the gas rationing of World War II, met some resistance when he sought to bring big bands to the Terrace Room at Newark's Mosque Theatre. "I served four million people at the Meadowbrook in 12 years and had only one charge against me," he replied to concerns about minors attracted to the dance bands in 1943.

"Burlesque bid," read another headline. The "appeal for peel" to lift legal prohibitions dating to 1957 against burlesque came in 1966 when a "willowy blonde" who produced shows on Long Island sought to replicate them in Newark. "Is it burlesque?" asked Councilman Philip E. Gordon. "Yes, it is burlesque," came the reply, "the same burlesque that gave birth to great entertainers. Burlesque is one name, but I also think of it as live vaudeville." The councilman's retort: "It's still burlesque."

"Theaters changing," read yet another headline atop a 1953 story about the arrival of 3-D features, namely *Bwana Devil* and *House of Wax*. It was all about keeping up with the latest technology. "In fact, we've got a CinemaScope installation in the works right now," said Edgar Goth, with Newark's Branford Theatre. "We're going to be equipped for all the new processes, wide screen or three-dimensional."

It was no different in other North Jersey locales. In Paterson, a rededication of the c. 1925 Fabian Theatre was front-page news in 1962. The palace sat 2,900 patrons, fewer than the original, but with roomier legroom. The $500,000 renovation led to a proclamation in honor of "Fabian Day." Simon H. Fabian, the honoree at a black-tie banquet, told of his commitment to the city: "We cannot sit wistfully by and hope that a good fairy godmother from one of the governments will pull us out of our troubles."

In their heyday, movie houses seating thousands were the place to be. Today, many are long-since gone, in ruins, or converted into small multi-screen venues or even retail space. But they live on in the memories of so many.

"The Trivoli was a place of dreams for mere mortals," said filmmaker and Newark native Ron Merk, "and one in which we felt as if we were part of the adventure going on up on the screen."

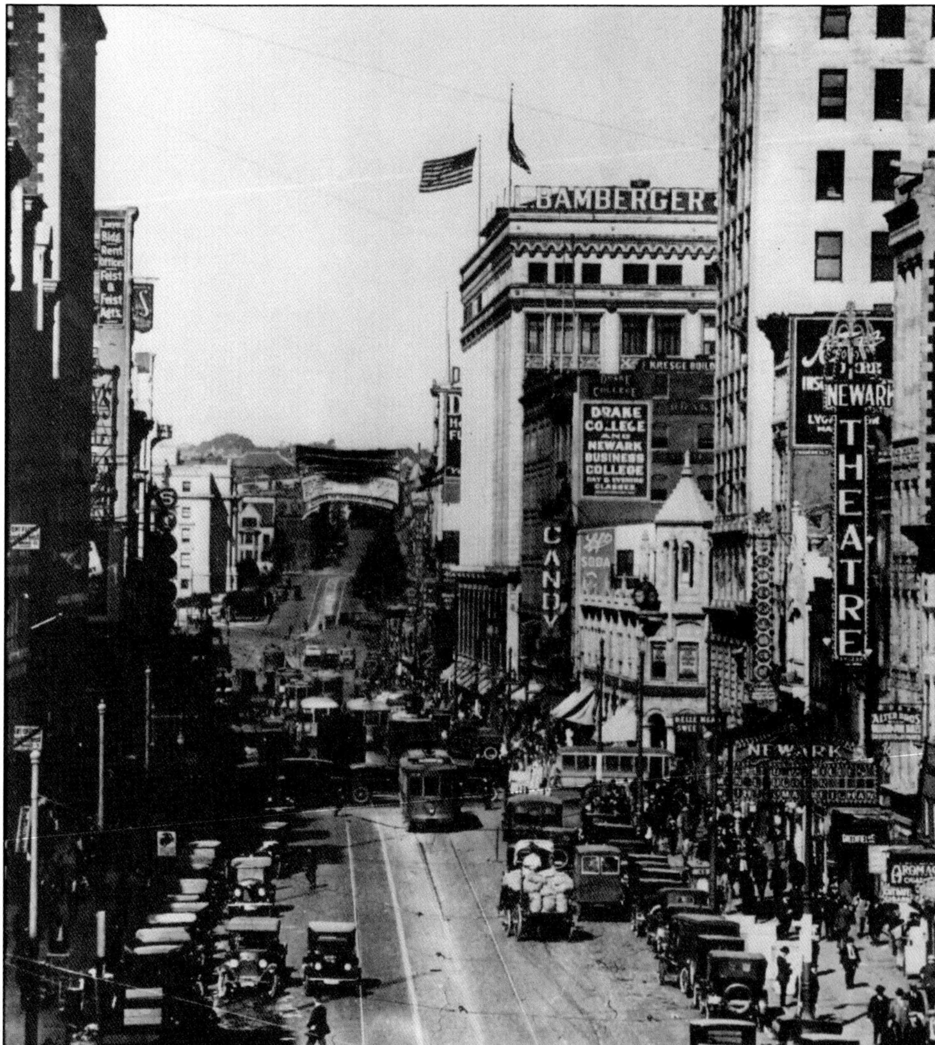

Seen here around 1922, the Newark Theatre, later renamed the Paramount, was centrally located on Market Street, with Bamberger's, the Strand, Drake College, Bell Mead Sweets, Greenfield's, and other merchants making for a busy shopping district. One of the shows then playing at the Newark was Cecil B. DeMille's 1922 silent *Manslaughter*, starring Thomas Meighan, a matinee idol whose career went into a downward spiral after the advent of "talkies." The DeMille film was said to highlight the debauchery of the Jazz Age as a warning to wayward youth, with its story of a reckless, speed-loving socialite, played by Leatrice Joy, who causes the death of a motorcycle cop. (Courtesy of the Newark Public Library.)

One

Newark

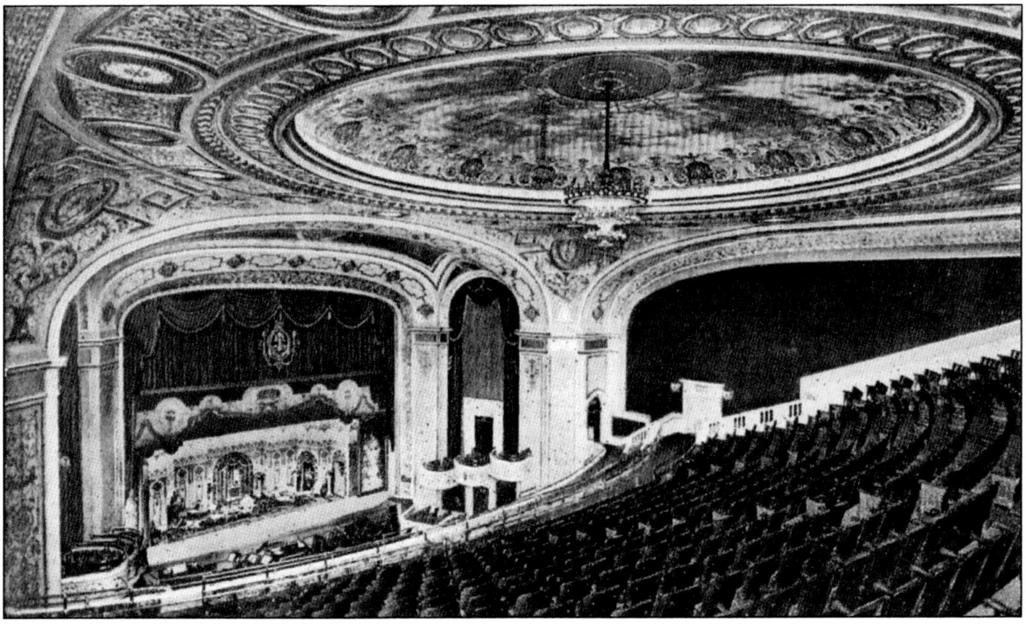

Loew's State Theatre, the handiwork of architect Thomas W. Lamb of New York, was estimated to cost $500,000 to erect—far more than the more typical $80,000—when building plans were approved by Newark's building department on February 11, 1921. (Author's collection.)

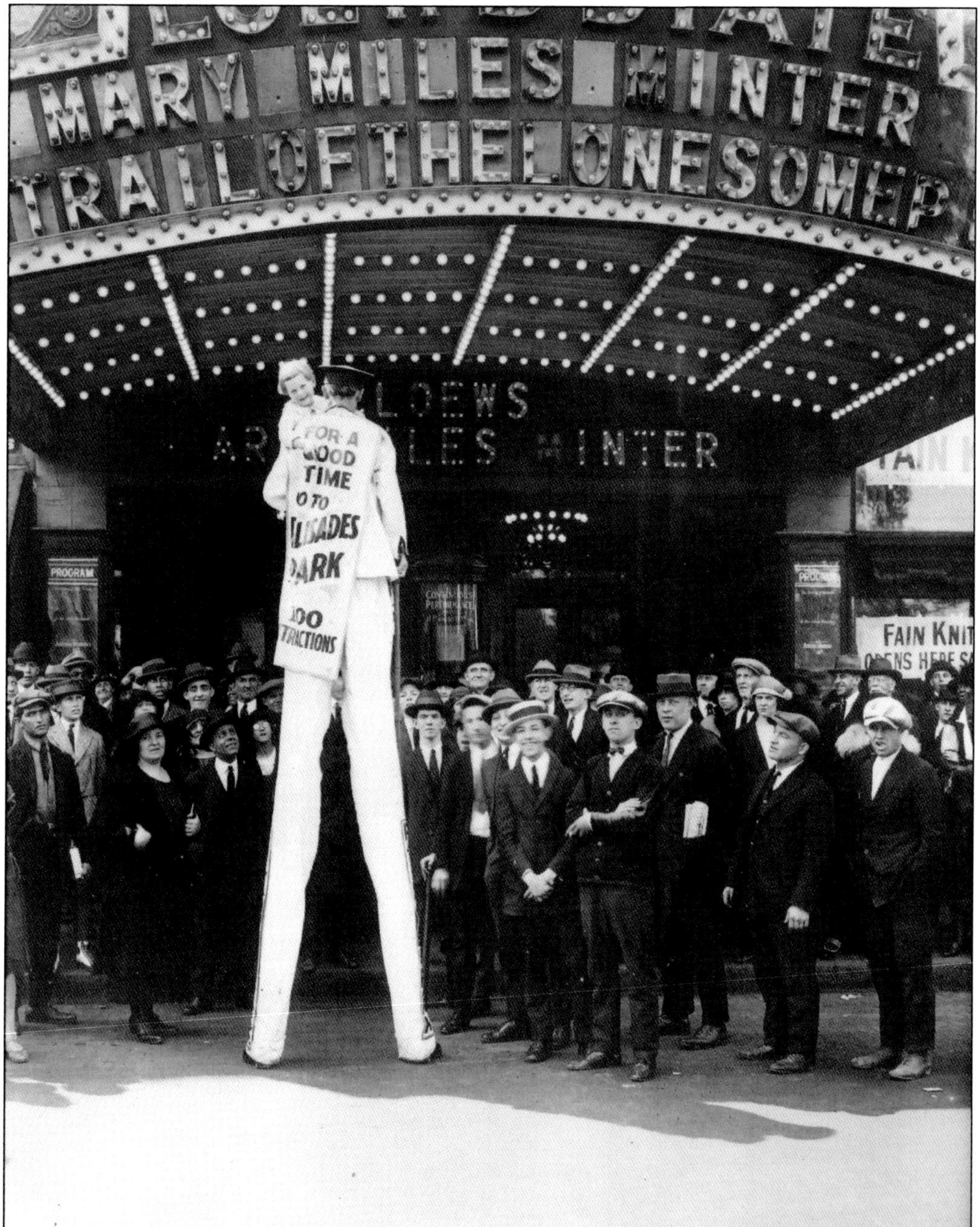

In 1923, Loew's State was showing *The Trail of the Lonesome Pine*, starring Mary Miles Minter in the last of her silent movie roles. From its December 1921 opening until 1927, Loew's was managed by William A. Downs, who had made a name for himself as a songwriter. He was credited with writing the lyrics for "I'm Going Back to Carolina," "Sail on Silv'ry Moon," "Down in Melody Lane," and "The Charlie Chaplin Walk." Some of the recordings can be listened to today on the Library of Congress's free National Jukebox. (Courtesy of the New Jersey Historical Society.)

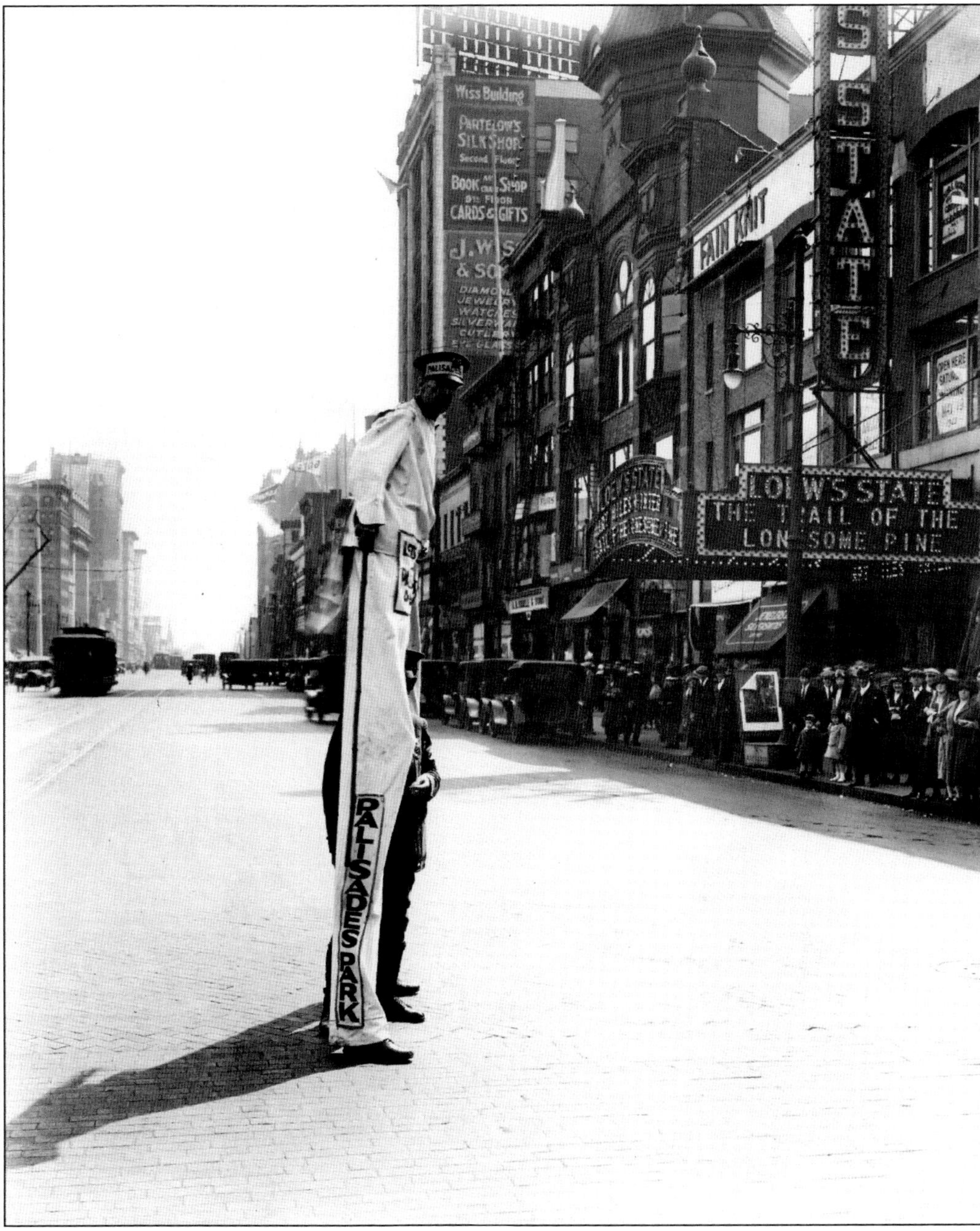

In 1923, a crowd gathered outside Loew's State on Newark's Broad Street as a man on stilts promoted the attractions found elsewhere, namely at Palisades Amusement Park, which by then was already well promoted with a jingle titled "Palisaders," composed by Ernest Luz. It would not be until 1965 when young baby boomers heard "Come on Over" and these memorable lyrics by Steve Clayton: "Palisades from coast to coast, where a dime buys the most / Palisades Amusement Park/ swings all day and after dark / (bumm, baa, dumm, bumm, bummmm) / ride the coaster / get cool / in the waves in the pool / you'll have fun . . . so / come on over / (dumm, de dum, da dum . . . dum)." (Courtesy of the New Jersey Historical Society.)

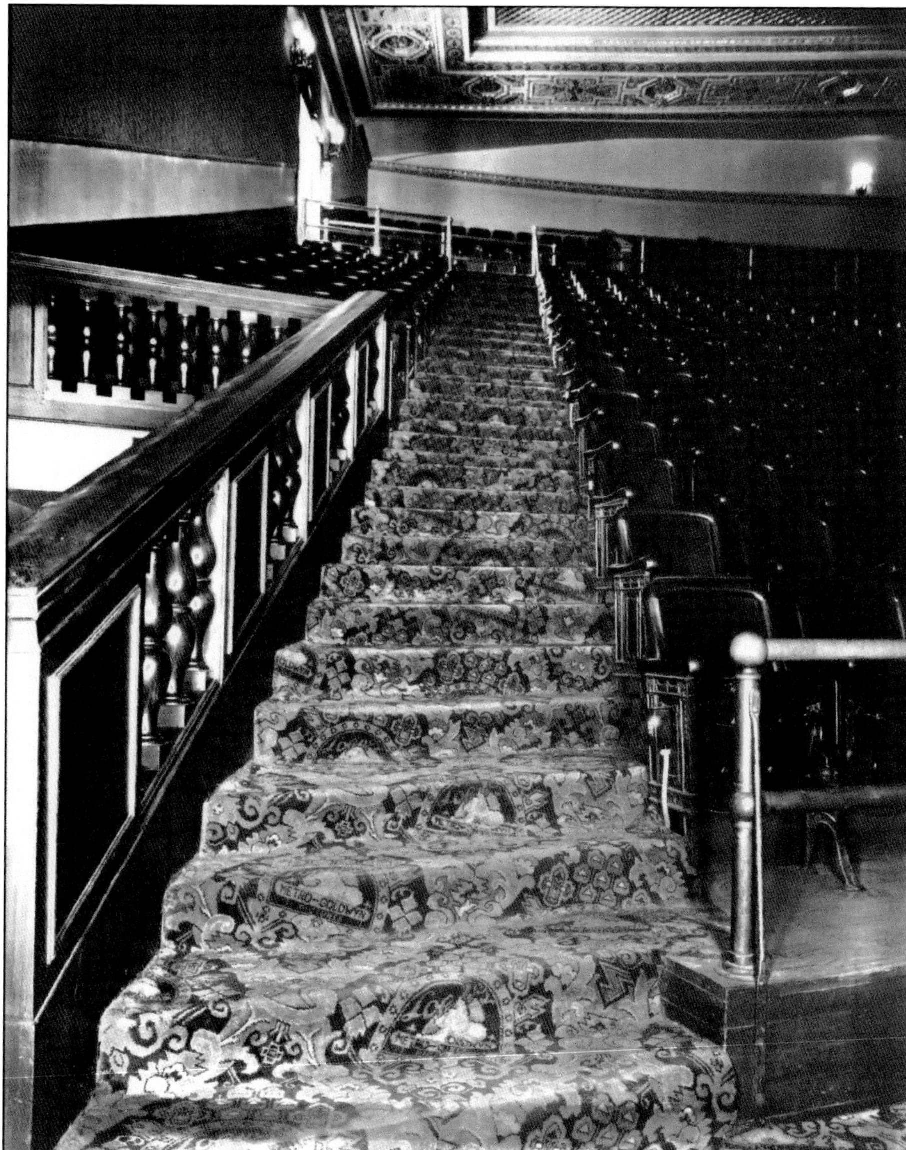

The ultimate in personalized carpeting announced "Loew's" and "Metro-Goldwyn Pictures" at Loew's State in Newark. On the chilly morning of January 25, 1940, crowds could not wait to warm up in those seats after lining up along New Street to Halsey Street for the Newark run of *Gone with the Wind*. "Long Line Shivers While Waiting for Movie Classic" read the newspaper headline. First to get his ticket that day was a young Frank Michelli of 241 North Fifteenth Street in Bloomfield, undaunted by the prospects of sitting through a four-hour-long film. "Did you bring your lunch?" he was asked. "No," he answered. "I had a good breakfast. I can stick it out. I think it will be worth seeing." The film had what was described as a "seven-week siege," with 270,000 patrons passing through the theater till. William S. Phillips, the theater manager, summed it up this way: "There were no lost children, no requests for refunds, no enraged Yankees demanding justice for the North," he said. "A few of the veterans of the Civil War didn't relish the way Sherman's march was shown. A very few walked out on the film; maybe they had another appointment." (Courtesy of the New Jersey Historical Society.)

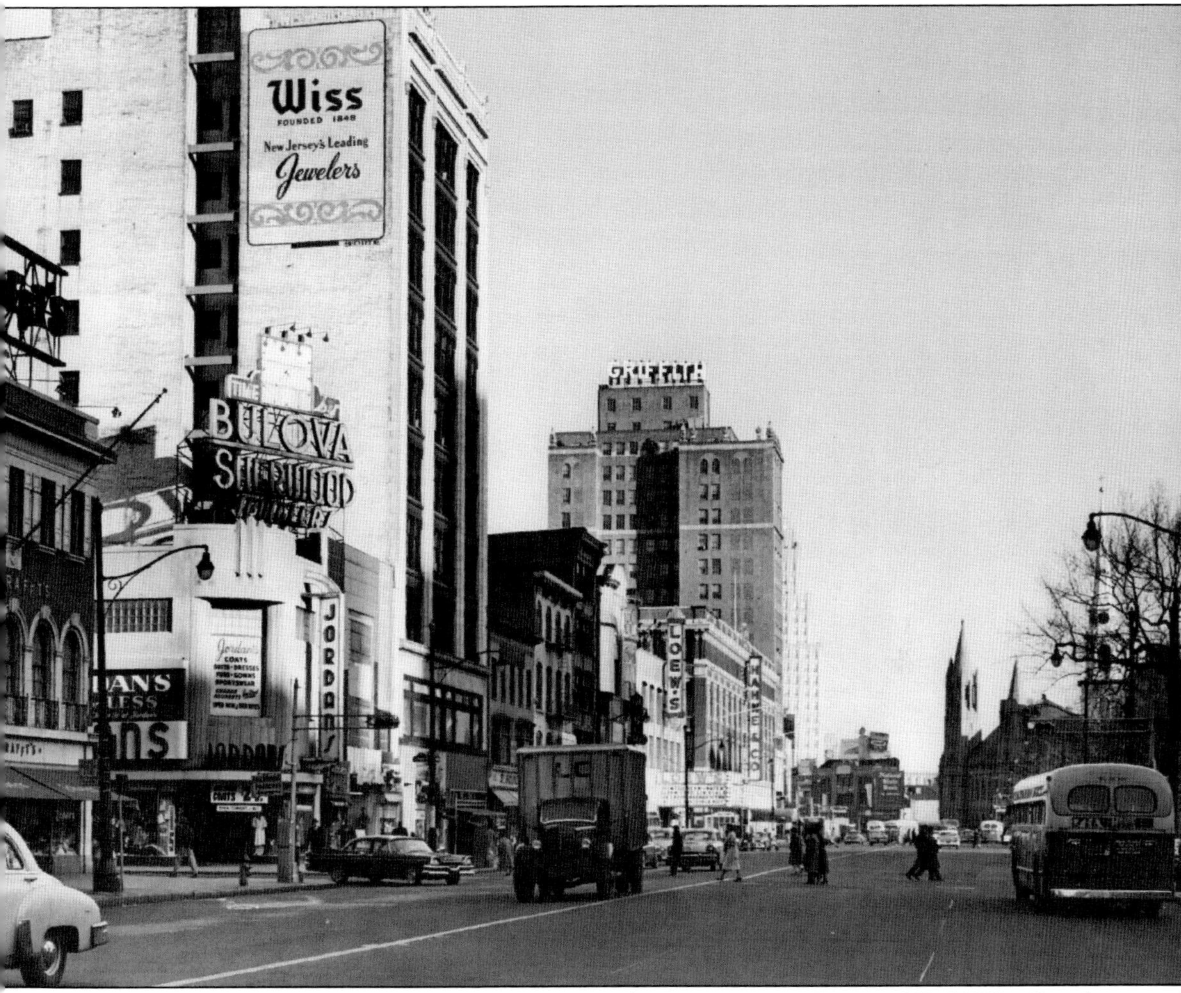

Loew's State in Newark was showing *Don't Go Near the Water*, a comedy set in World War II and starring Glenn Ford, in this 1957 street scene. Yet, it was the August 1964 debut of the Beatles movie *A Hard Day's Night* that really grabbed the attention of the press. "No Place to Hide, Covering The Beatles is War Correspondent's Job," read one headline. Gunter David, a reporter for the *Newark News*, started his story this way: "Memo: City editor. Subject: Combat pay for covering special showing of first Beatles movie, 'A Hard Day's Night.' I am battle scarred and weary. My knees are bruised and my ear drums still hurt. Last night I saw a mob in action. It was a mob of nice little girls. Two thousand of them. . . . They came to see their favorites, the Beatles, in a special showing at Loew's." (Courtesy of the New Jersey Historical Society.)

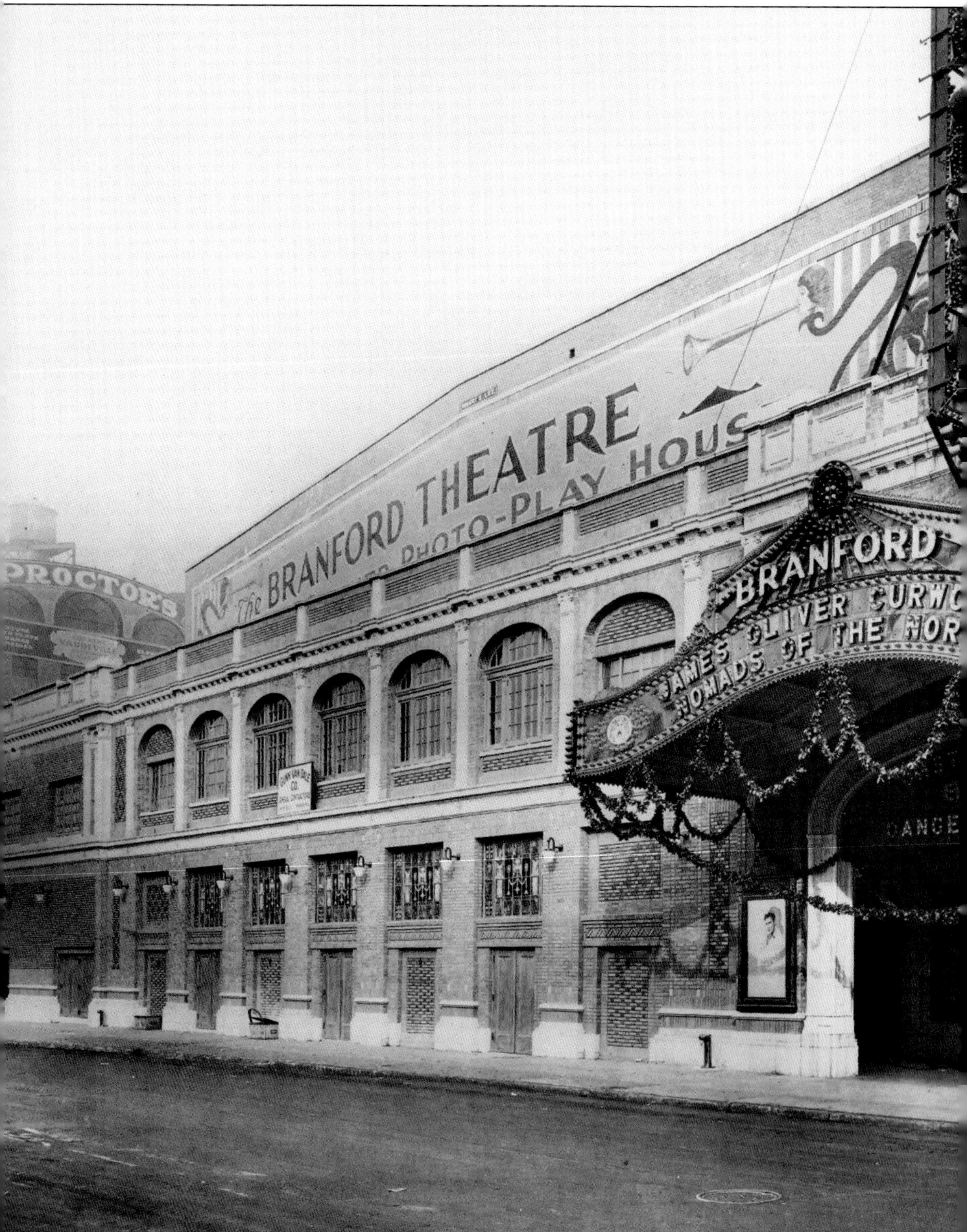
PROCTOR'S
The BRANFORD THEATRE
PHOTO-PLAY HOUS
BRANFORD
BRANFORD
JAMES OLIVER CURWO
NOMADS OF THE NOR

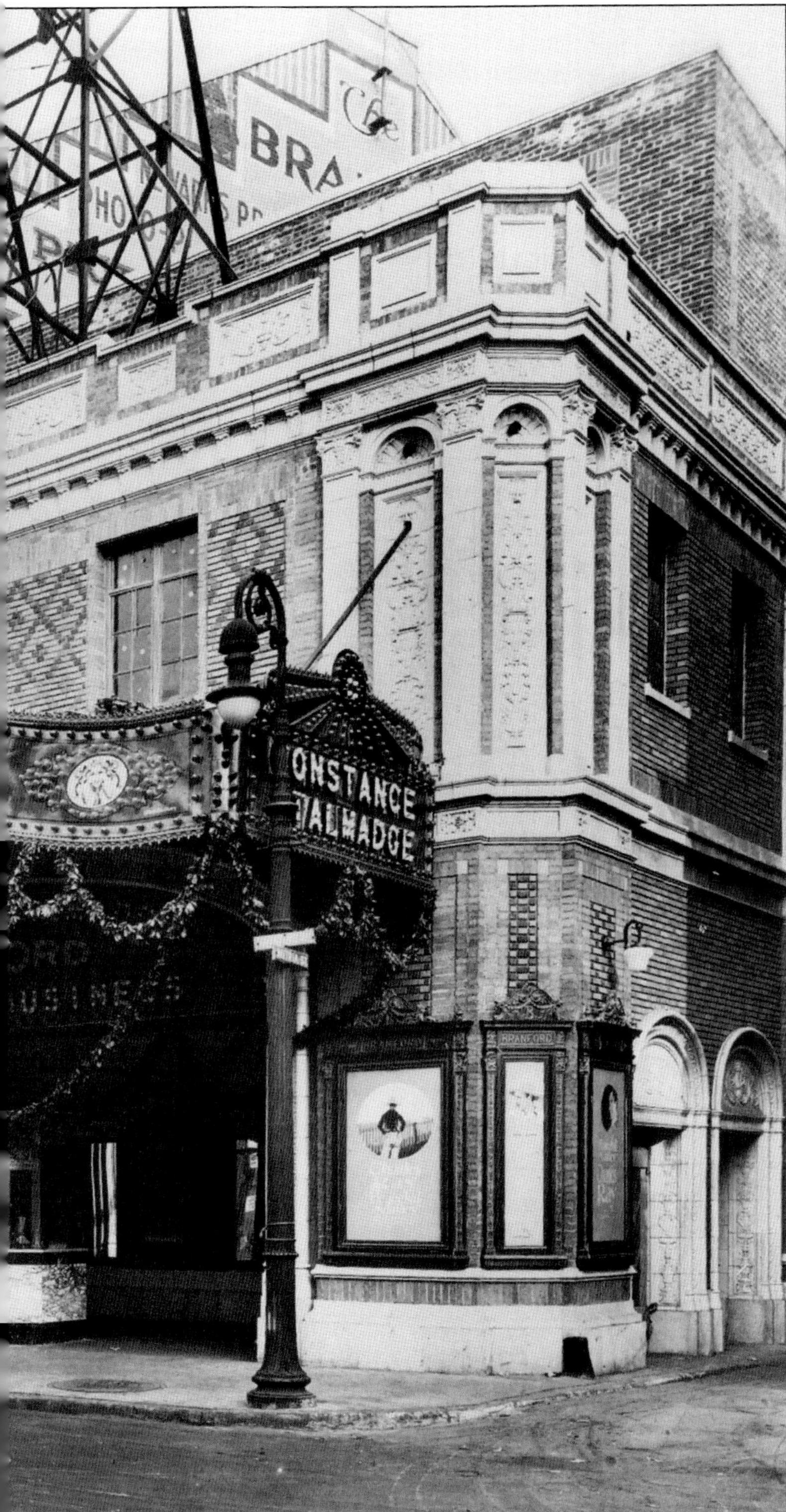

The feature film at the Branford Theatre, at Newark's 11 Branford Place, in 1920 was *Nomads of the North*, whose stars included Lon Chaney in the romantic lead portraying a suitor in novelist James Oliver Curwood's adventure tale. In the ensuing decades, there were other off-screen adventures. In 1957, police stopped the showing of *Reform School Girl* after a telephoned bomb threat. In August 1965, *Newark News* reporter Vincent DeP. Slavin met up with some 1,100 screaming teenagers who arrived at the Branford for an appearance by The Dave Clark Five, whose 1964 hit "Glad All Over" bested the Beatles's "I Want to Hold Your Hand" on the British pop charts. His report, headed "In Another Orbit," noted that the fans did not seem to care much about astronauts Gordon Cooper and Charles Conrad's launch on an eight-day Gemini 5 mission. "The mobs screeched, 'I love you, Dave' . . . 'touch me please' . . . 'here I am' . . . and other unintelligible endearments," he wrote. The Branford was one of three stops for the band, which also appeared in Paterson and Passaic. (Courtesy of the New Jersey Historical Society.)

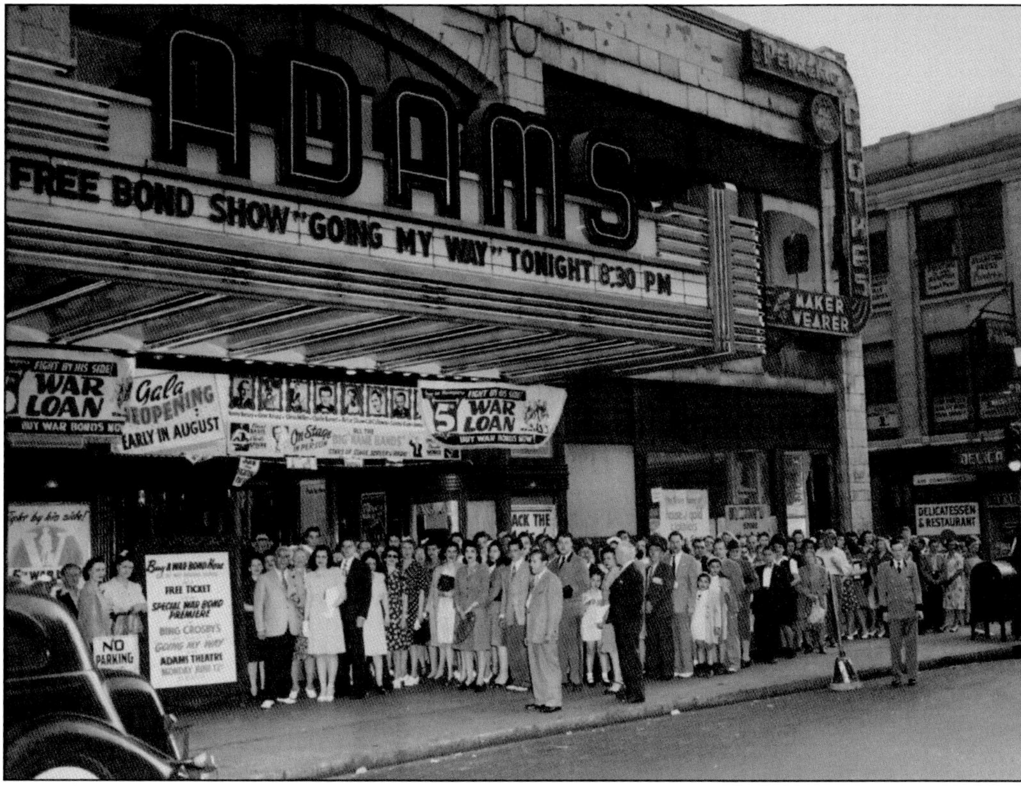

The Adams Theatre, on Newark's Branford Place, brought out crowds for the "Special War Bond Premiere" of Bing Crosby's *Going My Way* in June 1944 (above), with theatergoers backed up to Newark's Halsey Street. Note the sign on the right for Hobby's, the famed Newark delicatessen that continues to serve up classic Jewish pastrami sandwiches. The theater's namesake, Adam A. Adams, was there (below, center), along with his daughter Dorothea and son Peter. (Courtesy of the Newark Public Library, Hellenic Heritage Collection.)

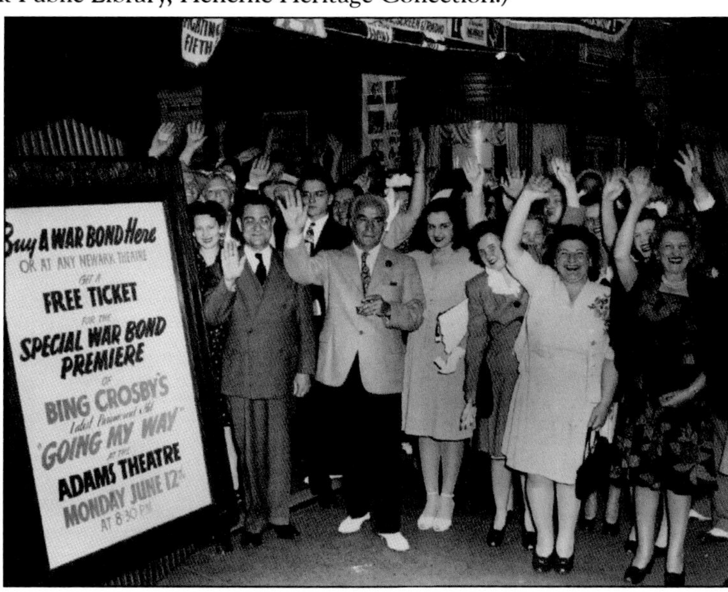

In the early 1940s, A.A. Adams (center group, far right) brought top big-band talent to the Adams, including Tommy Dorsey, Sammy Kaye, Gene Krupa, Artie Shaw, and Charlie Barnet. The hit parade also drew the likes of The Andrew Sisters, The Four Ink Spots, Ella Fitzgerald, and Cab Calloway. Here, he is joined by Teddy Powell (center group, far left), whose orchestra played such tunes as "Jersey Bounce" and "Blue Moon." (Courtesy of the Newark Public Library, Hellenic Heritage Collection.)

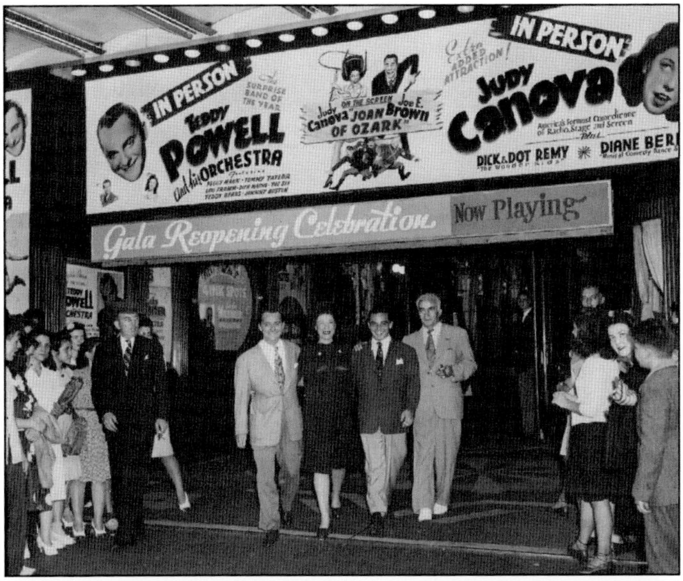

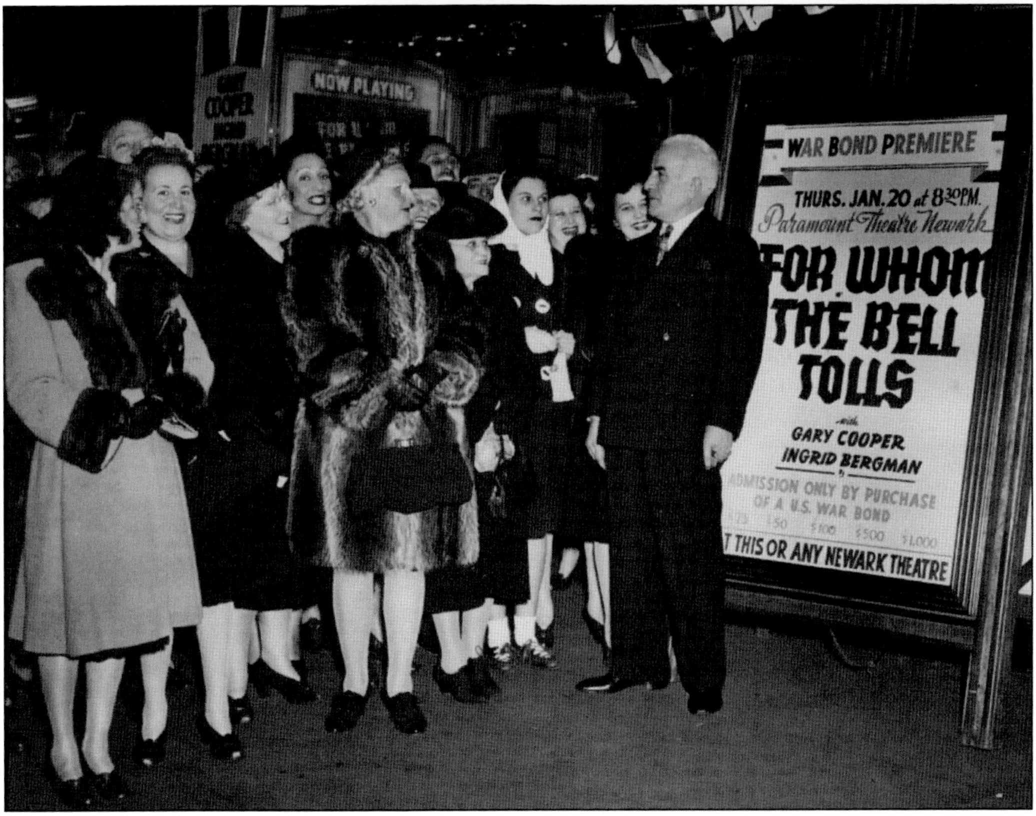

Admission was gained only by the purchase of a US War Bond at many shows at A.A. Adams's Newark theaters. Beside film premieres, the Adams Theatre in August 1943 was host to a beauty show featuring 125 young candidates hoping to be selected as Miss New Jersey and compete on September 6 at the Miss America finals in Atlantic City. (Courtesy of the Newark Public Library, Hellenic Heritage Collection.)

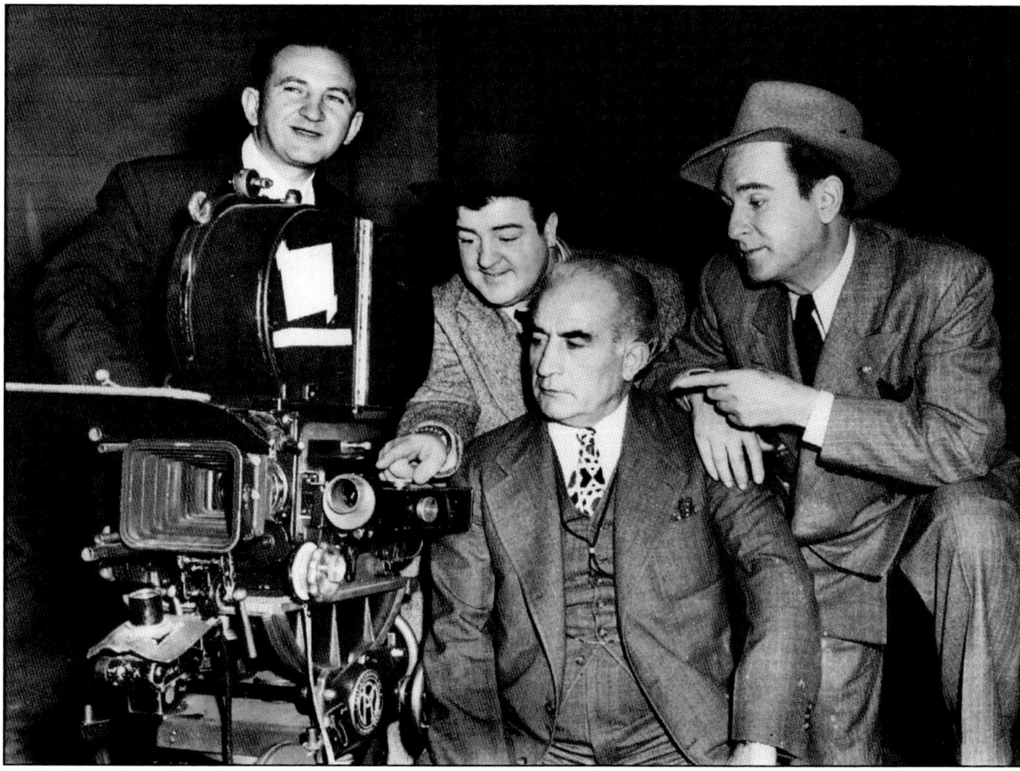

Big stars came to rub shoulders with Adam A. Adams at the Paramount. Above, the comedy team of Bud Abbott (far right) and Lou Costello (rear, center) are in the projection room with their agent and Adams. Below, comedian Jerry Lewis (dark suit), who once served as an usher at the Paramount, visits with his producer Hal Wallis (second from the right) and marvels at a billboard noting the showing of 1951's *A Place in the Sun*. The film debuted the same year Lewis teamed up with Dean Martin in *That's My Boy*. The stars were all Jersey: Lewis was born in Newark, Costello called Paterson home, and Abbott hailed from Asbury Park. (Courtesy of the Newark Public Library, Hellenic Heritage Collection.)

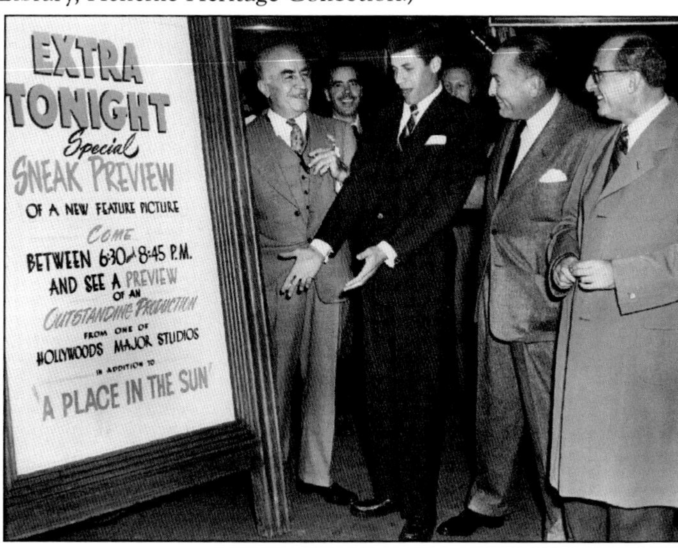

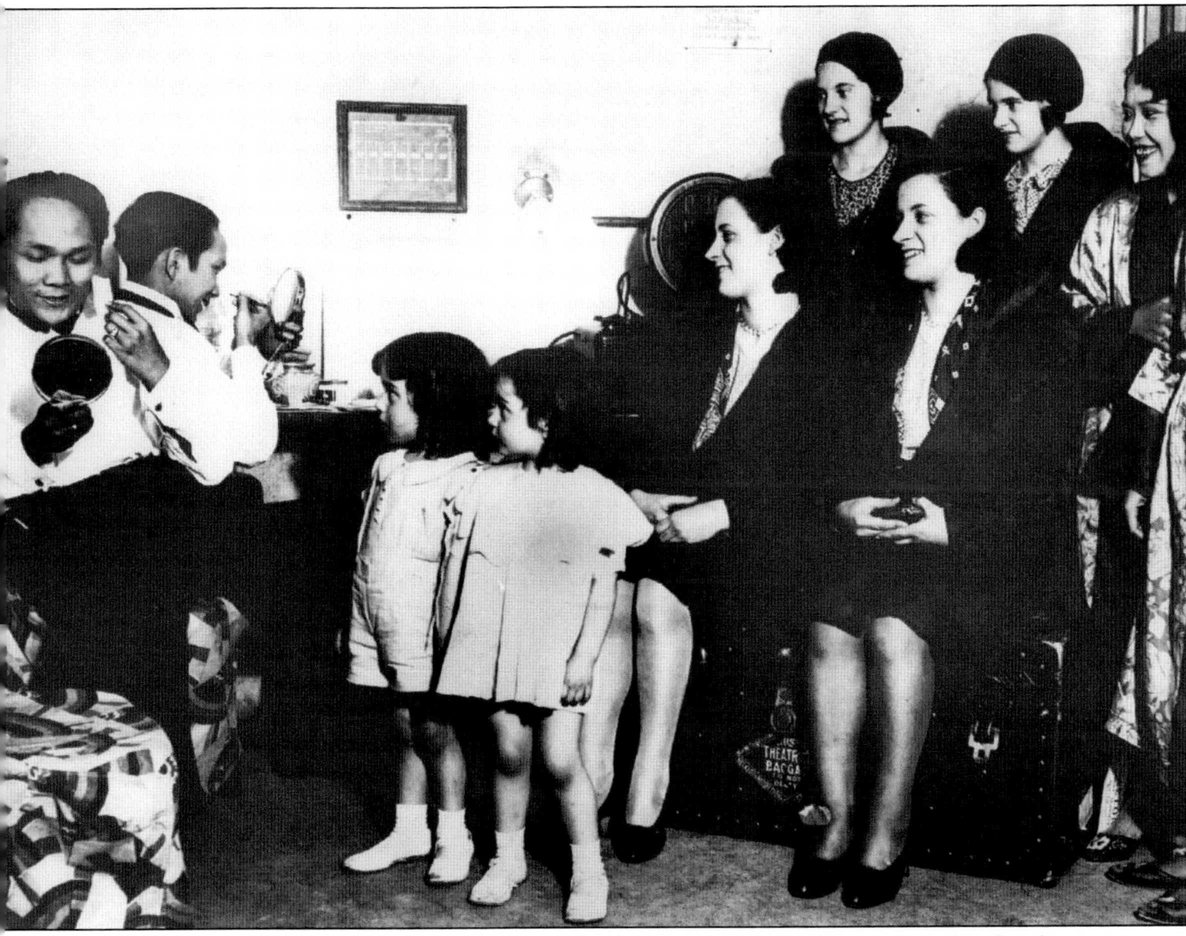

In the 1930s, a "Twins Day" promotion included Peter A. Adams and Dorothea Carol Adams, children of the Newark Theatre's owner. (Courtesy of the Newark Public Library, Hellenic Heritage Collection.)

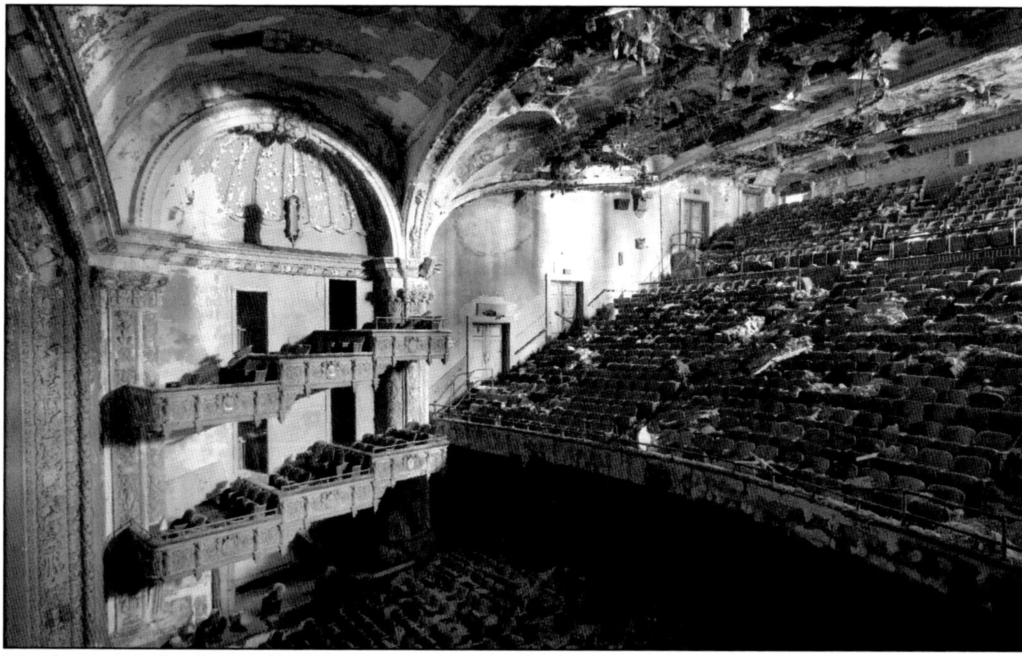

The long-closed Adams Theatre, on Newark's Branford Place, has a surreal quality. "The Paramount and Adams Theatres are still beautiful despite the decay and collapses," said Matt Lambros, the architectural photographer who captured this image. (Courtesy of Matt Lambros.)

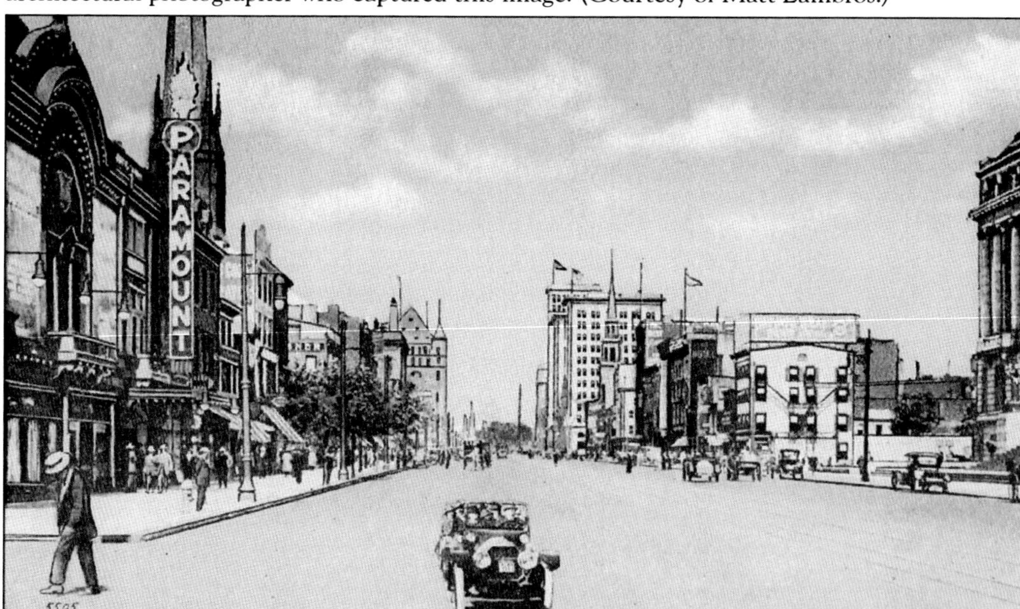

In 1915, an early incarnation of the Paramount stood across from Newark City Hall on Broad Street. Those who arrived at the 1,200-seat venue spotted these words, carved in stone, over the entrance: "Whatever You Do, Do It Well." One of the interior stairways was a replica of a staircase in the congressional library in the nation's Capitol, according to the April-June 1915 issue of *Moving Picture World*. Among the 100 feet of oil paintings of Paramount stars to grace the lobby were two life-size depictions of "America's sweetheart," silent film star Mary Pickford. (Author's collection.)

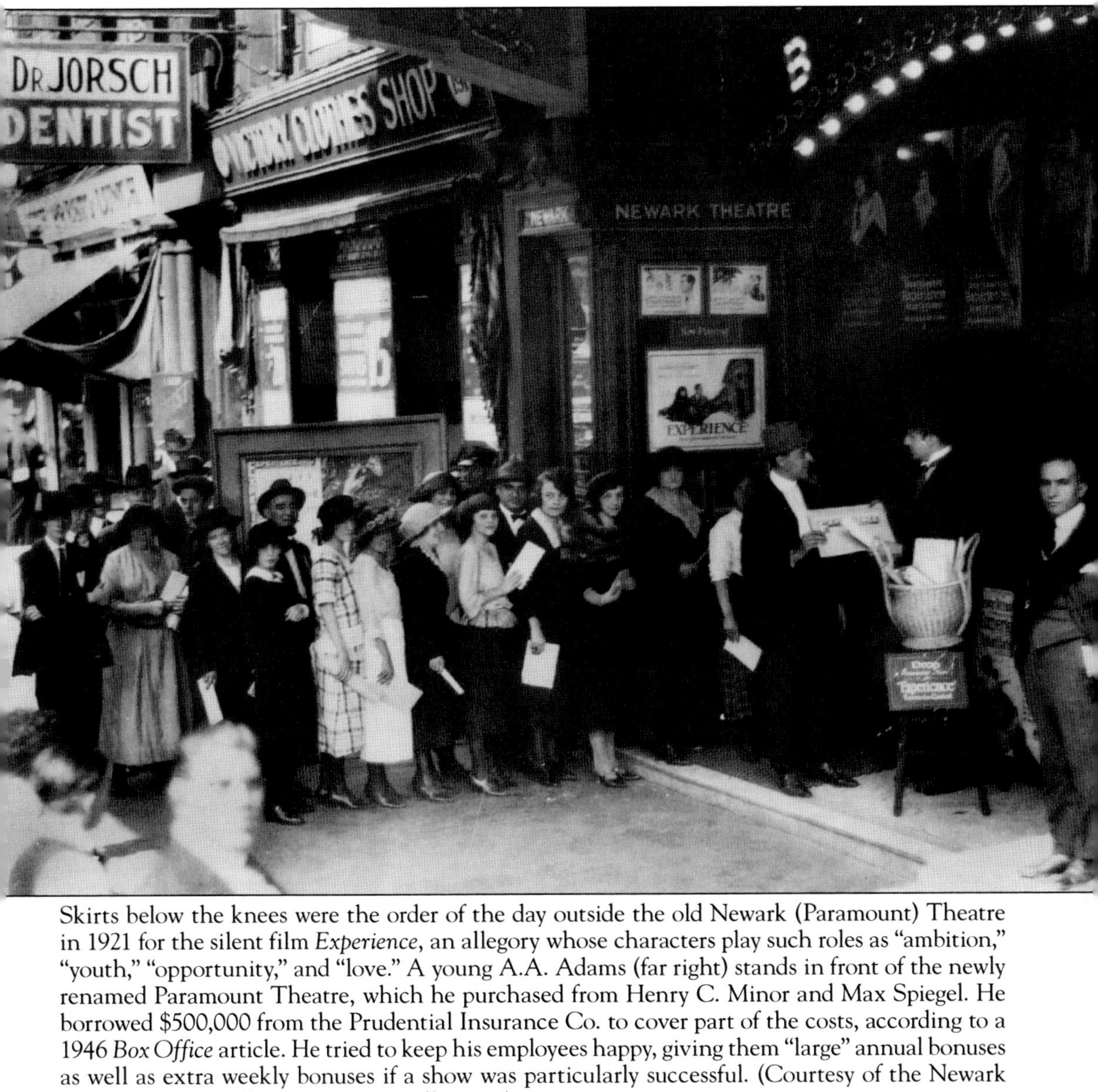

Skirts below the knees were the order of the day outside the old Newark (Paramount) Theatre in 1921 for the silent film *Experience*, an allegory whose characters play such roles as "ambition," "youth," "opportunity," and "love." A young A.A. Adams (far right) stands in front of the newly renamed Paramount Theatre, which he purchased from Henry C. Minor and Max Spiegel. He borrowed $500,000 from the Prudential Insurance Co. to cover part of the costs, according to a 1946 *Box Office* article. He tried to keep his employees happy, giving them "large" annual bonuses as well as extra weekly bonuses if a show was particularly successful. (Courtesy of the Newark Public Library, Hellenic Heritage Collection.)

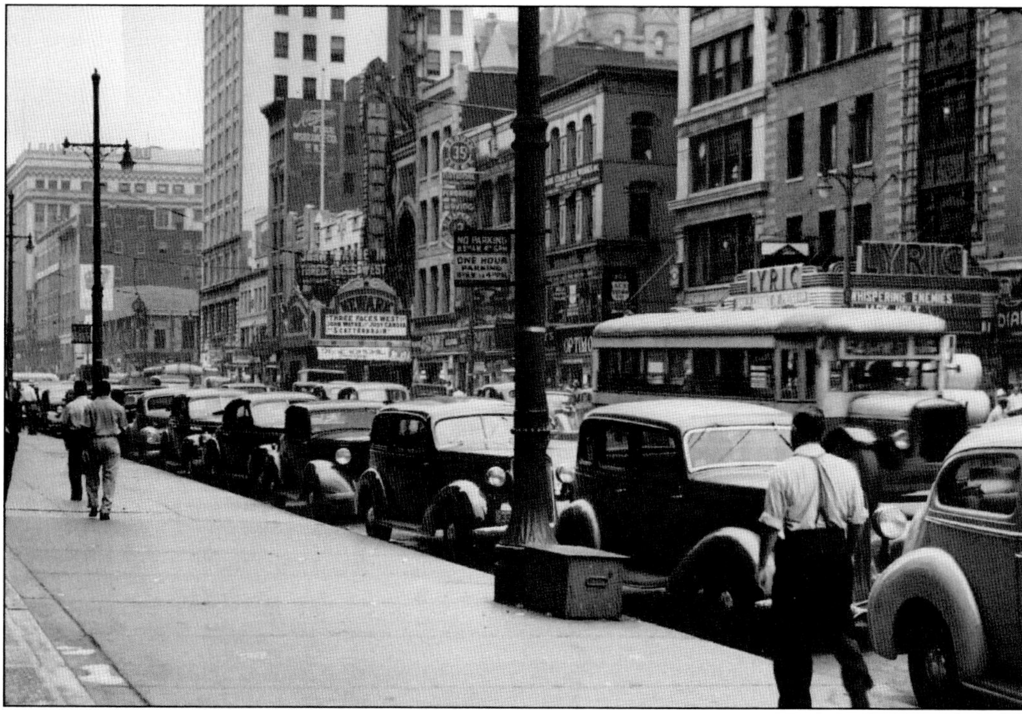

The first-run Paramount was showing John Wayne's 1940 wartime drama *Three Faces West*, while the fare at the Lyric was 1939's *Whispering Enemies*, a tale of corporate intrigue in the cosmetics industry. (Courtesy of the Newark Public Library.)

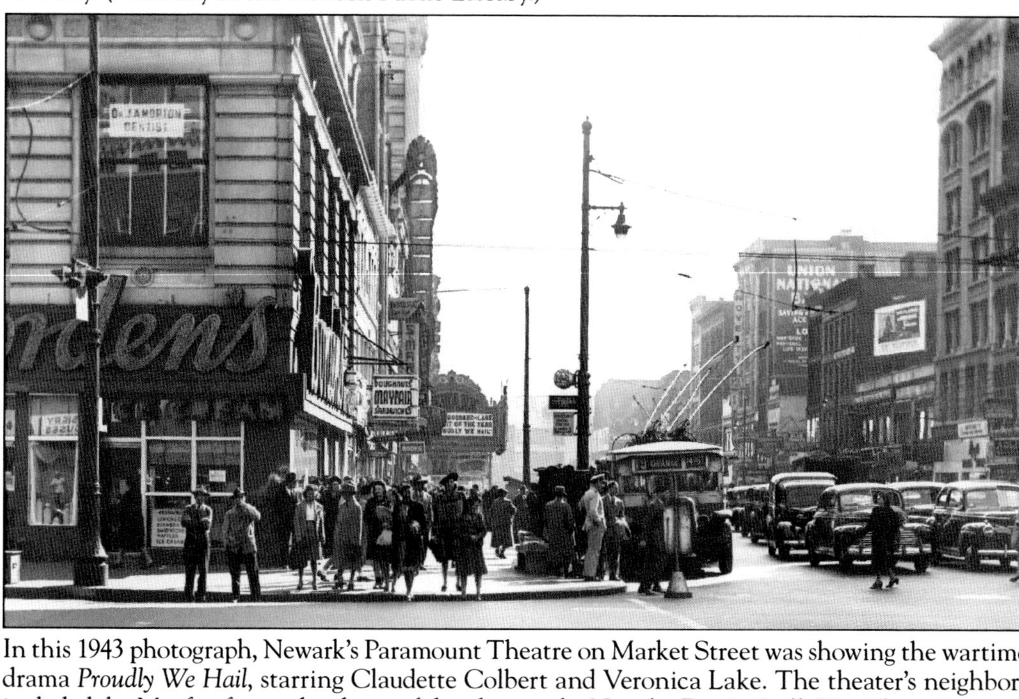

In this 1943 photograph, Newark's Paramount Theatre on Market Street was showing the wartime drama *Proudly We Hail*, starring Claudette Colbert and Veronica Lake. The theater's neighbors included the Mayfair for sandwiches and doughnuts, the Novelty Bar & Grill, E.N. Plates Printing, and the ever-present Army & Navy Store. (Courtesy of the Newark Public Library.)

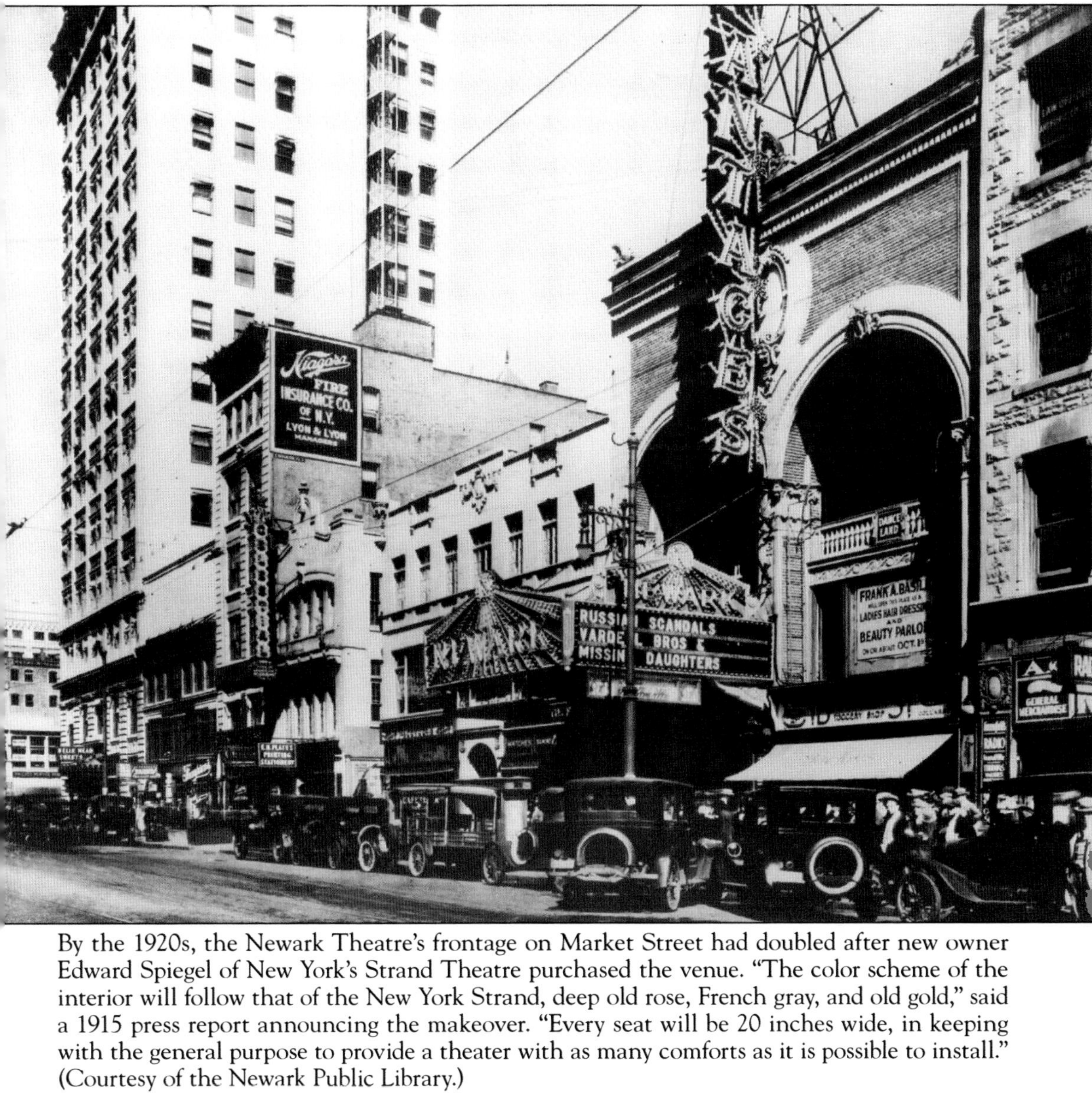

By the 1920s, the Newark Theatre's frontage on Market Street had doubled after new owner Edward Spiegel of New York's Strand Theatre purchased the venue. "The color scheme of the interior will follow that of the New York Strand, deep old rose, French gray, and old gold," said a 1915 press report announcing the makeover. "Every seat will be 20 inches wide, in keeping with the general purpose to provide a theater with as many comforts as it is possible to install." (Courtesy of the Newark Public Library.)

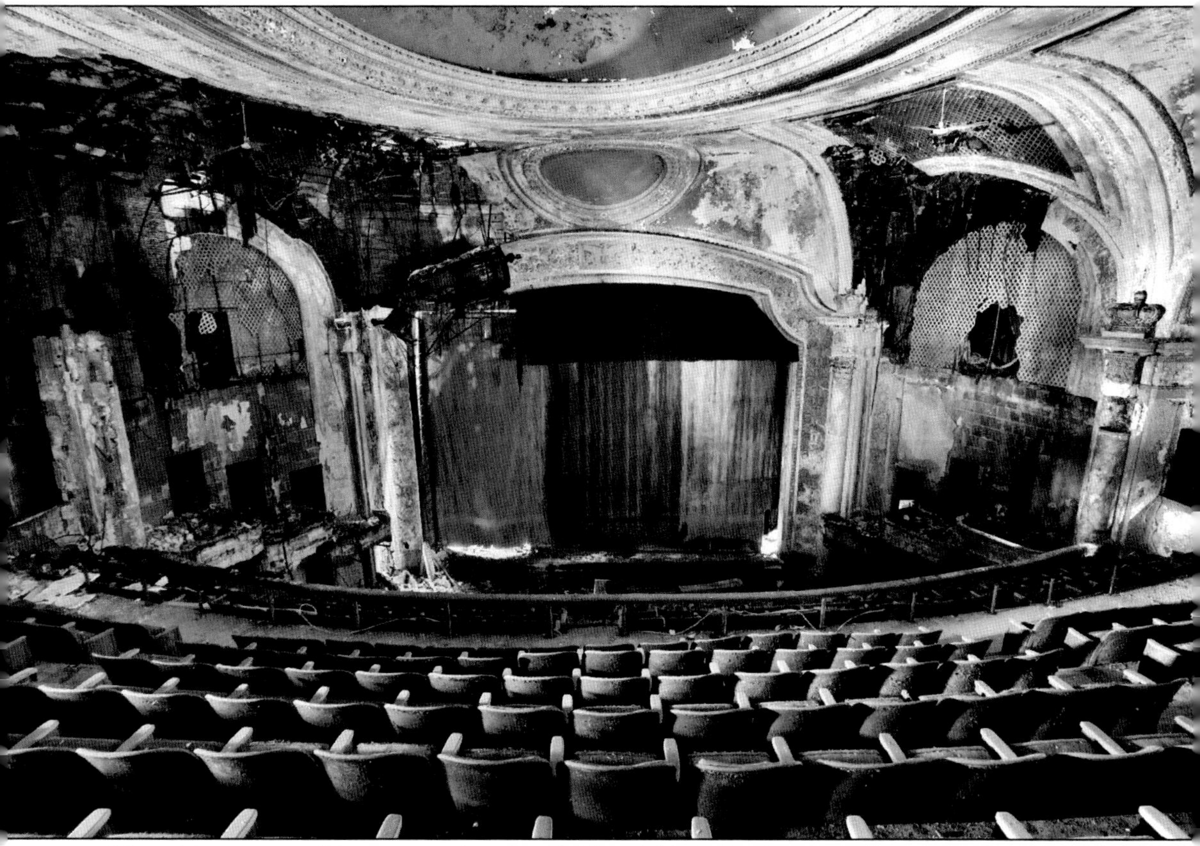

Newark's once grand Paramount closed in 1986, its lobby leased on and off to various small retailers. Inside, the remains of the Newark movie house were captured in this image by Matt Lambros, a New York–based architectural photographer who chronicles the state of many of the nation's old palaces on his website afterthefinalcurtain.net and on Facebook. (Courtesy of Matt Lambros.)

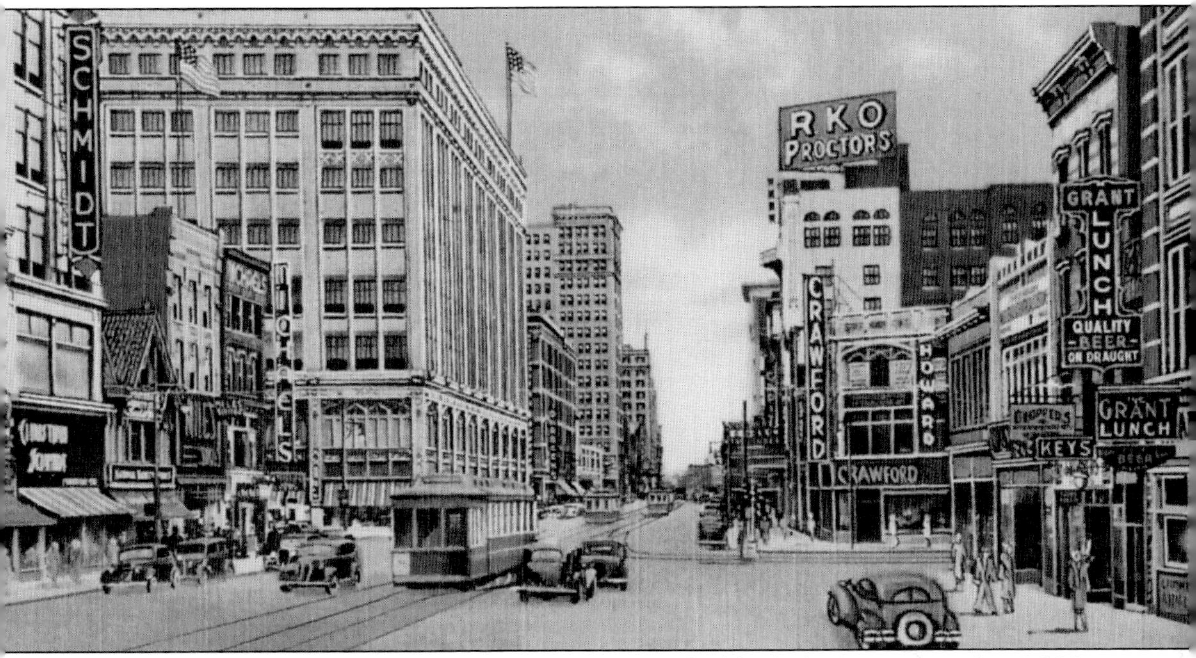

RKO Proctor's on Newark's Market Street was a rare "double-decker" venue, with a 2,300-seat theater on the ground level topped by a four-story 900-seat theater beneath the roof. (Author's collection.)

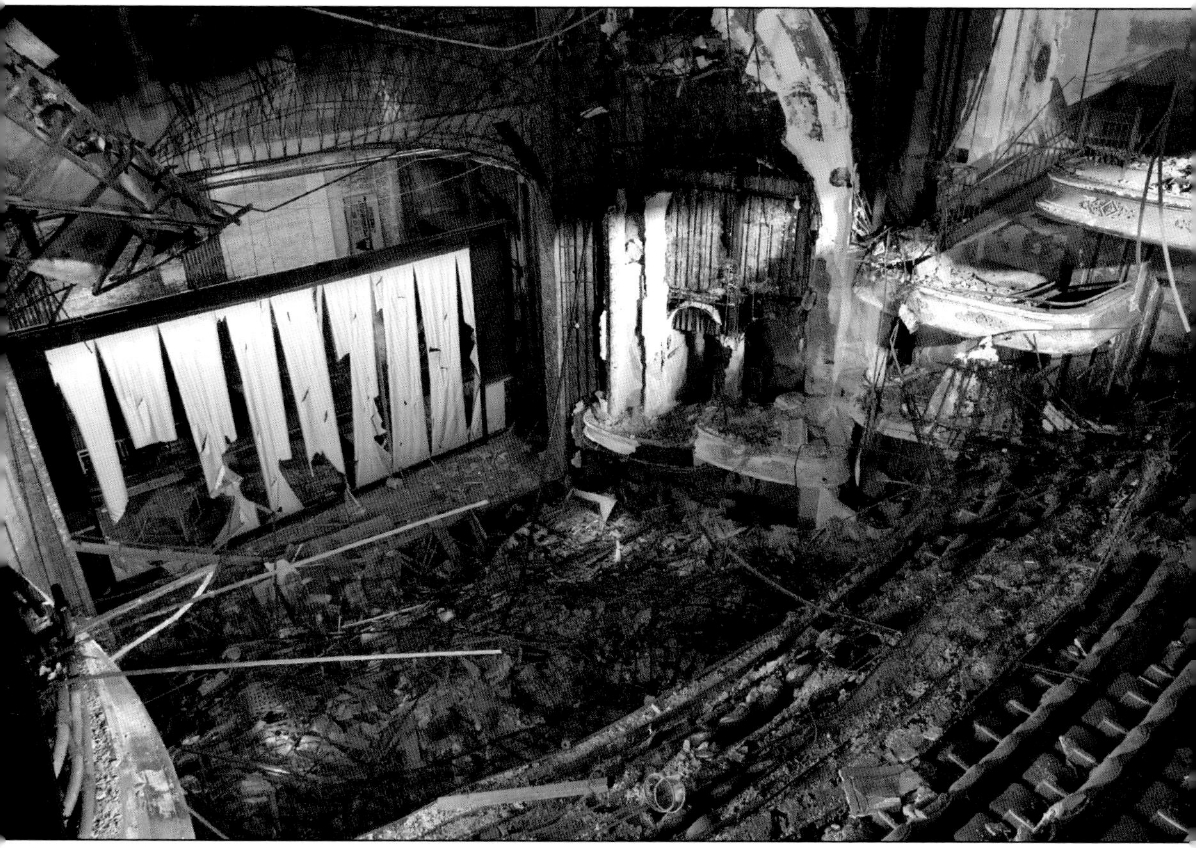

RKO Proctor's was designed by architect John W. Merrow, the nephew of theater circuit owner Frederick F. Proctor. In 1916, the locale was prominent enough that it was used by Newark to mark its 250th anniversary celebration. (Courtesy of Matt Lambros.)

The massive stage of the Newark Symphony Hall, once known as the Mosque Theatre, has seen—and heard—the likes of Frank Sinatra, the Rolling Stones, the Supremes, the Temptations, Chuck Berry singing "Maybellene," Bob Dylan, and Sarah Vaughn, the jazz singer whose name now graces its hall. The 2,743-seat theater is a New Jersey treasure built from 1922 to 1925 with Neo-Classical, Greek, Roman, and Egyptian design elements. By World War II, with gas rationing in full swing, the famed Frank Dailey brought his Meadowbrook roadhouse shows from the far-to-reach countryside of Cedar Grove to the theater's Terrace Room. (Author's collection.)

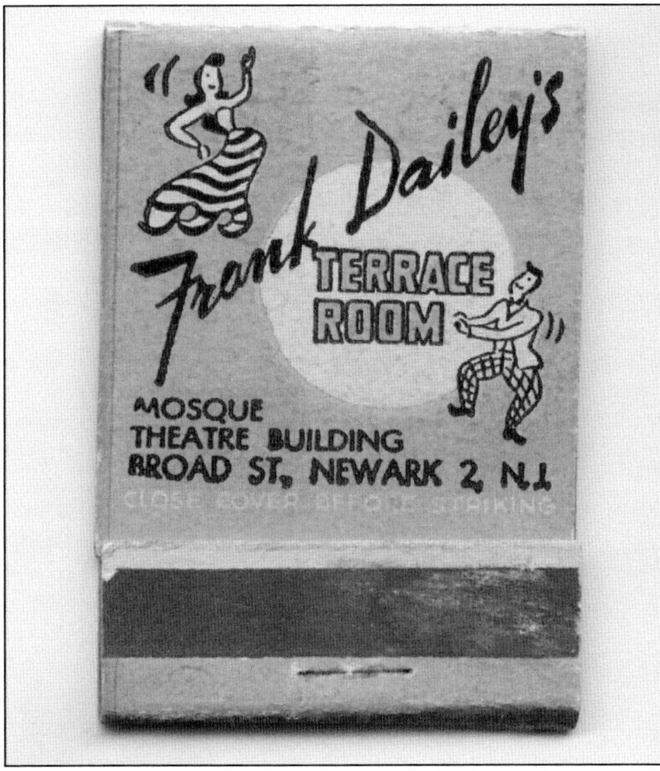

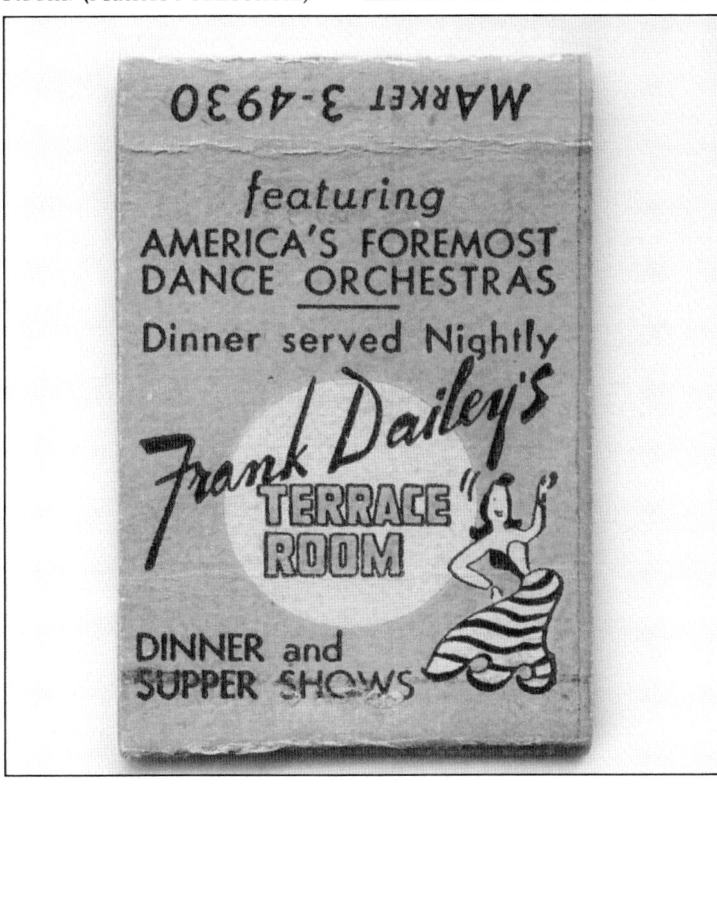

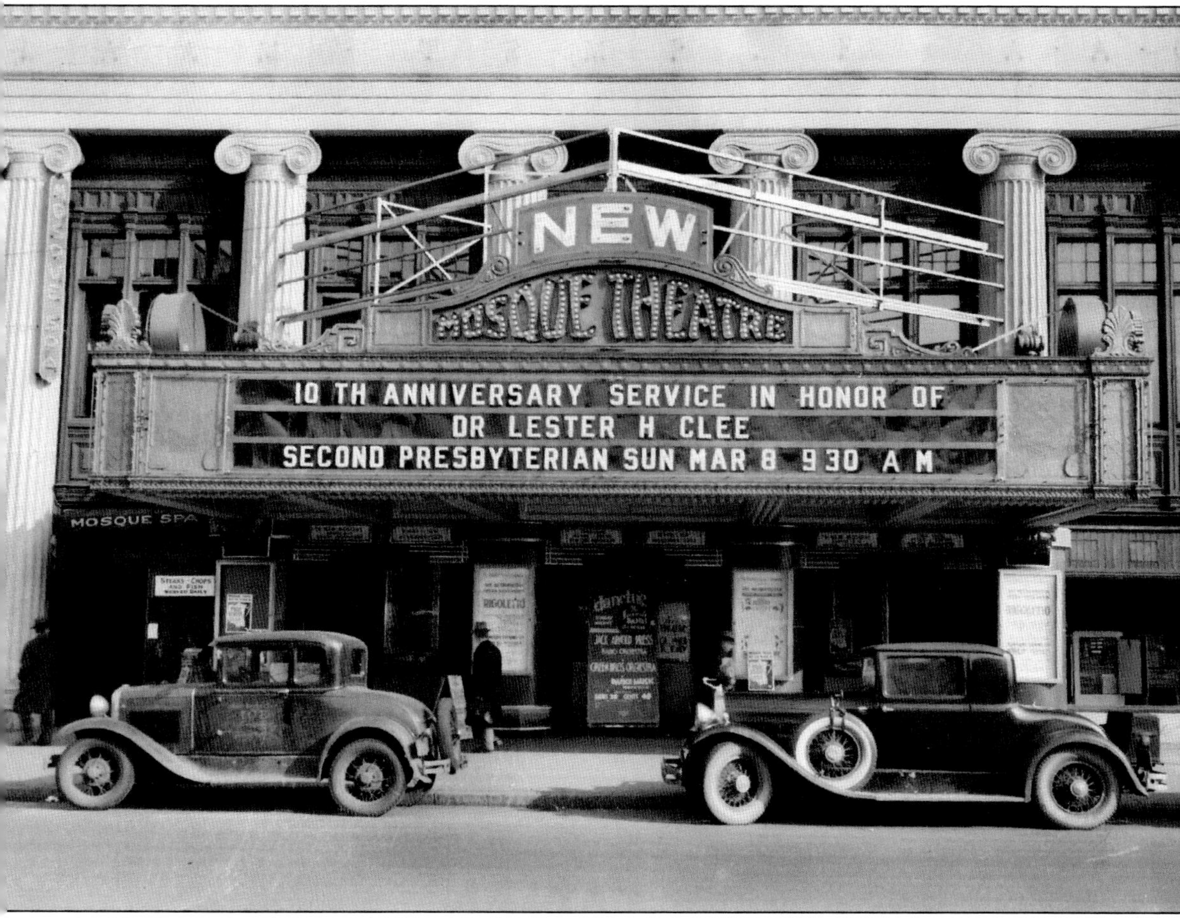

The Mosque Theatre, which opened on March 27, 1925, hosted dancers, singers, and movies in the 1930s. By 1936, it reopened as the New Mosque, debuting with the Buddy Rogers film *Dance Band*, a romance about a bandleader falling in love with the leader of an all-female orchestra during a band contest. (Courtesy of the New Jersey Historical Society.)

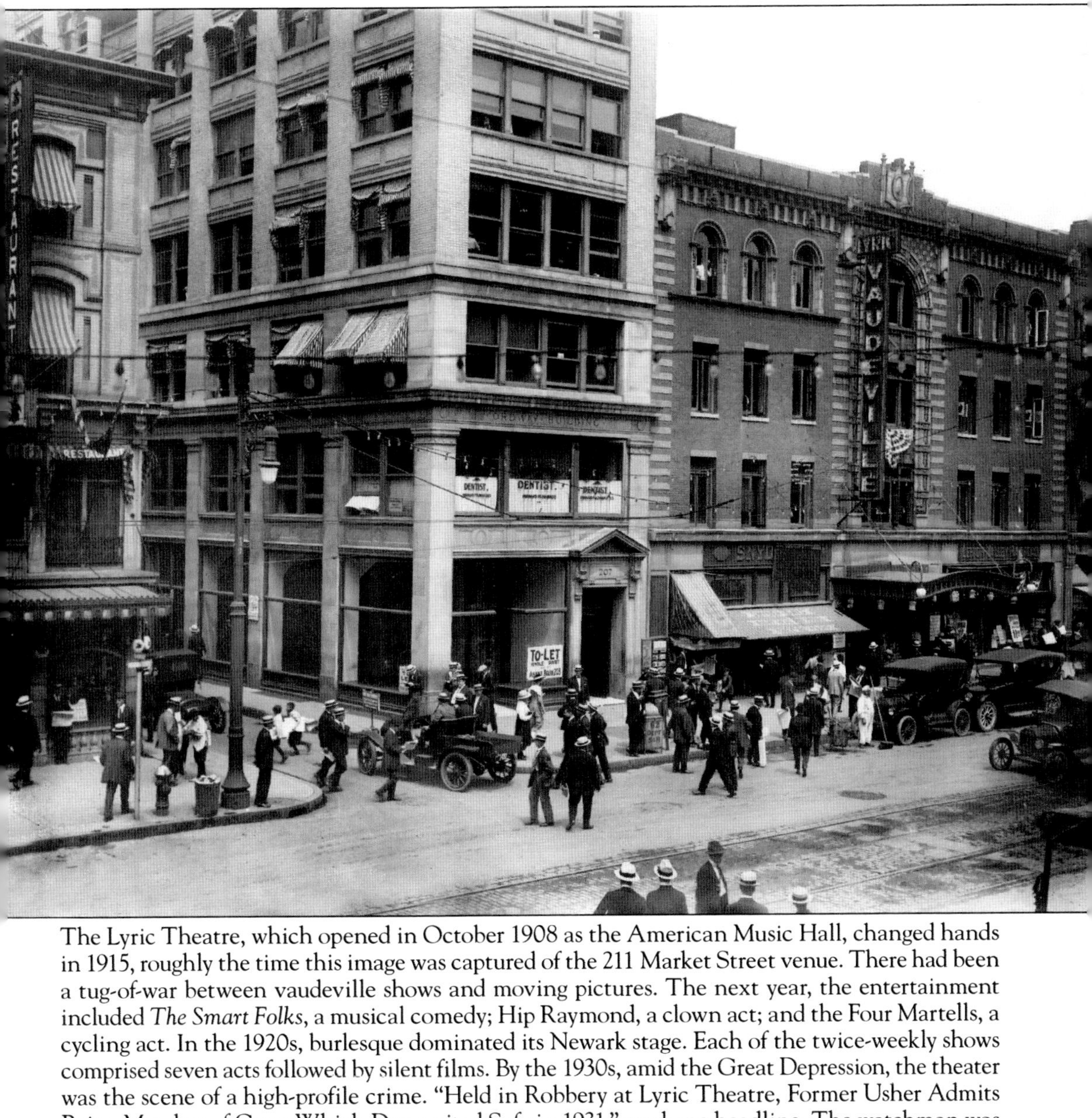

The Lyric Theatre, which opened in October 1908 as the American Music Hall, changed hands in 1915, roughly the time this image was captured of the 211 Market Street venue. There had been a tug-of-war between vaudeville shows and moving pictures. The next year, the entertainment included *The Smart Folks*, a musical comedy; Hip Raymond, a clown act; and the Four Martells, a cycling act. In the 1920s, burlesque dominated its Newark stage. Each of the twice-weekly shows comprised seven acts followed by silent films. By the 1930s, amid the Great Depression, the theater was the scene of a high-profile crime. "Held in Robbery at Lyric Theatre, Former Usher Admits Being Member of Gang Which Dynamited Safe in 1931," read one headline. The watchman was bound, and $900 was stolen. (Courtesy of the New Jersey Historical Society.)

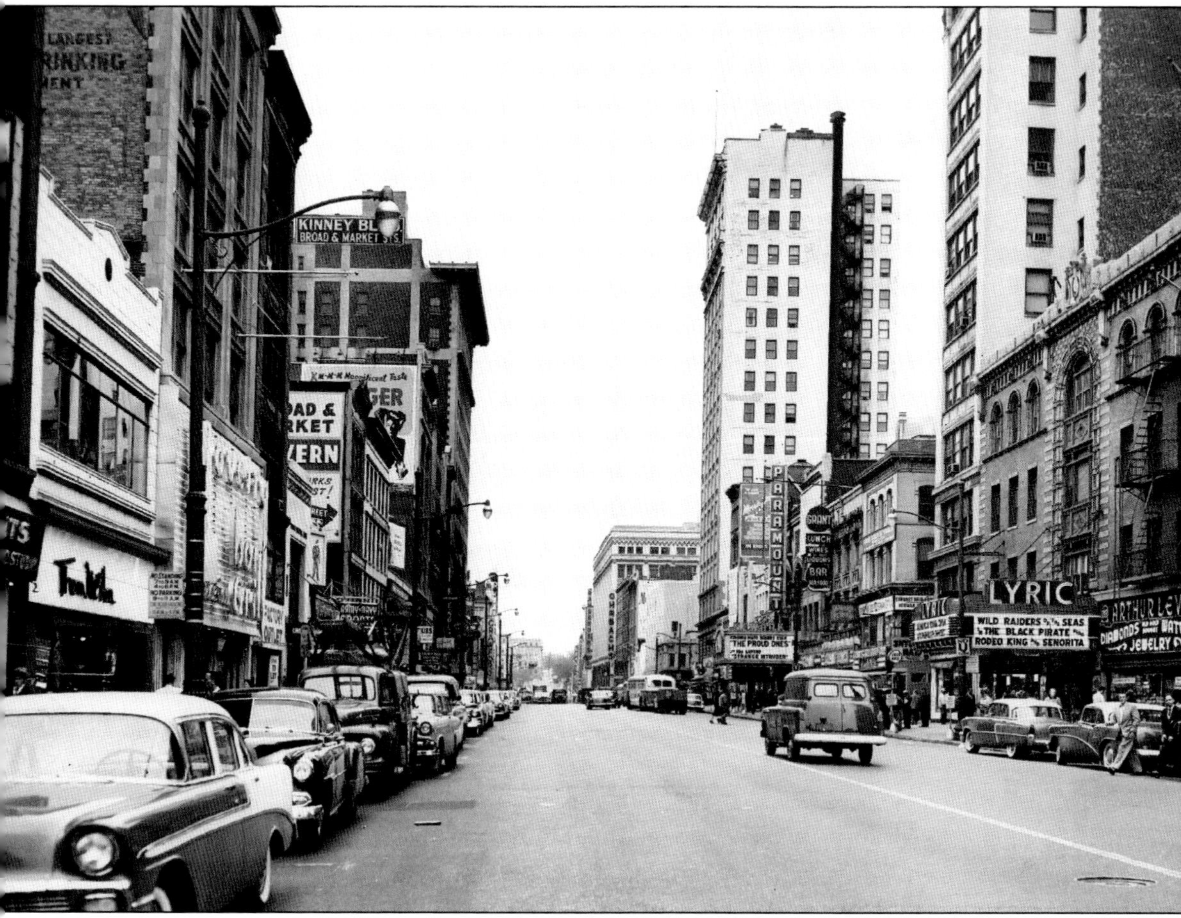

The 1,200-seat Lyric, then just a few doors down from the Paramount on Market Street, was near the end of its long run as the 1950s wore on. Still, it made headlines. The *Newark News* carried a photograph of a feline named Tiger, a familiar figure to daytime patrons as they approached its perch inside the ticket window. "It was born in the theater two years ago," read the press report, "and has never ventured beyond the box office, though it appears to enjoy watching the people and traffic from a distance." Come 1956, the theater was purchased by the *Newark News*, which intended to expand there. Films continued to be shown until 1964, and by January 1965 the wrecking crews arrived. Journalist Peter Carter, reporting on the event, recalled one of its last "live dramas," a 1950 fire that forced the evacuation of about 100 patrons watching the film *Perilous Waters*. "The fire was put out with only slight damage to a wall," he wrote, "the patrons, who had filed out, took their seats once more, and the movie resumed." (Courtesy of the Newark Public Library.)

In 1902, the old Proctor's Theatre was featuring the wall-scaling feats of the Imperial Japanese Guards. Also on the playbill was the act of McCue & Cahill, dubbed "thc best singing act of its kind in vaudeville." Before long, they were singing Burt and Solman's 1905 hit "Little Girl You'll Do," whose lyrics included the lines "Listen to me, little girl! / You, with the eyes of blue / There's only one little girl / And that little girl is you!" (Courtesy of the New Jersey Historical Society.)

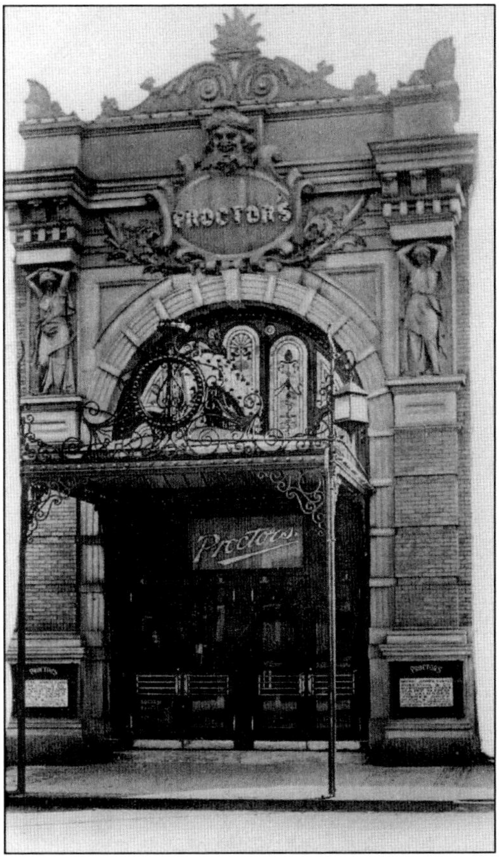

In this c. 1914 image, Proctor's Theatre is overshadowed by the three-story S. Scheuer & Sons grocery store building, topped by such advertisements as one toting "Madam Butterfly" at New York's Garden Theatre. At the time, the lead role in that show was played by Clara Blandick, who would go on to play opposite Judy Garland as Auntie Em in 1939's *The Wizard of Oz*. (Courtesy of the New Jersey Historical Society.)

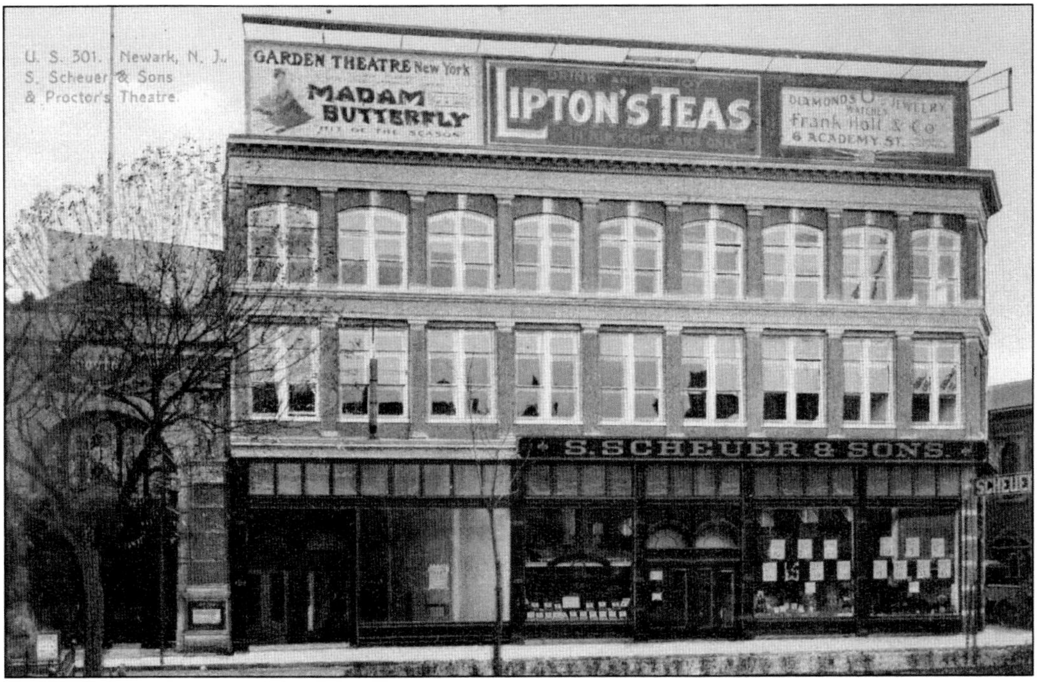

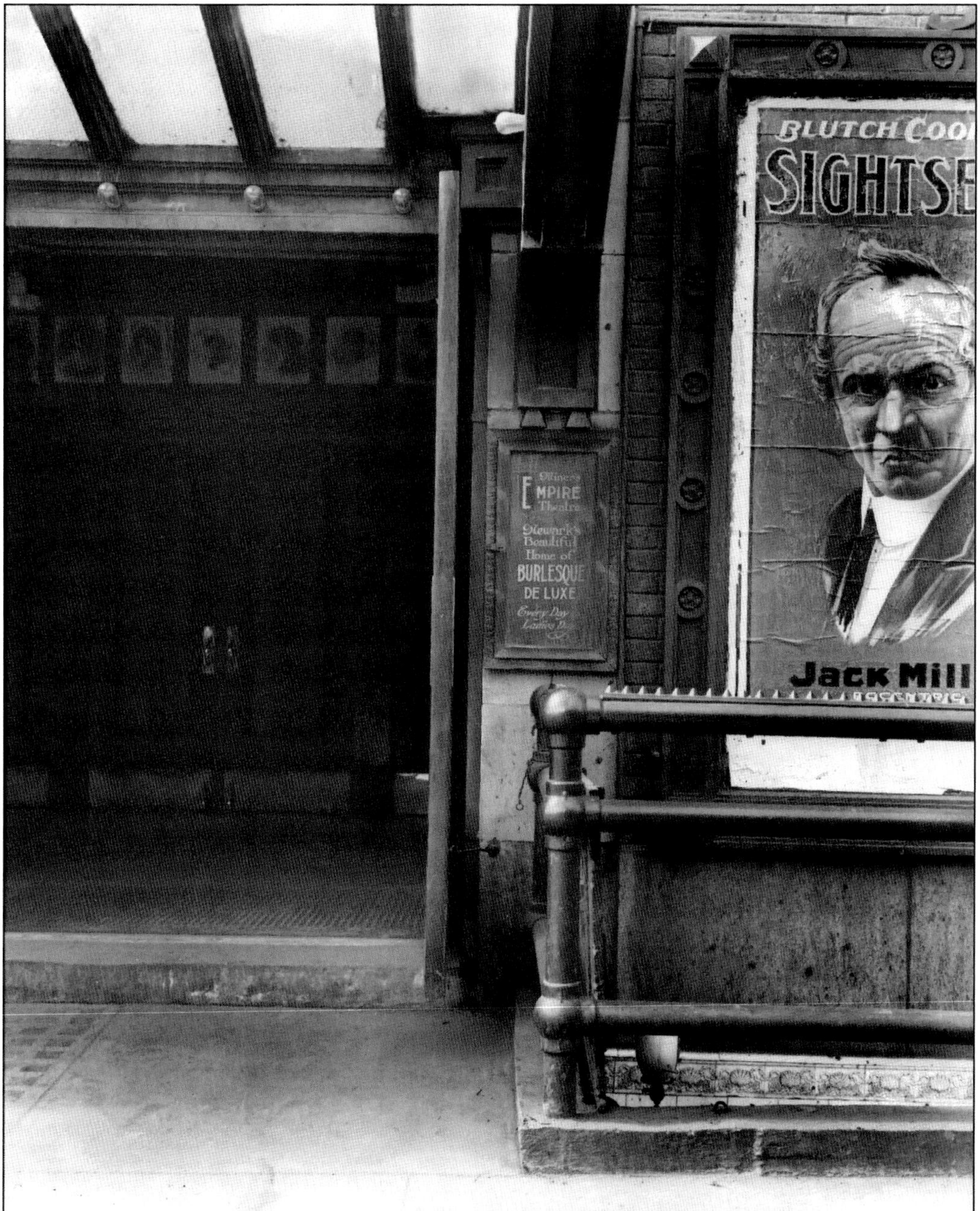

Miner's Empire Theatre, dubbed "Beautiful Home of Burlesque Deluxe," noted, "Every Day is Ladies Day" in Newark. Henry C. Miner, who in the words of a press report "covered himself with glory at Miner's Bowery Theatre," opened the Newark venue in 1886. Among the performers at the showplace was Lillian Russell, whose career performances had such titles as "Twirly Whirly" and "Fiddle-dee-dee." She was so popular that by 1940 a Hollywood version of her life, titled simply *Lillian Russell*, was released, starring Alice Faye. (Courtesy of the New Jersey Historical Society/ William Cone Collection.)

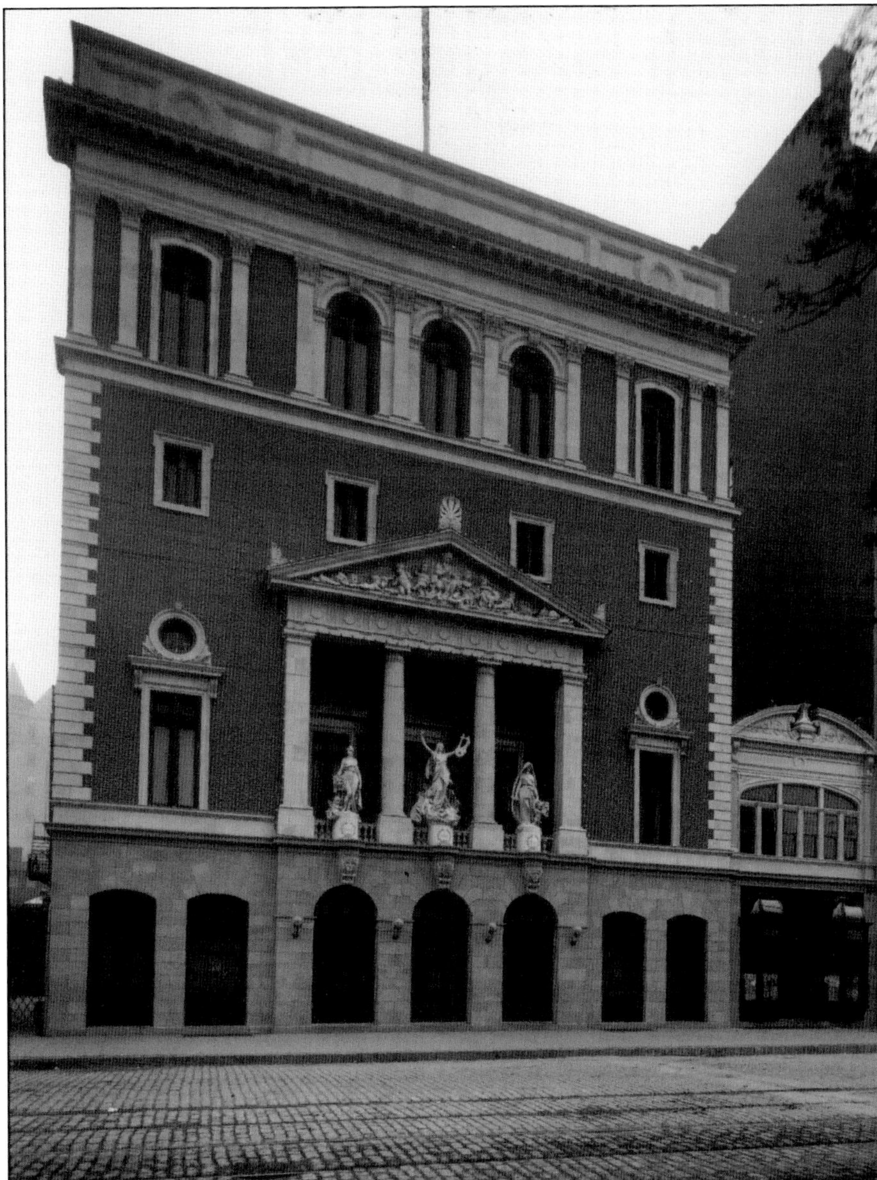

Newark's newest version of the Empire Theatre was once, along with Minsky's, one of the city's top burlesque houses. In the late 1930s, the 2,000-seat Washington Street venue featured such headliners as "Bozo" Snyder and Hinda Wassau. The accompanying feature flick was 1933's *Hallelujah, I'm a Bum*, by then re-released under the title *The Heart of New York*. By 1957, headlines read, "Bye, Bye Burlesque," after the US Supreme Court upheld Newark's ban on stripping. The next year, the one-time palace was being readied for demolition to make way for parking. One reporter had particular fun with the story: "There will be different greases and paints, with tail fins and monstrous headlights to replace body adornments of yesteryear that never failed to elicit gasps of unbelief and whistles of sheer admiration. Where rafters once rang with cries of 'take it off,' attendants will command patrons to 'leave it right there.' Gone forever will be the hawker whose boxes of popcorn always contained 'valuable' prizes, invariably those mysterious glasses through which one could 'see anything.' " (Courtesy of the New Jersey Historical Society.)

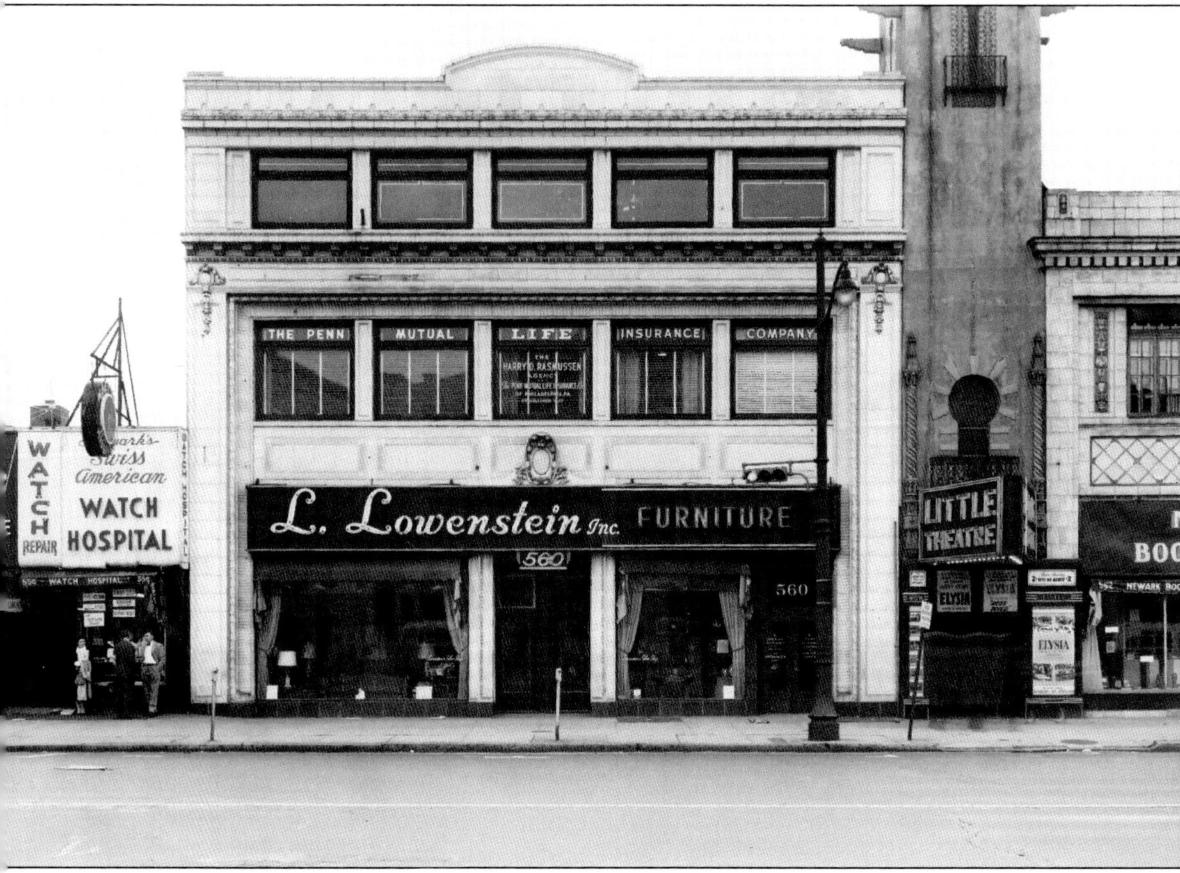

On August 22, 1928, an artist's illustration of the Little Theatre appeared in newspapers, heralding the arrival of the Broad Street venue across from Newark's Washington Park. The 299-seat theater, said to be patterned on the style of the Fifth Avenue Playhouse in New York, is credited to architects Harris & Sohn. The creation of the theater for "photoplays" was spearheaded by the Newark Motion Picture Guild. The features were to be of foreign origin, in particular from Germany, and "will be of a character that will appeal, it is believed, to patrons because of their unusual subjects and artistic quality," stated a press report. (Courtesy of the New Jersey Historical Society/William Cone Collection.)

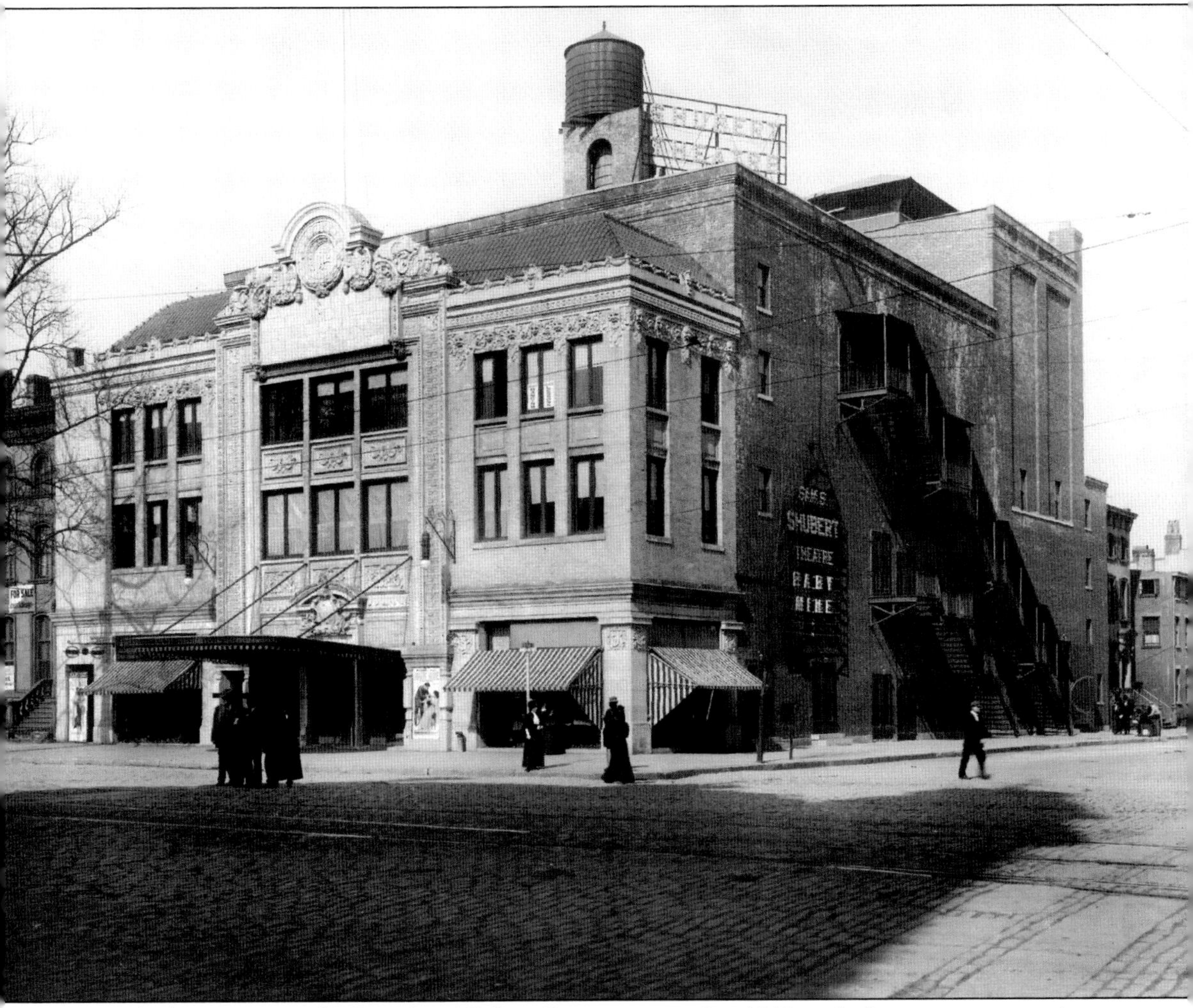

The Schubert, at Newark's Broad and Fulton Streets, opened in 1912, with the stage presentation *The Henpecks*, starring Lew Fields. In its day, famed actress Helen Hayes, early in her career, took to its stage in *Coquette*, as Ethel Merman did later in the musical *Take a Chance*. As it was being built, it was dubbed the "most beautiful and costliest" theater in the region and in a few years was showing *Baby Mine*, a silent film based on Margaret Mayo's 1910 Broadway comedy. By the next decade, the venue had been renamed the Broad Street Theatre, which in 1922 during the administration of Pres. Warren Harding was the locale of an anti-lynching rally intended to sway the president to "use all the powers of the presidency to immediately bring to an end all the persecutions that innocent citizens were subjected to," according to a 1970 newspaper retrospective. By late 1952, the headlines revealed its fate: "Exit Broad Theater, Old Showhouse, Host to Stage Greats, Making Way for Parking Lot." (Courtesy of the New Jersey Historical Society/William Cone Collection.)

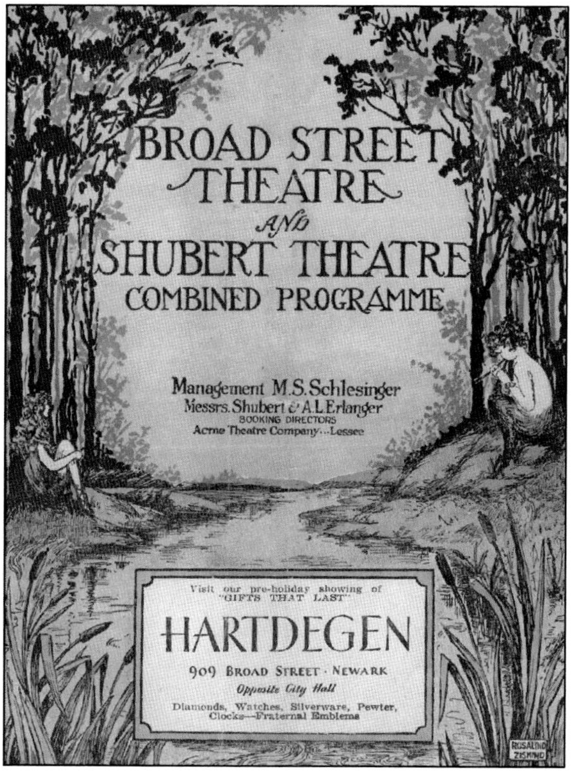

The Broad Street Theatre in Newark featured silent-film notable Elsie Ferguson on stage in *The Last Lover* during the 1928–1929 season. Its stage also featured a pre-Broadway performance of *Luckee Girl*, starring famed actress Irene Dunn. (Author's collection.)

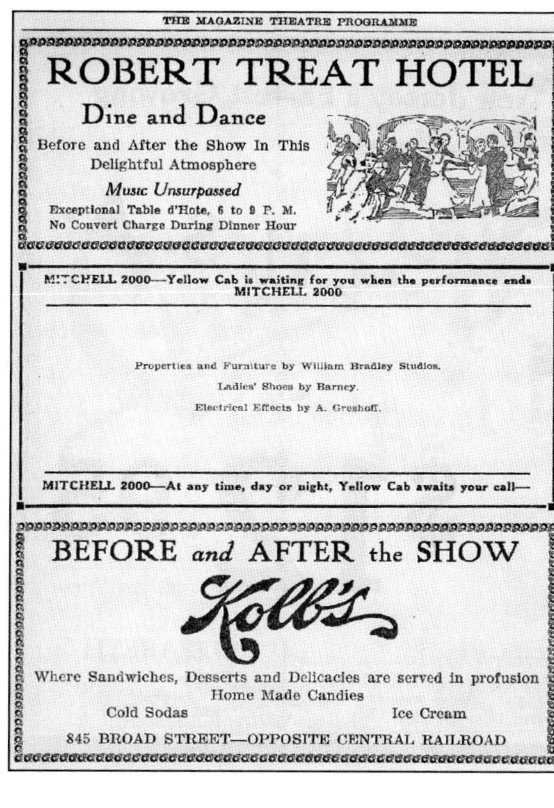

THE MAGAZINE THEATRE PROGRAMME

ROBERT TREAT HOTEL

Dine and Dance

Before and After the Show In This Delightful Atmosphere

Music Unsurpassed

Exceptional Table d'Hote, 6 to 9 P. M.
No Couvert Charge During Dinner Hour

MITCHELL 2000—Yellow Cab is waiting for you when the performance ends MITCHELL 2000

Properties and Furniture by William Bradley Studios.

Ladies' Shoes by Barney.

Electrical Effects by A. Greshoff.

MITCHELL 2000—At any time, day or night, Yellow Cab awaits your call—

BEFORE *and* AFTER the SHOW

Kolb's

Where Sandwiches, Desserts and Delicacies are served in profusion
Home Made Candies
Cold Sodas Ice Cream

845 BROAD STREET—OPPOSITE CENTRAL RAILROAD

The program for the season was a reflection of commerce in Newark's downtown. The Robert Treat Hotel featured "music unsurpassed" before and after the show. Among the others were Palais Joy, dubbed "Newark's Most Beautiful Chinese-American Restaurant," at 807–813 Broad Street, and the Washington Restaurant, with its tearoom and soda shop directly opposite the Broad Street Theatre. (Author's collection.)

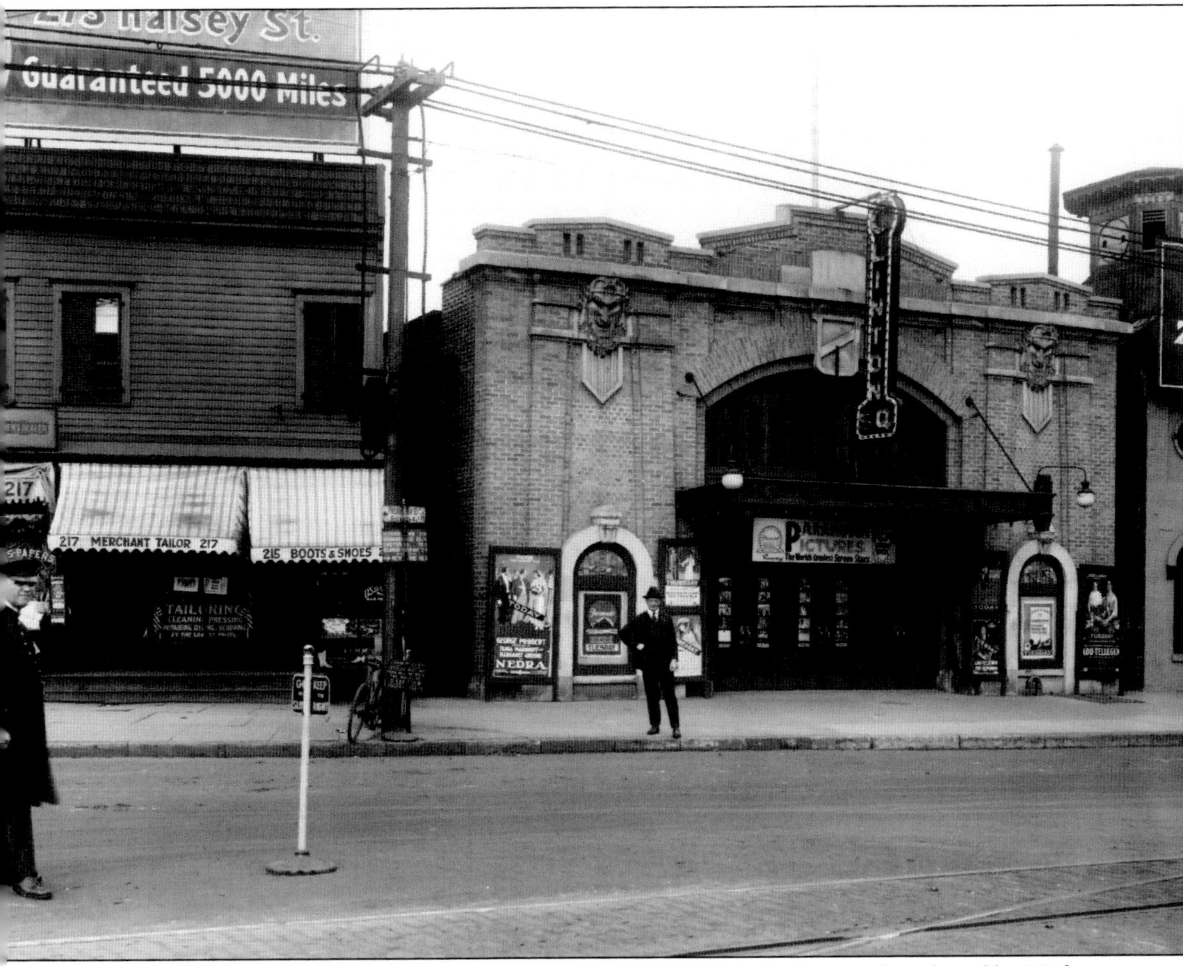

In 1915, the Clinton Square Theatre in Newark featured George Probert in the silent film *Nedra*, a melodrama that lands an engaged couple on an isolated island after their ship goes down in a storm. The film was based on a popular novel by George Barr McCutcheon. The directional sign on the telephone pole notes that New York is just 10 miles away. (Courtesy of the New Jersey Historical Society.)

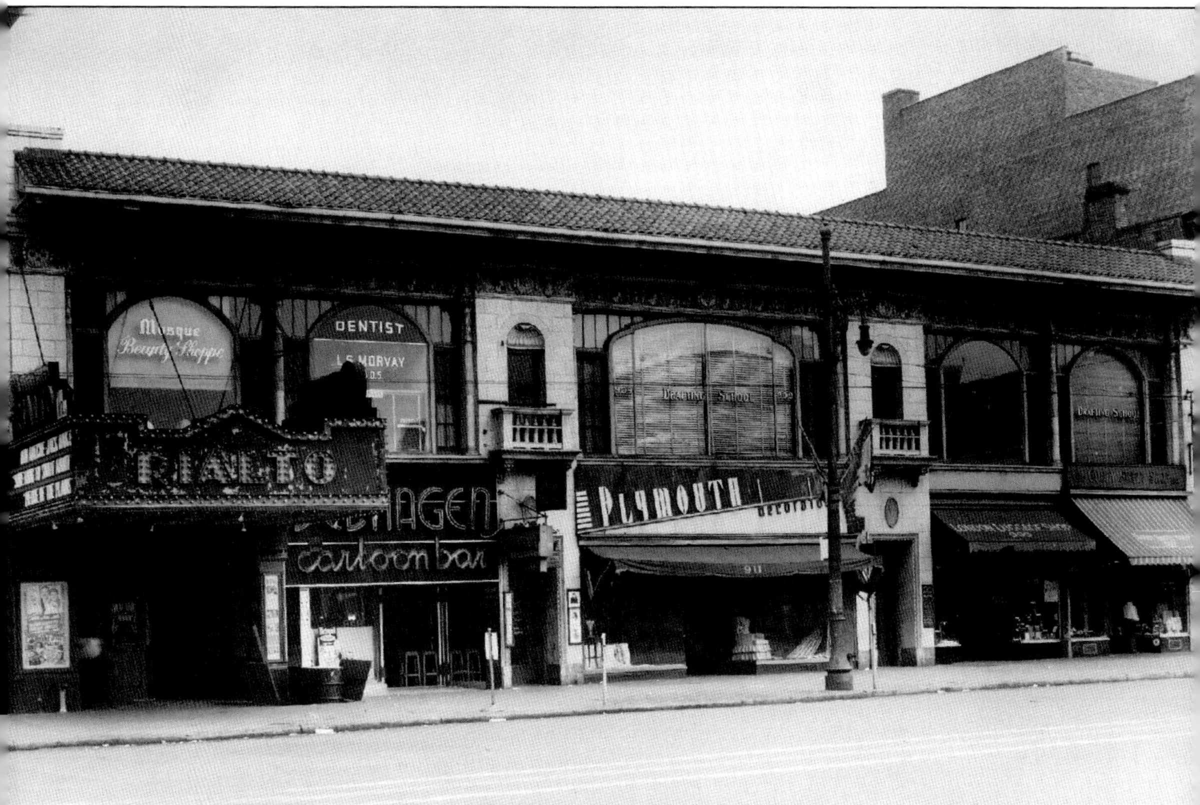

The 2,000-seat Rialto on Newark's Broad Street was dedicated in 1920 with manager Max Spiegel at one point taking the stage. The applause was so great, wrote a newspaper reporter, that it "must have warmed the cockles of his heart." A half-century later, the theater, at 863 Broad Street, was referred to as a "hangout for school truants" until its transformation into a bargain store. (Courtesy of the Newark Public Library.)

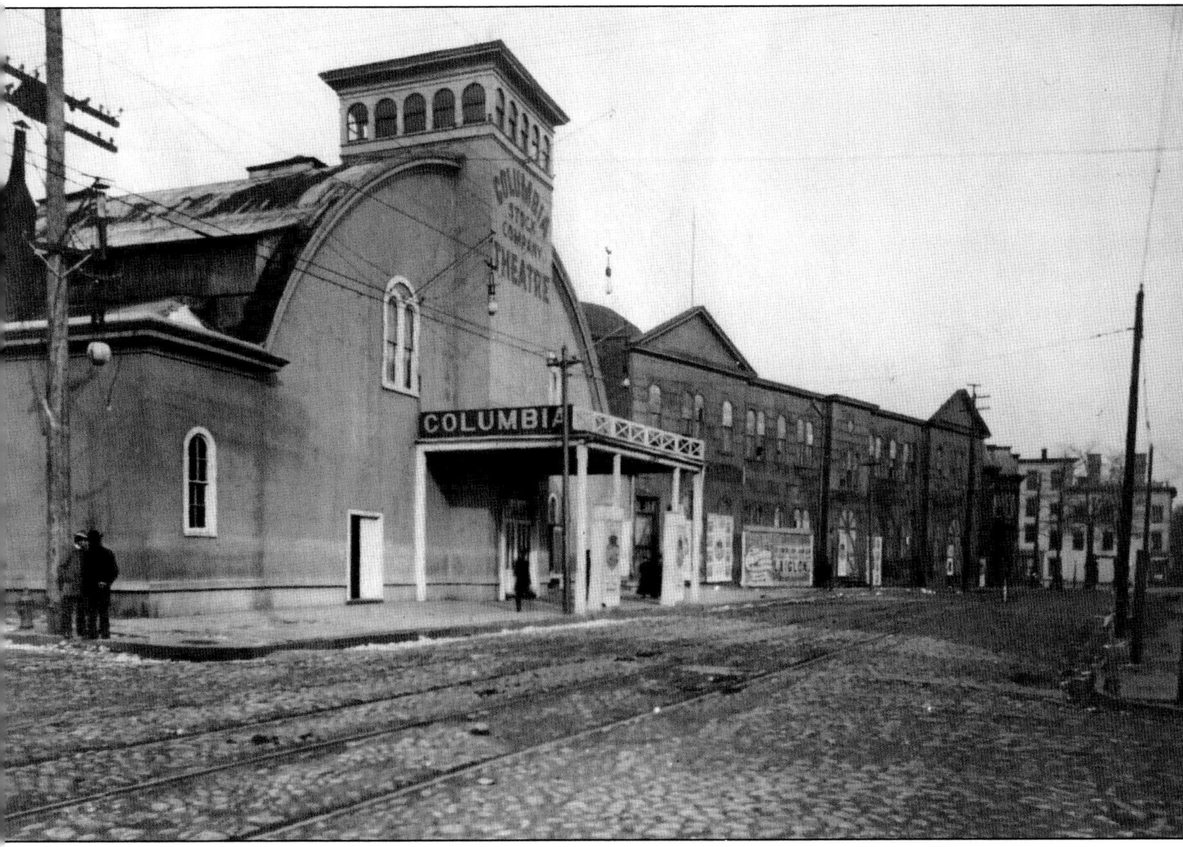

The Columbia Theatre on Newark's Washington Street was converted to the Grand Opera House in 1878 but by 1910 was reopened as the Orpheum, according to a 1959 *Newark News* article. In 1915, it was showing the silent film short *She Took a Chance* and feature *The Scarlet Sin*, starring Hobart Bosworth as a minister who aims to put the fear of God into residents of a wide-open mining town. At the time, its orchestra pit was concealed by foliage and a Japanese garden in front of the newly installed screen. During film intermissions, a 15-piece band, a soprano, and a vocal quartet entertained the audience. In August 1963, the c. 1873 theater was abandoned and ready to be demolished. "Now the phantom of opera departs" read the newspaper article in an account ended with the words "Goodbye honey!" A skating rink was erected in its place. (Courtesy of the New Jersey Historical Society/William Broadwell Collection.)

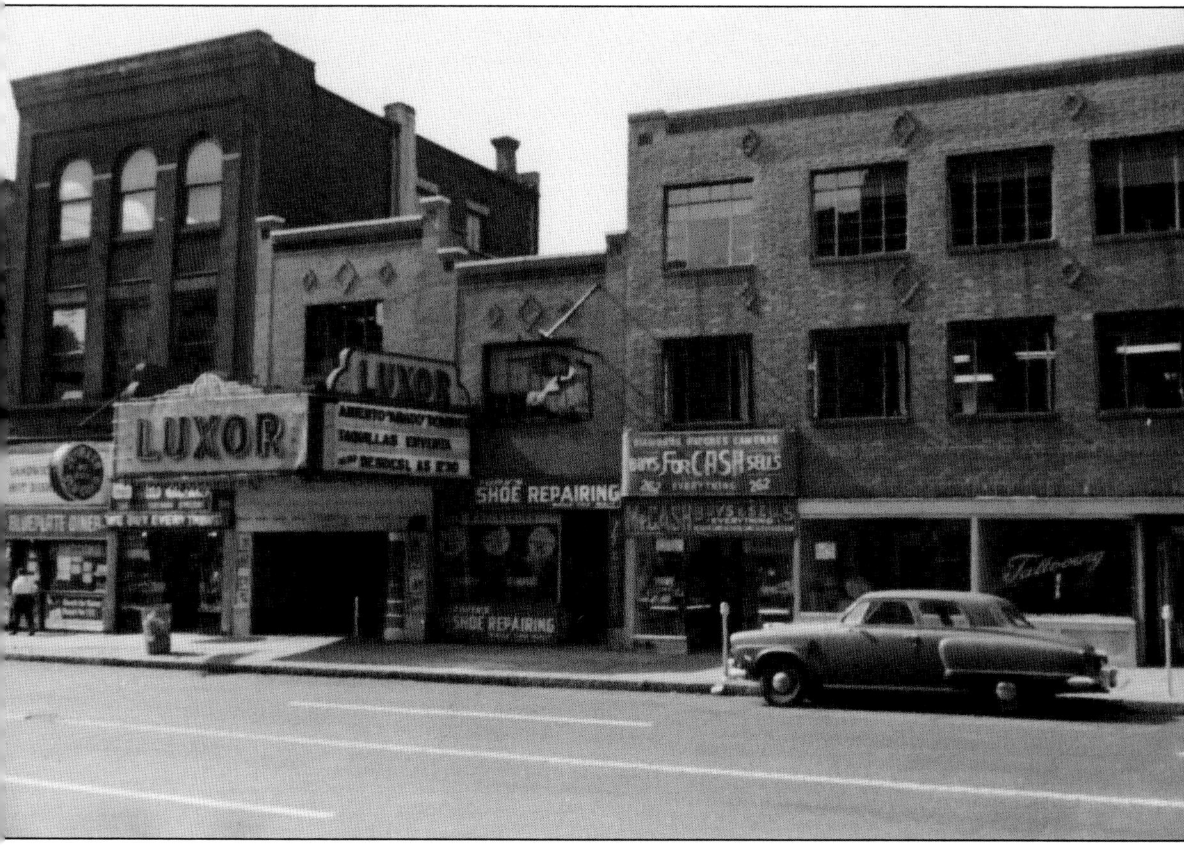

The Luxor Theatre, at 266 Market Street in Newark, opened in the early 1930s but was making headlines in the mid-1960s as the "Luxor Follies." Detectives repeatedly raided the locale on charges of showing obscene movies, such as *Super Dreams* and *Erotica.* In fact, the fallout resulted in a trial for the theater manager and, as evidence, the showing of the films to an Essex County jury during a four-day trial in March 1965. The verdict was guilty. The next month, the manager of the 500-seat movie house was fined $1,000 and given a one-year suspended jail sentence. Still, come October, detectives were back, posing as theatergoers in a "study" of a pre-show performance by the star of the about-to-be-shown film *Secrets of a Cover Girl.* The "bumps and grinds" performance, according to a press report, was determined to be simply too much. The performer and, again, the theater manager were arrested. "Police stressed that the week's activities by the detectives at the Luxor were strictly in the line of duty," read the news article. Before long, however, the 500-seat theater was deemed a prime target for demolition to make way for an urban renewal project around Newark's Penn Station. (Courtesy of the Newark Public Library.)

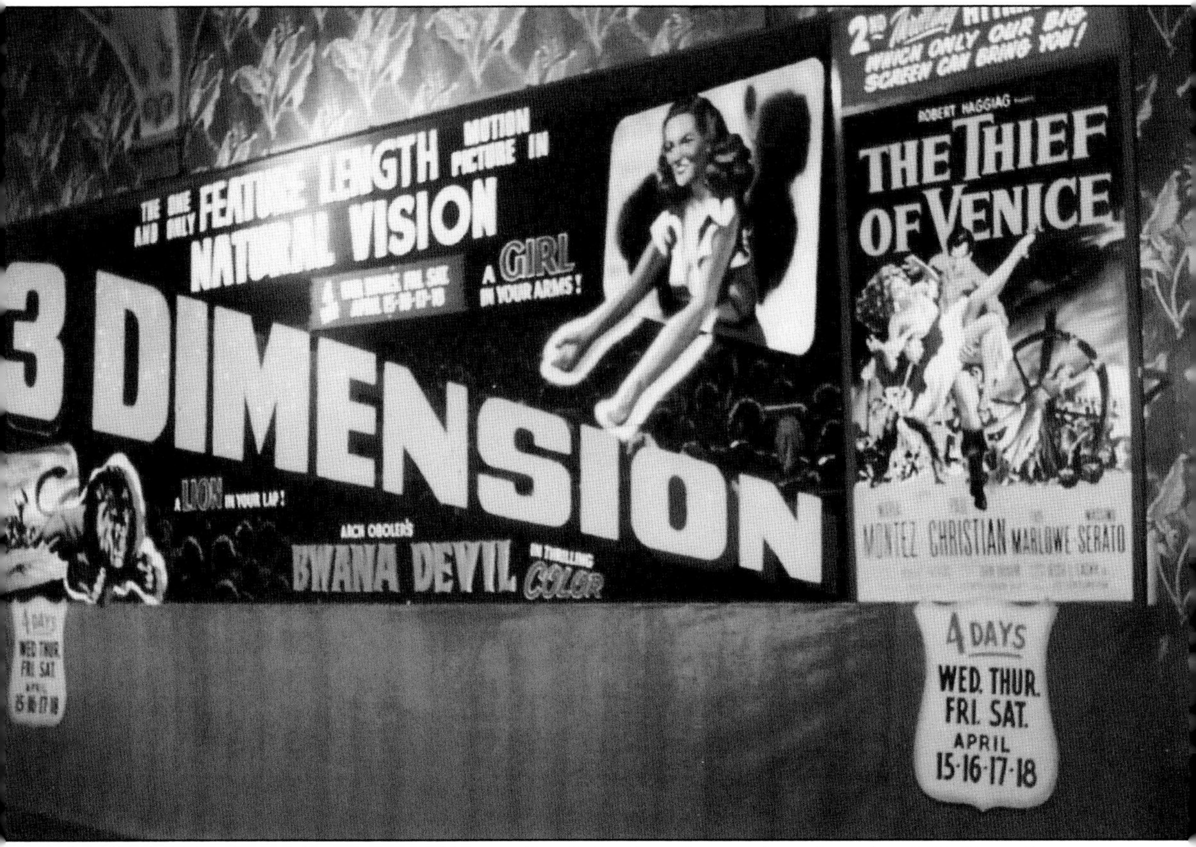

One had to don special eyewear for *Bwana Devil*, the first feature-length, color, 3-D film, when it was projected on the screen at the Trivoli in 1953. The poster promised "A Girl in Your Arms!" and "A Lion in Your Lap!" The matinee also included *The Thief of Venice*, a 1950 Italian-made adventure film. (Courtesy of Skip Borsos.)

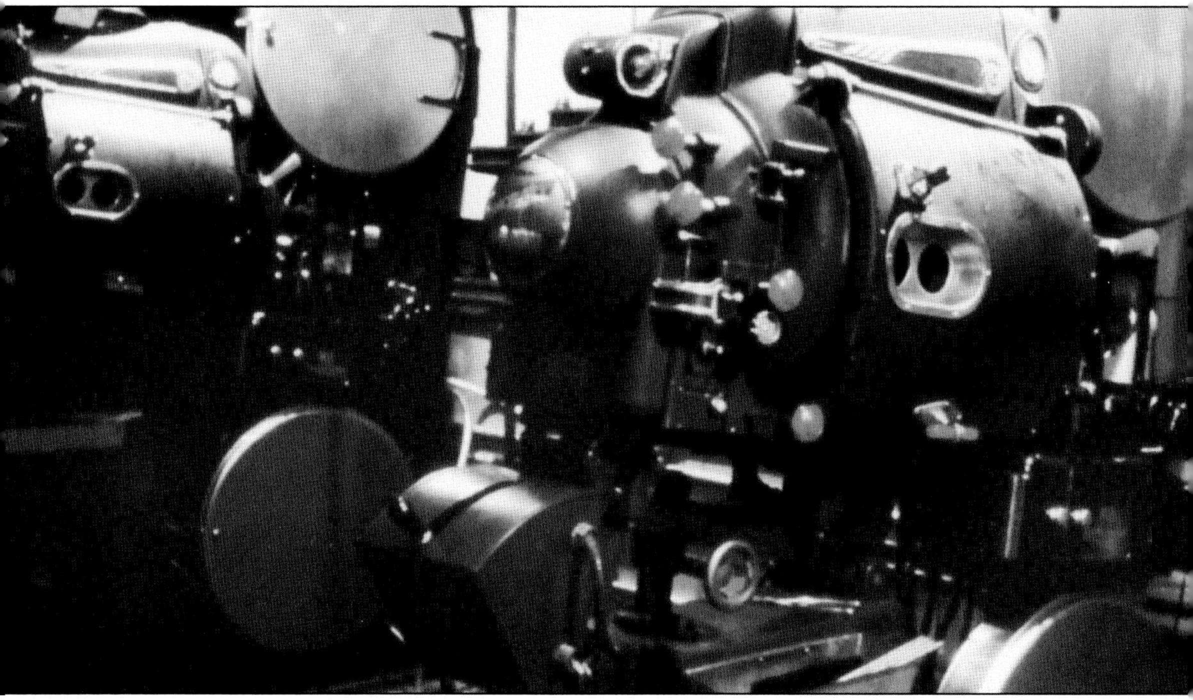

This projector is seen at work at the Trivoli, but it was not the only essential equipment. "The Tivoli also had a Wurlitzer organ, and I'm not sure why, but it was never played when I was there," said filmmaker Ron Merk. "When the theater was torn down to be replaced by an ugly building, I don't know what happened to that organ, but I hope it was saved and living someplace else." (Courtesy of Skip Borsos and Ron Merk.)

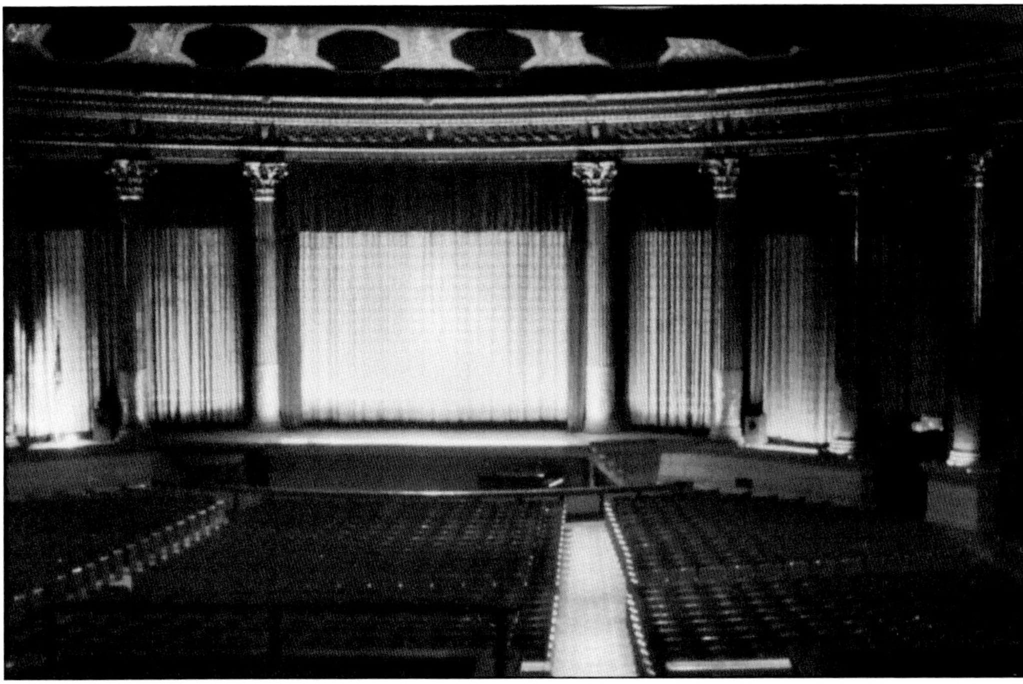

The Trivoli's lounge and auditorium were something to behold in the 1950s, recalls Ron Merk. "It was quite an awesome sight to watch the curtain open and close over the big screen, which it did at the beginning and end of every film. I remember watching the effects of people smoking in the loge as the light beams from the projector went through them. You could see the smoke whirling on the screen." (Courtesy of Skip Borsos and Ron Merk.)

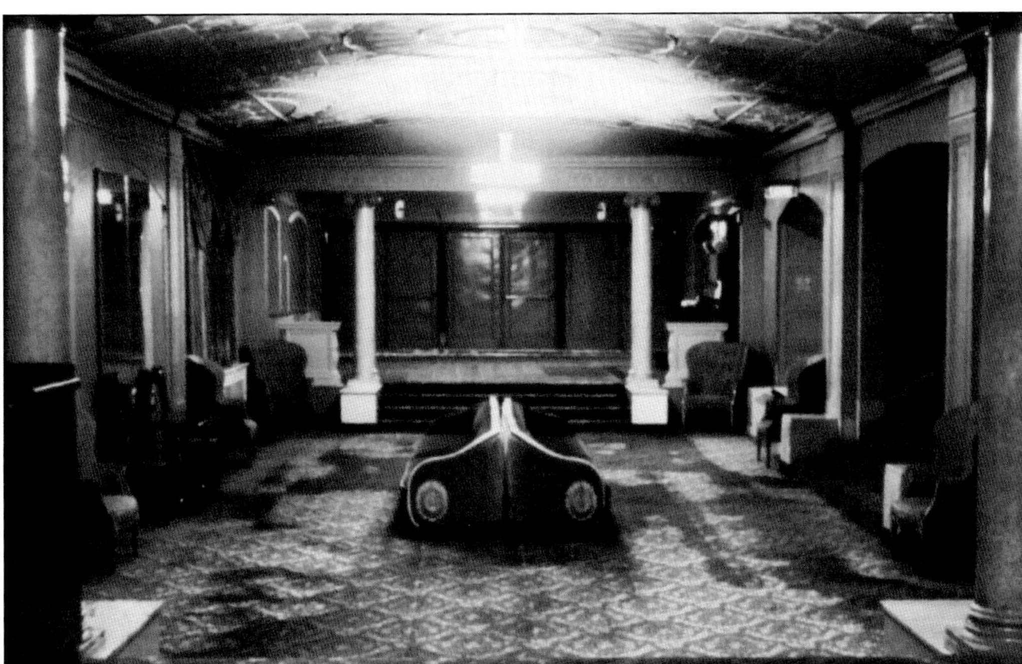

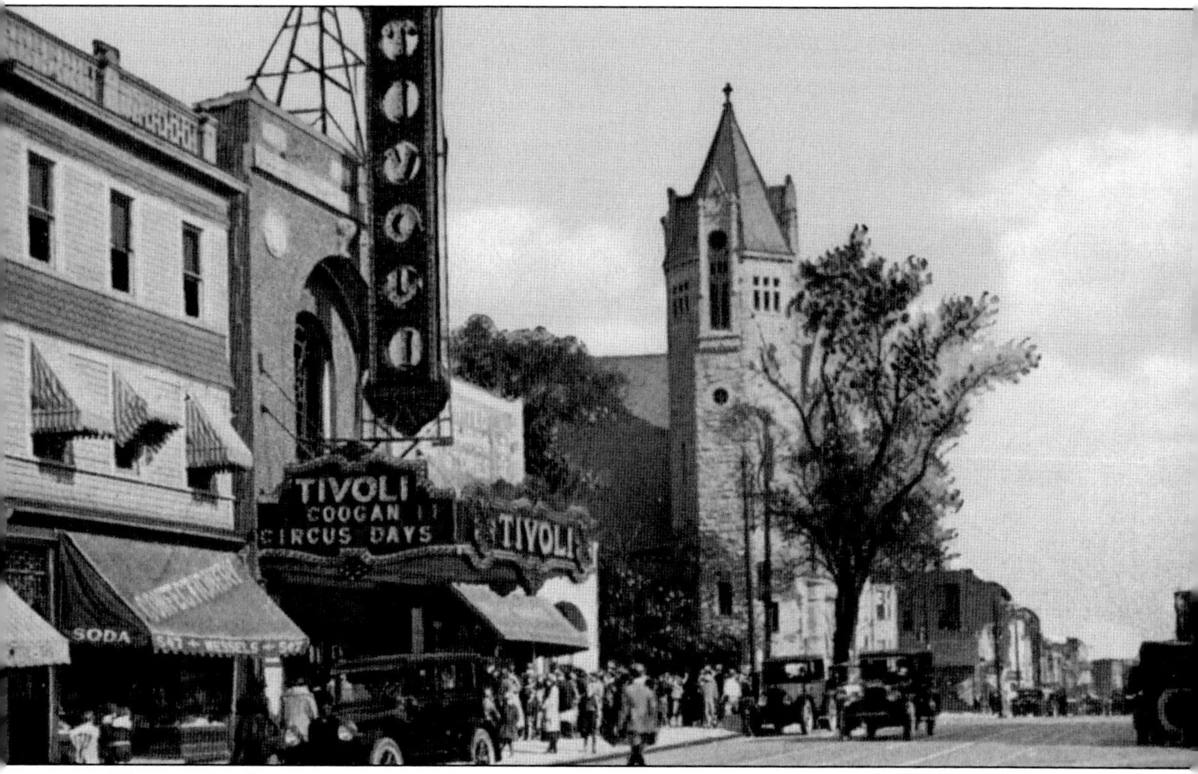

The Tivoli Theatre, on Orange Street in Newark's Roseville section, was one of the many movie houses operated by Joseph Stern, whose long list of properties included the Castle Theatre in Irvington and the Lincoln Theatre in Bloomfield. In 1923, his Tivoli featured *Circus Days*, starring child star Jackie Coogan as Toby Tyler. In later life, Coogan portrayed Uncle Fester in the television series *The Addams Family*, which ran from 1964 to 1966. (Author's collection.)

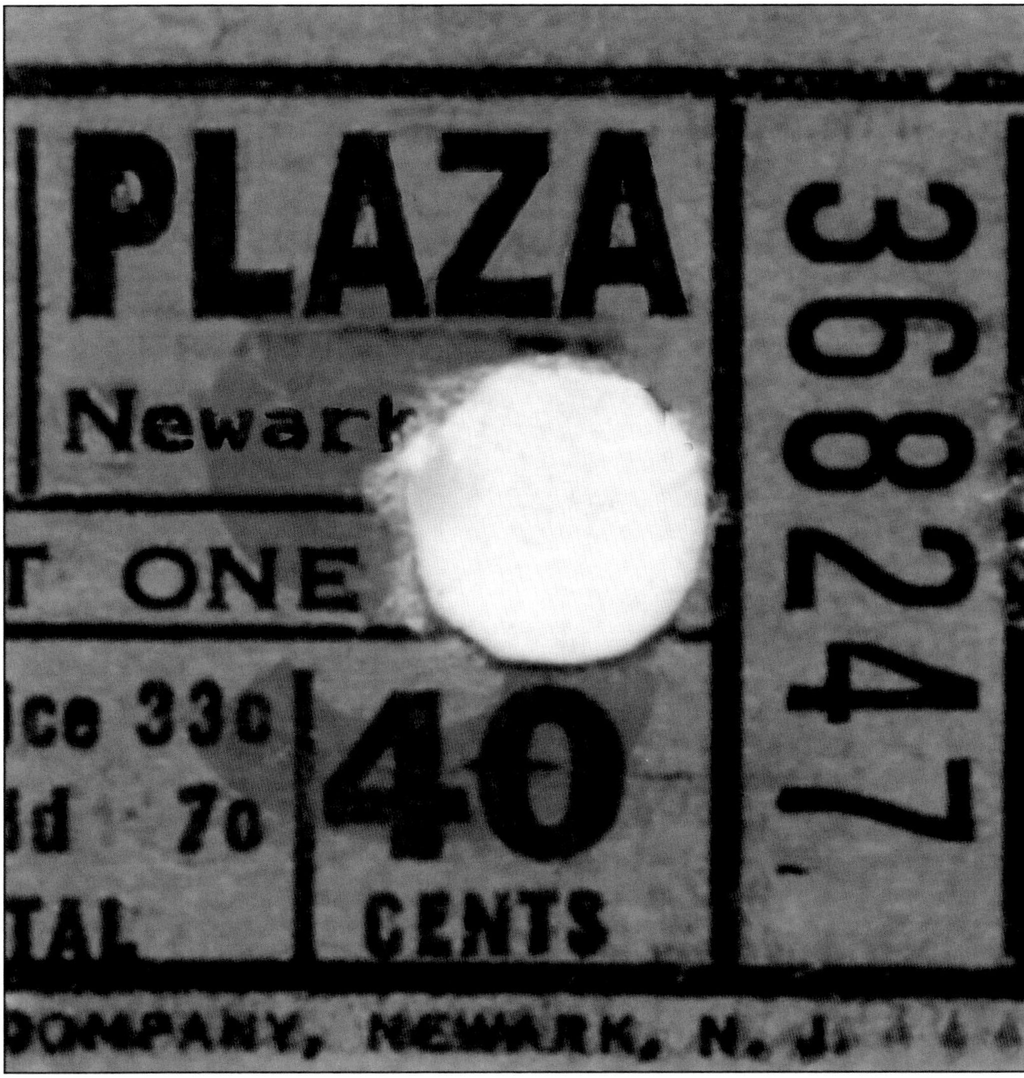

Theatergoers could get into the Plaza for a mere 40¢ in the 1950s in Newark's Roseville neighborhood. (Courtesy of Skip Borsos.)

PLAZA

THEATRE

"The Littlest Theatre Around the Corner

129 NO. 7th ST., NEWARK, N. J.

HUmboldt 3-9717

Free Parking — cor. 7th St. & 7th Av

The Plaza was known as "The Littlest Theatre around the Corner." (Courtesy of Skip Borsos.)

Two

SUBURBAN ESSEX

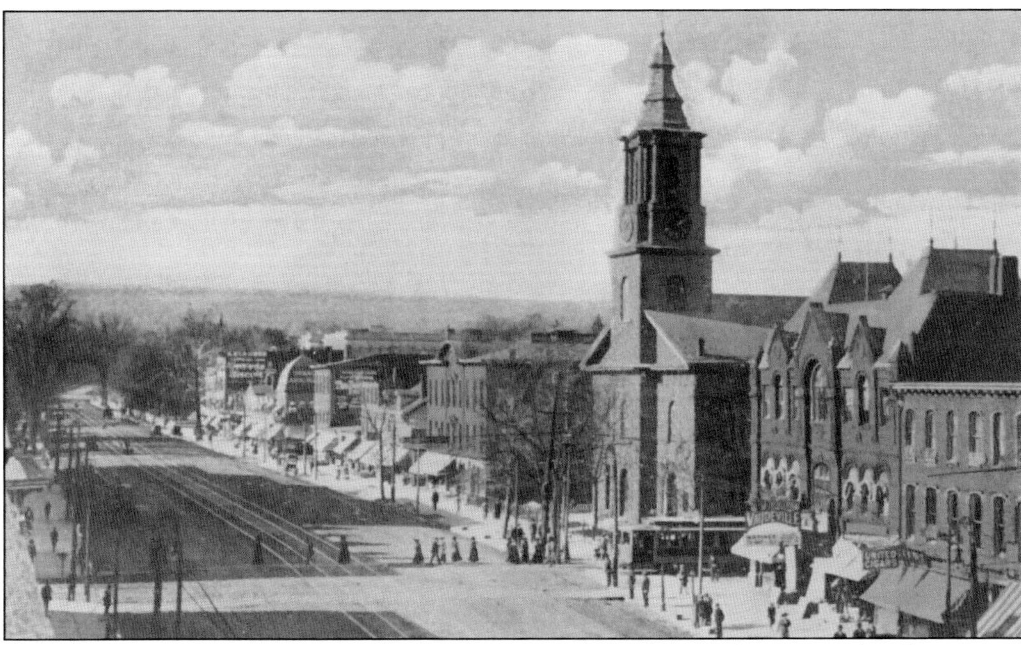

In 1906, the entire ranks of the Princeton Alumni Association went by train and trolley to arrive at the Orange Music Hall for a benefit performance of the Triangle Club's staging of *Tabasco Land*, whose musical numbers included "I'm All Alone," "My Parasol," and "Shifty Sadie." The performance benefited the Orange Scholarship Fund. The theater also had a minor connection to early filmdom, when in 1888 a British photographer named Eadweard Muybridge, fresh from giving an Orange theater lecture titled "Animals in Motion," met with Thomas A. Edison to discuss pairing Edison's photograph with Muybridge's system of projecting rapid images on to a screen to give the impression of motion. (Author's collection.)

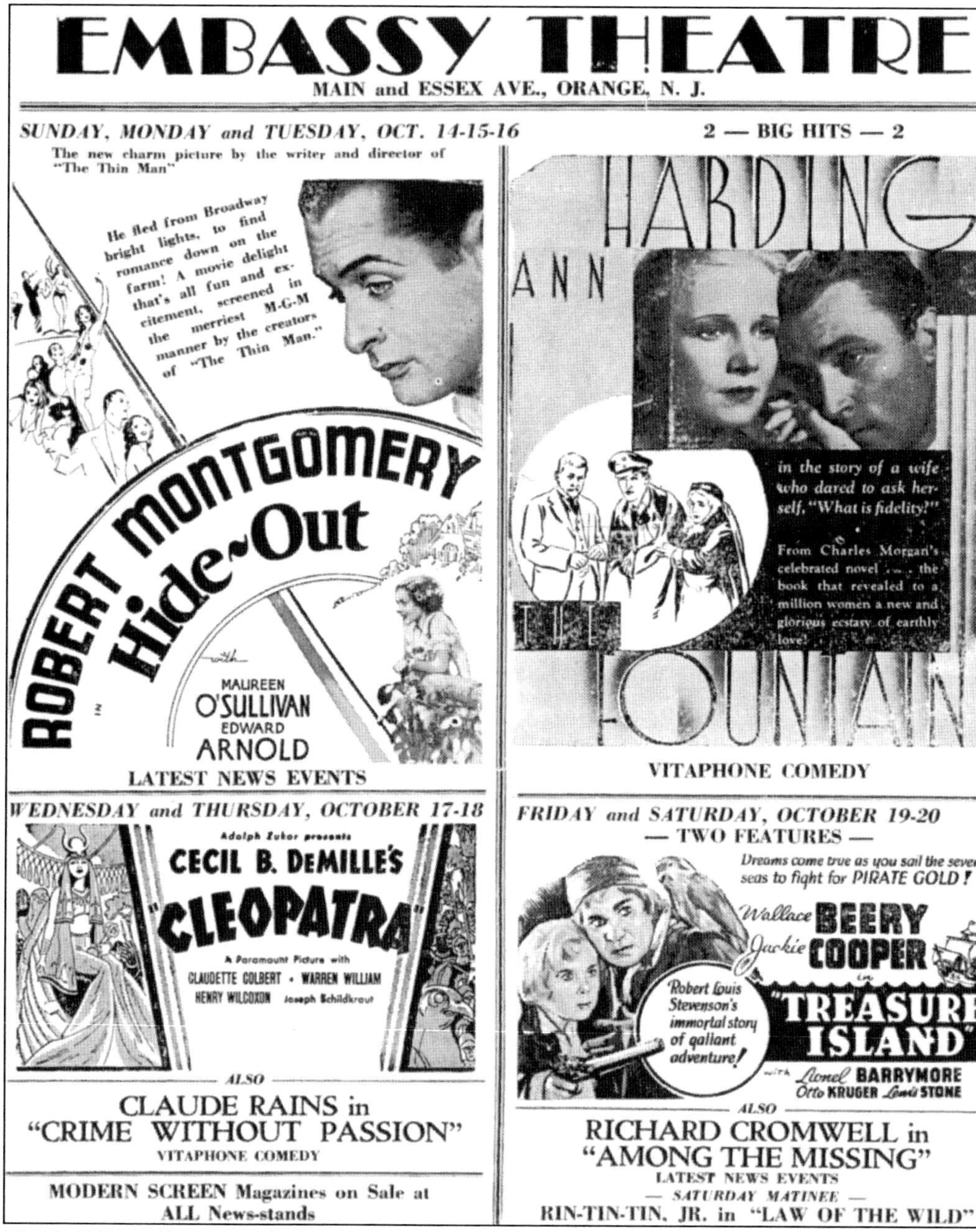

The 2,073-seat Embassy Theatre in Orange, which opened in 1925, was plugging the newest film releases in 1934, including Cecil B. DeMille's *Cleopatra*, starring Claudette Colbert. As an added bonus, the flip side of this advertisement included a seductive glossy of the actress, compliments of *Modern Screen Magazine*. The theater, though, like so many others, fell on hard times and closed in the 1970s, followed by the removal of its marquee at 349 Main Street in 1990. By 2005, the theater was no more. "It was very attractive, but it was functionally obsolete," owner Dennis Monasebian told *Star-Ledger* staff writer Kevin Dilworth in an October 8, 2005, article. "Many people have stopped by to point out a spot in the theater where they had their first date and where they shared a kiss." (Author's collection.)

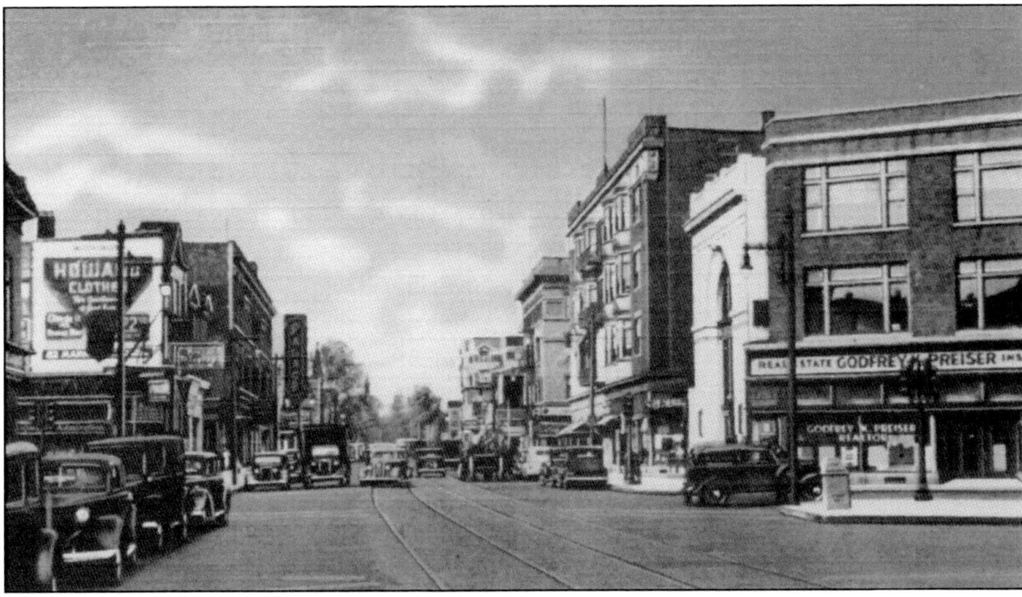

New Jersey downtowns were typical locales for movie houses, as seen in these postcard images from Orange, showing the c. 1880 Music Hall (below) and from neighboring East Orange, the marquee of the Palace in the distance (above). Among the many movie houses in the Newark suburb, the 2,073-seat Embassy on Orange's Main Street was demolished in 2005, years after the c. 1925 theater's last run. "It's kind of a shame. The inside was beautiful at one point," Dennis Monasebian, the property owner, said in a *Star-Ledger* newspaper story by Kevin Dilworth. Long before, one of the movie house's huge crystal chandeliers made it to the Highlawn Pavilion restaurant in nearby West Orange, as did the mural that once towered over the balcony. As for the Music Hall, it was renamed the Bijou and then the Royal before it was lost to a fire in 1927. (Author's collection.)

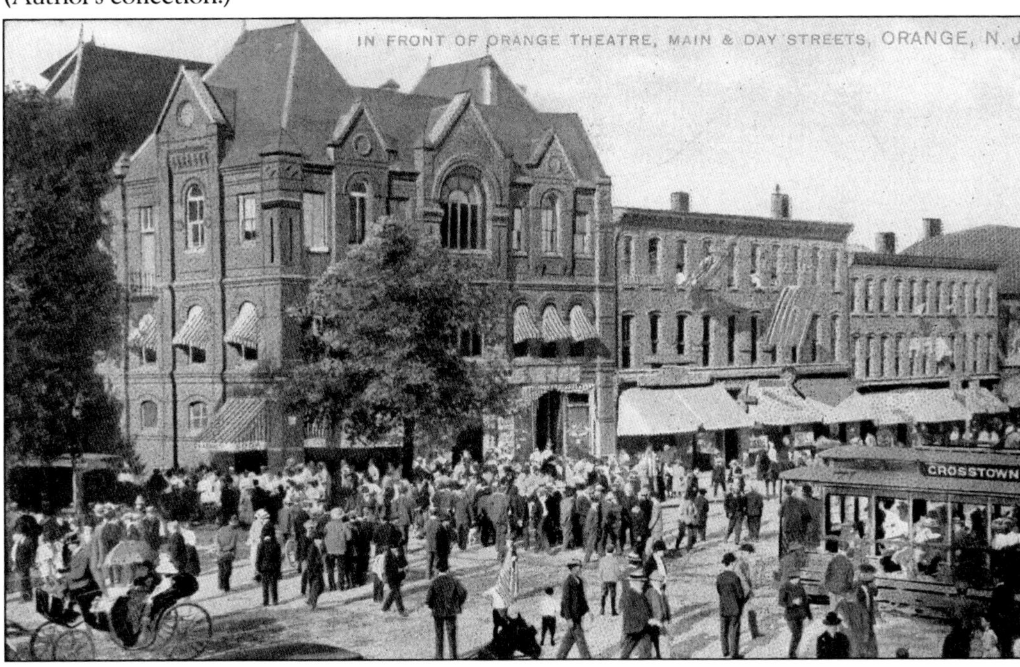

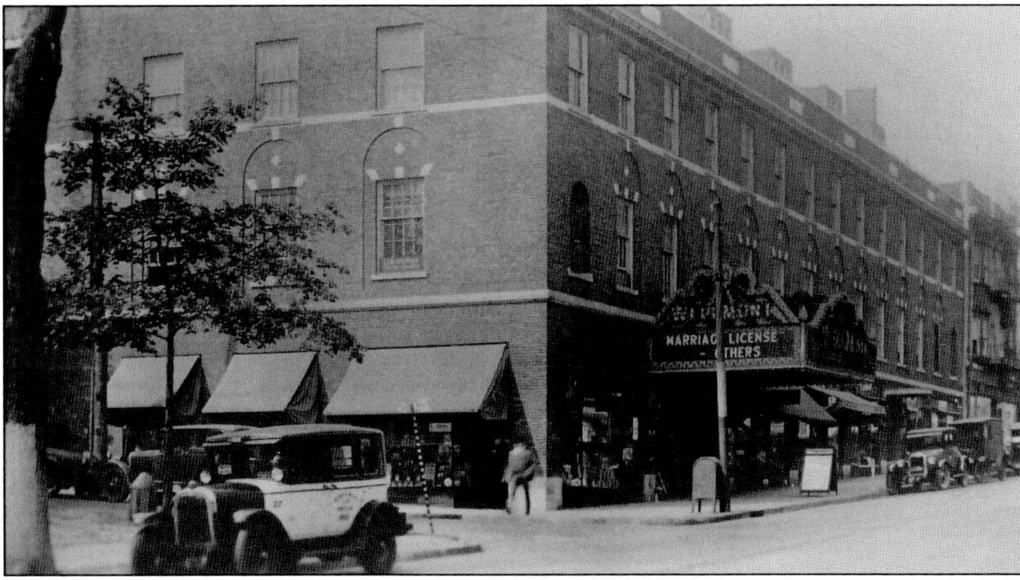

The Wellmont Theatre once fronted Montclair's busy Bloomfield Avenue before the main entrance was switched to a side street. Rare Italian marble was used in the construction of the lobby, according to an April 5, 1930, *Montclair Times* article. By 2008, workers were tearing away at the latter-day interior walls, revealing a grand 1922 stage obscured for decades by the screens of a shuttered triplex. Also intact was the ceiling's dome, a full 48 feet in diameter. Today, the restored theater features such talent as Crosby, Stills & Nash, as well as singer Tony Bennett and R&B artist Al Green. Yet, back in 1926, it was showing the silent film *Marriage License*, directed by Frank Borzage and starring, among others, young Walter Pidgeon, who in later life was featured in the 1956 matinee classic *Forbidden Planet*. (Courtesy of the Montclair Public Library, Newark Public Library.)

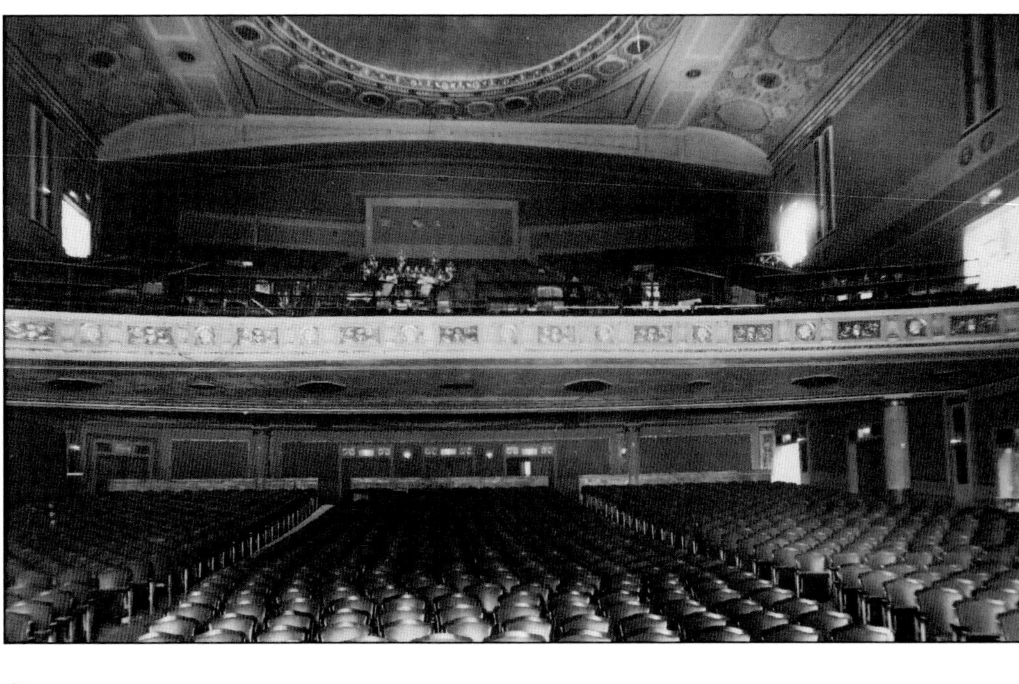

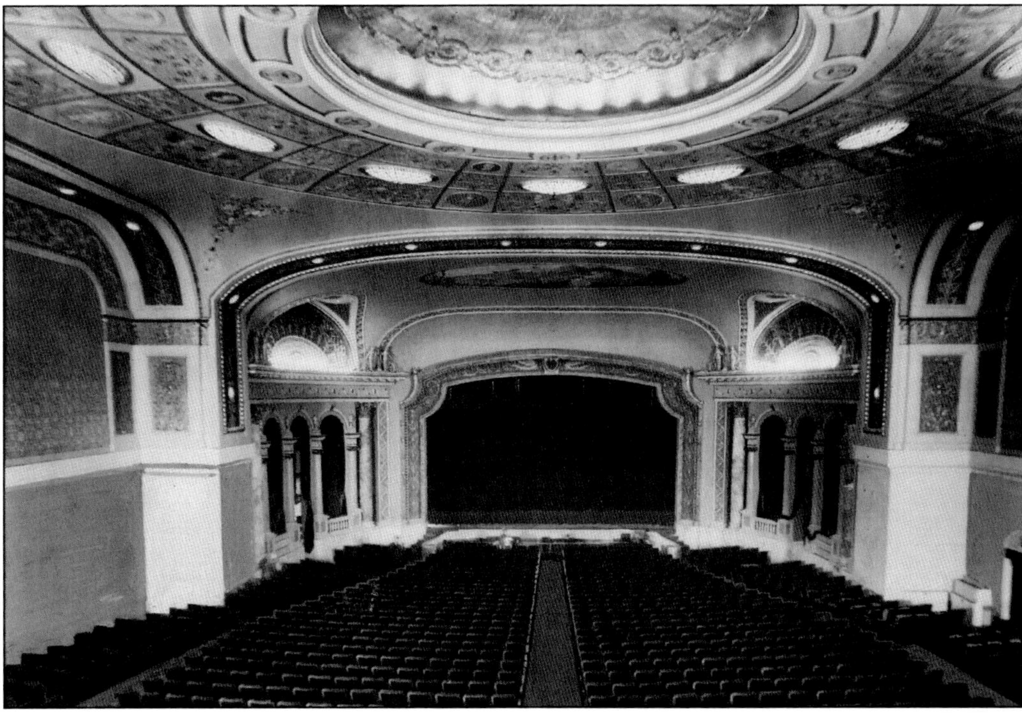

Just up the street from the Wellmont is the Clairidge, whose transformation to a multiplex in 1982 hid its ceiling from view in the landmark block-long Hinck Building at Montclair's "Six Corners." At the time, the theater's two-manual, 10-rank Wurlitzer organ, which occupied the Clairidge from 1923 before going silent with the arrival of "talking pictures," was donated to the New York Theater Organ Society. It is now on permanent loan to the Paramount in Middletown, New York. (Courtesy of the Newark Public Library.)

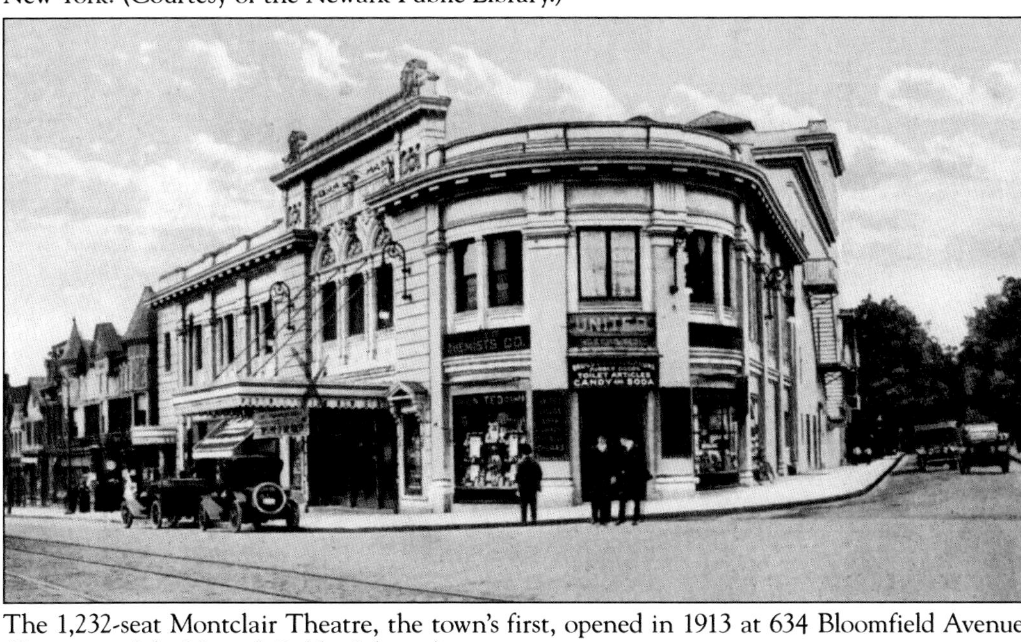

The 1,232-seat Montclair Theatre, the town's first, opened in 1913 at 634 Bloomfield Avenue. (Courtesy of the Newark Public Library.)

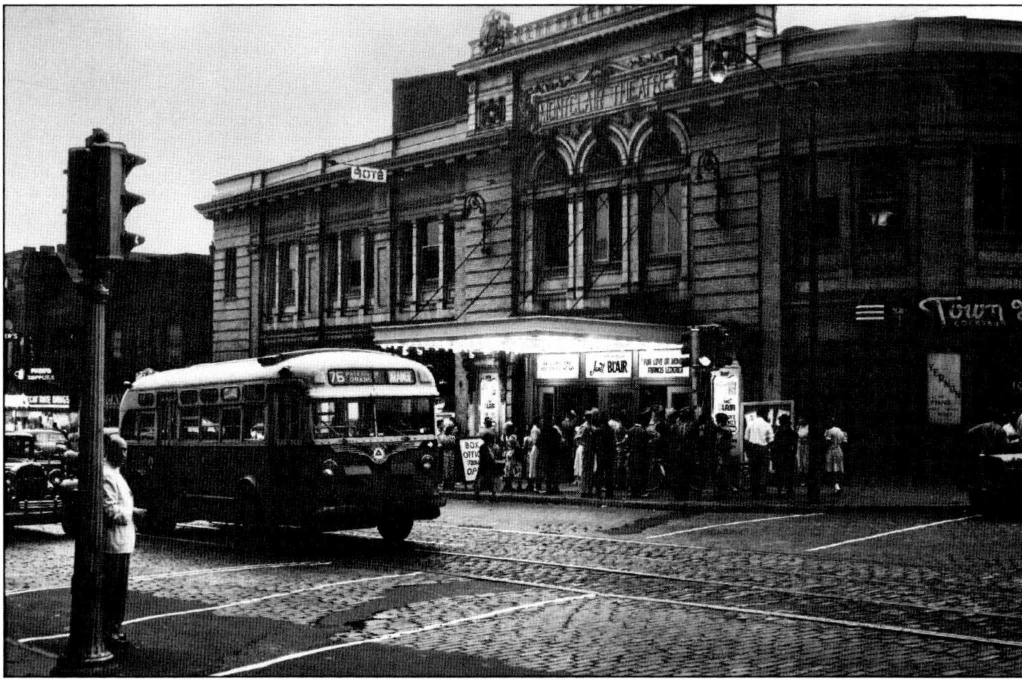

By the 1940s, as a No. 76 Orange-to-Paterson commuter bus rolled by, patrons lined up under the Montclair Theater marquee, whose lighted displays toted "Broadway and Hollywood Stars" and an appearance by Janet Blair, the vivacious star of Hollywood musicals. According to her 2007 obituary in *USA Today*, Blair played the love interest in *The Fabulous Dorseys*, starring bandleaders Jimmy and Tommy Dorsey, and appeared opposite Red Skelton in the 1946 sleeper hit *The Fuller Brush Man*. In 1948, she came to Montclair while on a national road tour with Francis Lederer in the F. Hugh Herbert stage comedy *For Love or Money*. (Courtesy of the Newark Public Library.)

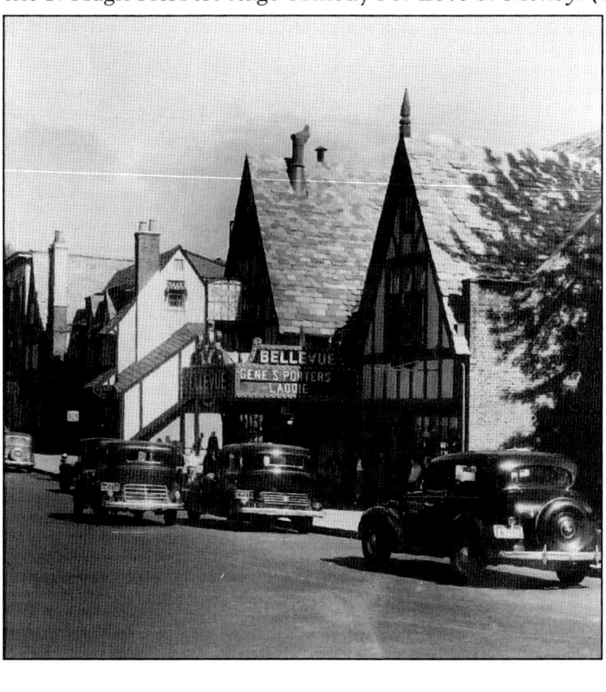

The marquee of the Bellevue Theatre in Upper Montclair Village features the 1935 film *Laddie*, a retelling of the Gene Porter novel featuring a romance between an Indiana farm boy and an English girl. The 1935 film version starring Gloria Stuart was described in a *New York Times* review as "a great bore but helpful as a sort of brief spiritual convalescence." The film was remade just five years later. (Courtesy of the Montclair Public Library/George French Collection.)

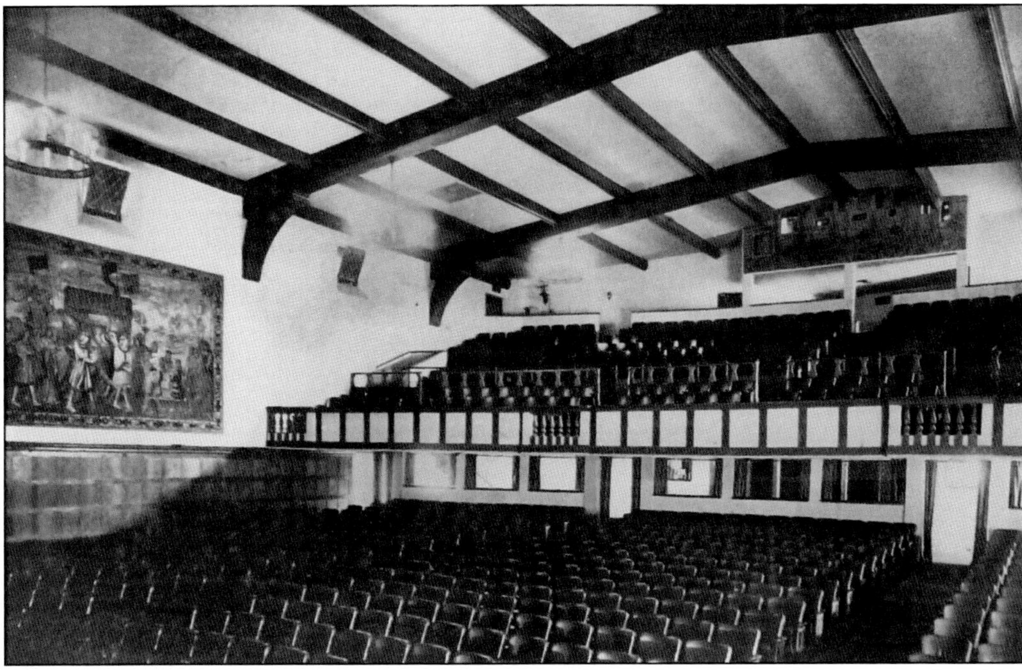

The Bellevue was designed by architect J.H. Phillips, whose offices were at 681 Fifth Avenue in New York. Photographs of the Tutor Revival–style theater, which cost $200,000 to erect, were featured in the June 1926 issue of *The Architect* magazine. Back in the 1960s, the theater's special attributes were said to include ushers in bright yellow blazers and tickets that actually got patrons an assigned seat. (Courtesy of the Montclair Public Library.)

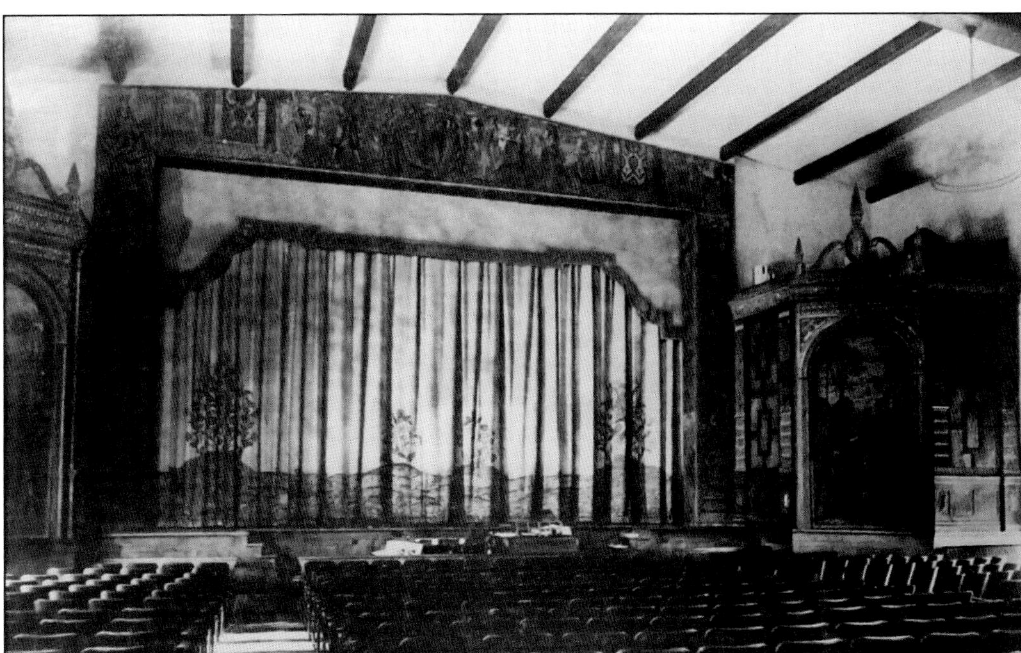

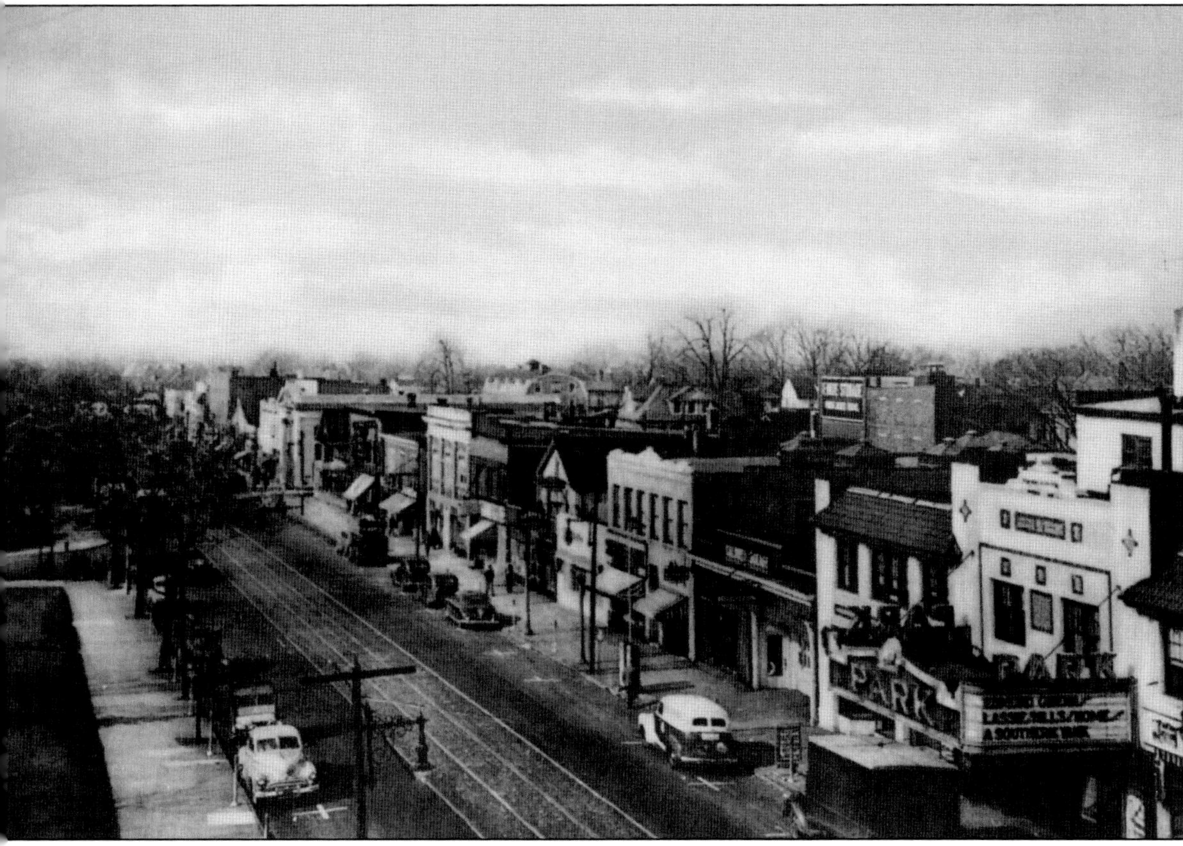

The feature *A Southern Yank*, a comedy starring Red Skelton, and an MGM production titled *Hills of Home*, starring the famous film canine Lassie, were the double billing at the Park Theater on Caldwell's Bloomfield Avenue back in 1948. Fast forward to 1973, and the theater's days were numbered. A spectacular fire on July 14, 1974, put an end to the venue, so fondly remembered by a one-time usher named Jeff Grimshaw. So much so that he published "Park Theater Confidential," a special, inside-story issue of his now defunct magazine, *Crystal Drum*. "I had few duties," he wrote, "and they rarely interfered with my movie watching, which after all was the raison d'etre of working as an usher. . . . From time to time you might be required to clean up spilled popcorn, or less frequently, mop up a mess in the bathroom; or stand in the lobby and rip tickets; or, once in great while, you might actually click on your flashlight and guide a late comer to a seat after the lights had gone down and the feature had started. That was about it." (Courtesy of the Newark Public Library.)

Three

Paterson

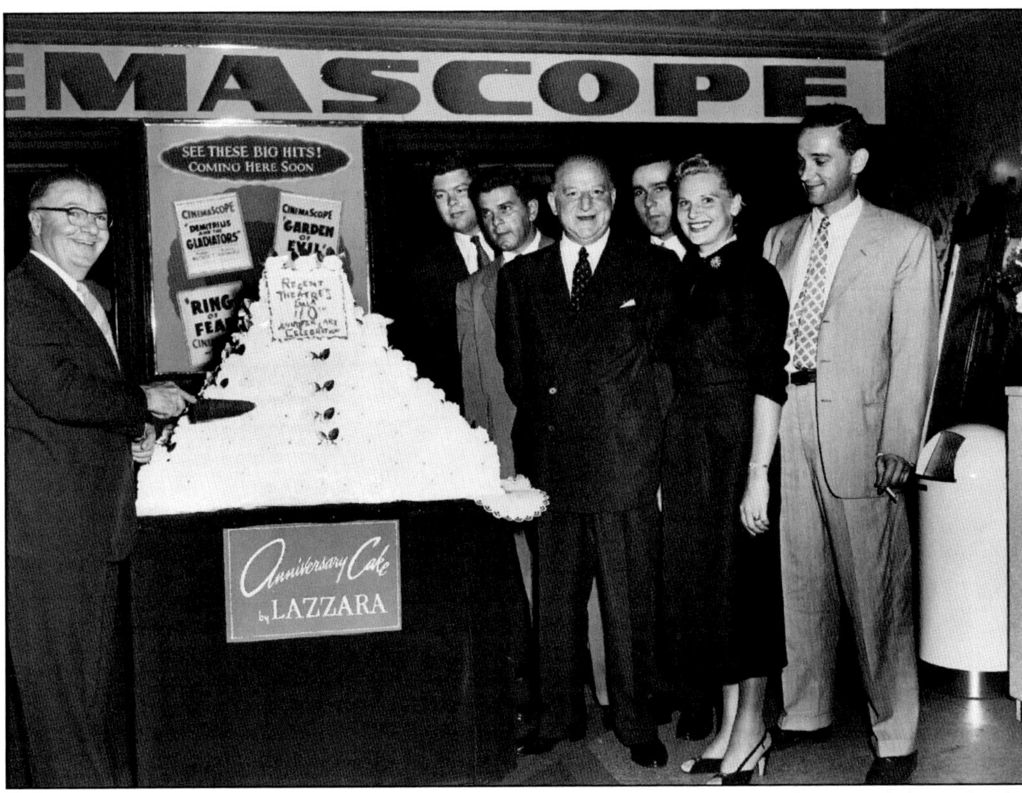

Outside the Regent Theatre in 1954, S.H. Fabian (center, son of Jacob Fabian and then chief of Stanley-Warner) came to mark 40 years since the Regent's opening. The "showman," as a newspaper headline described him, marked the event with an anniversary cake crafted by Lazzara Bakery, whose orange and green delivery trucks and "Tasty Crust Bread" sign were Paterson landmarks. One of the Cinema Scope ads on the "Coming Soon" board includes *Demetrius and the Gladiators*, the 1954 sequel to *The Robe*. The title role was played by actor Victor Mature, with costar Susan Hayward. (Courtesy of the Paterson Museum/Paterson News Collection.)

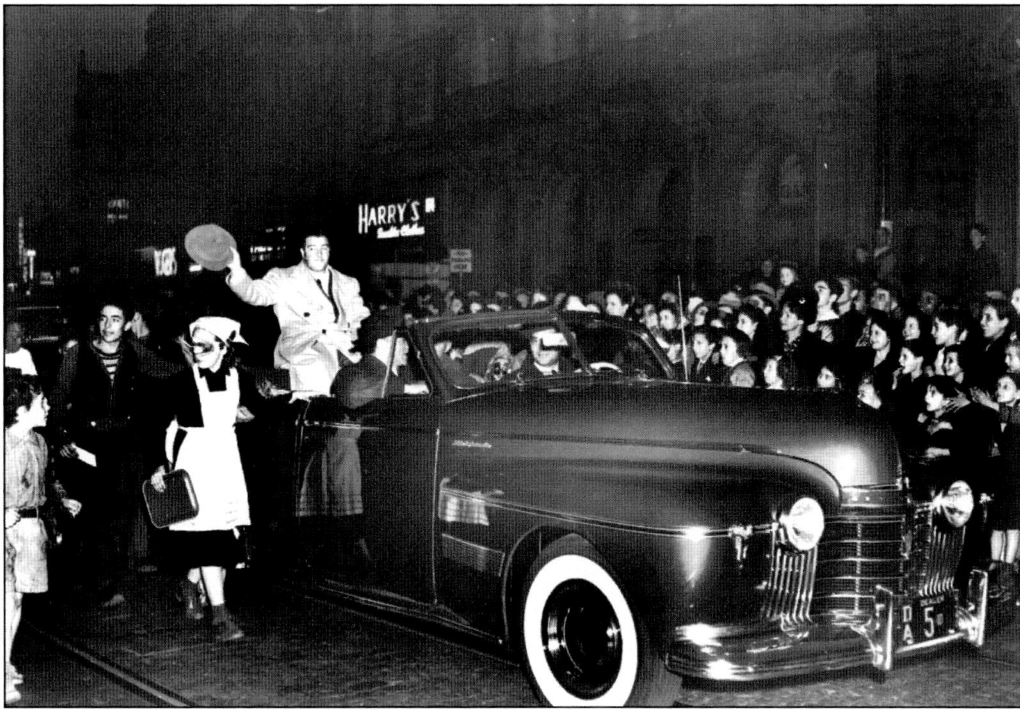

Lou Costello waves to his adorning fans during a motorcade to the Fabian Theatre for the premiere of the 1940 film *One Night in the Tropics*. Never one to forget his friends, Costello once asked Paterson's town fathers to give his old friend and one-time athlete John "Midge" Shields a six-week leave of absence from his job as a refuse truck driver so he could spend the time with Costello at his Van Nuys, California, home. "For six golden weeks, he visited every well-known place in Hollywood and was introduced to the celebrities on every movie location," wrote Fr. Anselm Krieger in an article in the Franciscan newspaper *Friar*. (Courtesy of the Passaic County Historical Society/Zito Collection.)

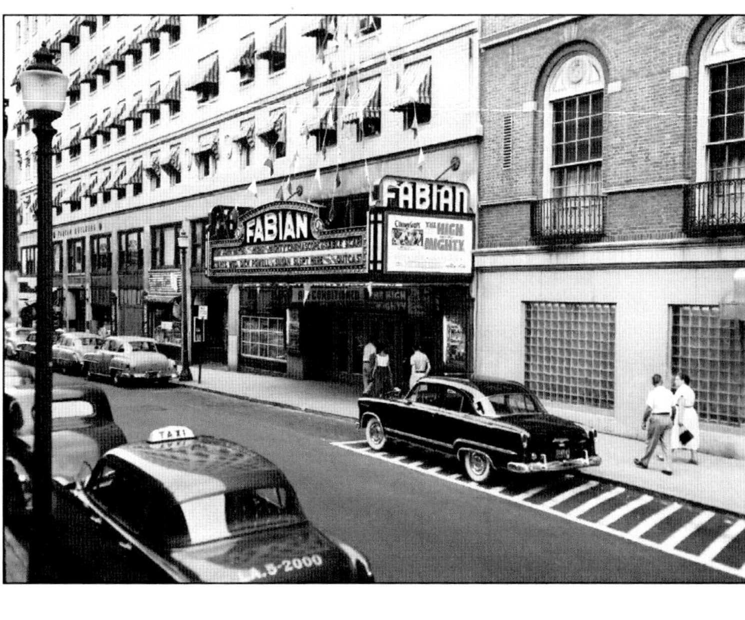

In August 1954, *Morning Call* photographer Russell Zito snapped this picture of the Fabian, then showing the airplane-disaster movie *The High and the Mighty*. The film, competing against the year's heavy favorite, *On the Waterfront*, was nominated for six Academy Awards but captured just one, for best score. (Courtesy of the Passaic County Historical Society/ Zito Collection.)

The Empire Theatre in Paterson, shown in this c. 1907 postcard, was at the time listed as being on B.F. Keith's vaudeville circuit, along with F.F. Proctor's in Newark. Among the stage acts was a young comedian by the name of Fred Allen, who later made a name in radio and film. In his 1956 autobiography, *Much Ado about Me*, Allen recalls "packing his juggling equipment" and heading to Paterson for a stage gig at the Empire. (Author's collection.)

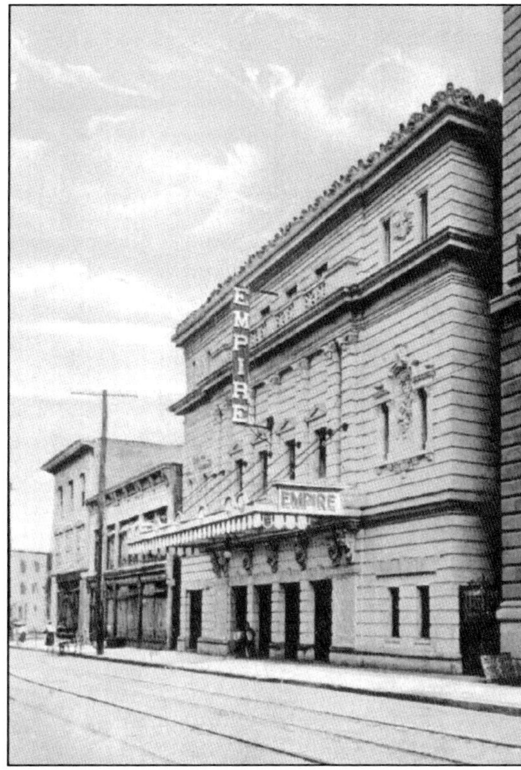

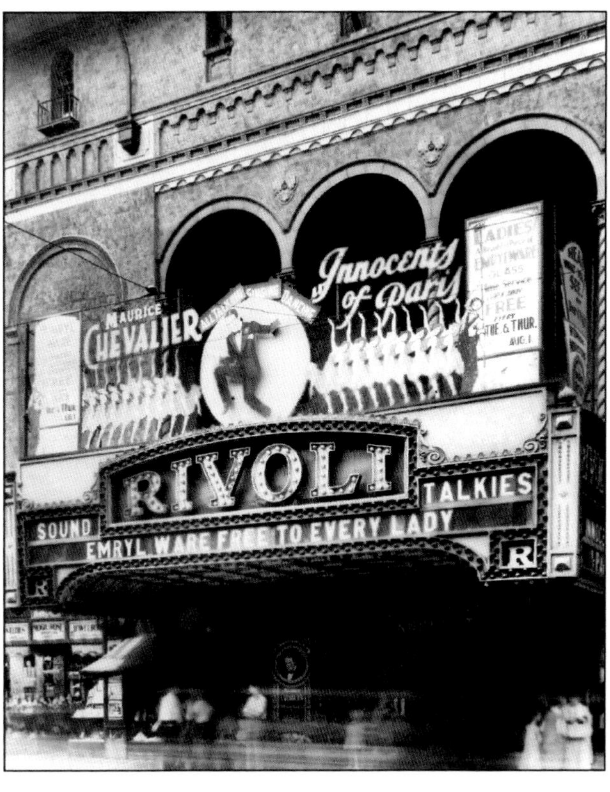

At the Rivoli Theatre on Paterson's Main Street, Maurice Chevalier's *Innocents of Paris* was the feature film. It was the French star's first Hollywood musical, coming just two years after Al Jolson's *The Jazz Singer*, the first all-talking picture. In the 1929 film, Chevalier sang "Louise," one of his signature songs. It ended with the refrain, "Anyone can see why I wanted your kiss / It had to be / But the wonder is this / Can it be true / Someone like you / Could love me Louise." In the 1950s, Chevalier would star in the Oscar-winning musical *Gigi*. His last work was the title song for the 1970 Disney film *The Aristocrats*. (Courtesy of the Paterson Museum.)

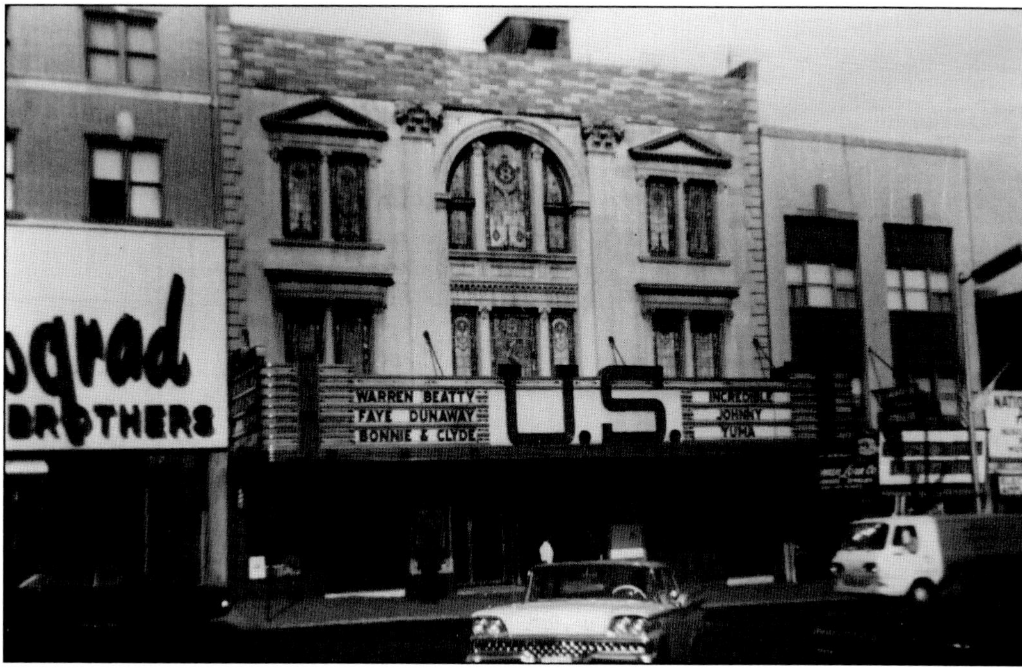

Just before its closing, the U.S. Theatre in Paterson was showing Warren Beatty and Faye Dunaway in *Bonnie & Clyde*, the story of the infamous Depression-era bank-robbery duo whose heists ended in a hail of machine-gun fire. The film was released on August 13, 1967, a time when the theater's retail neighbors included the likes of Bograd Brothers furniture and Donahue's floor coverings, longtime downtown mainstays. (Courtesy of the Paterson Museum.)

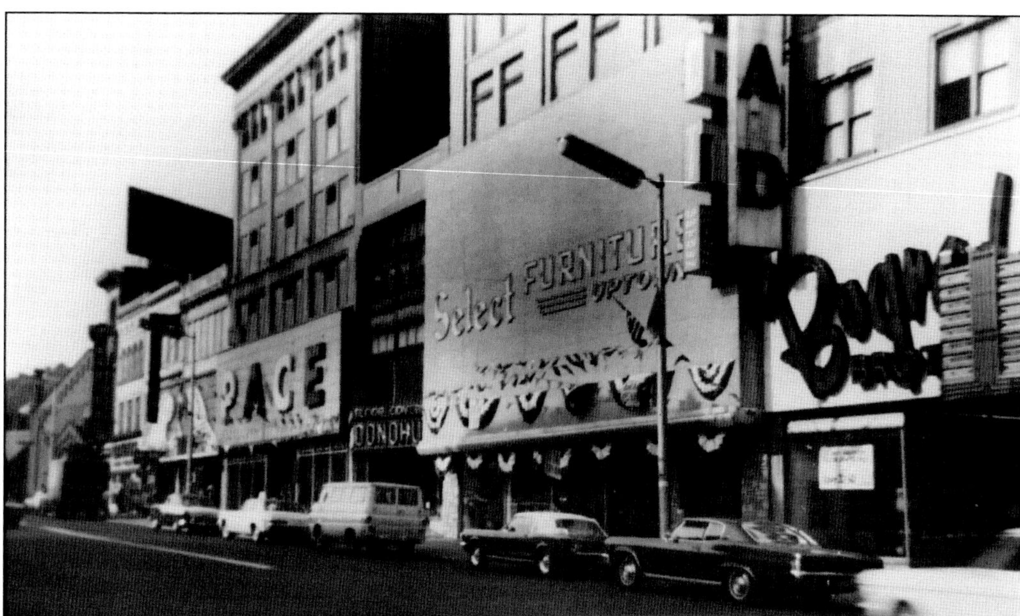

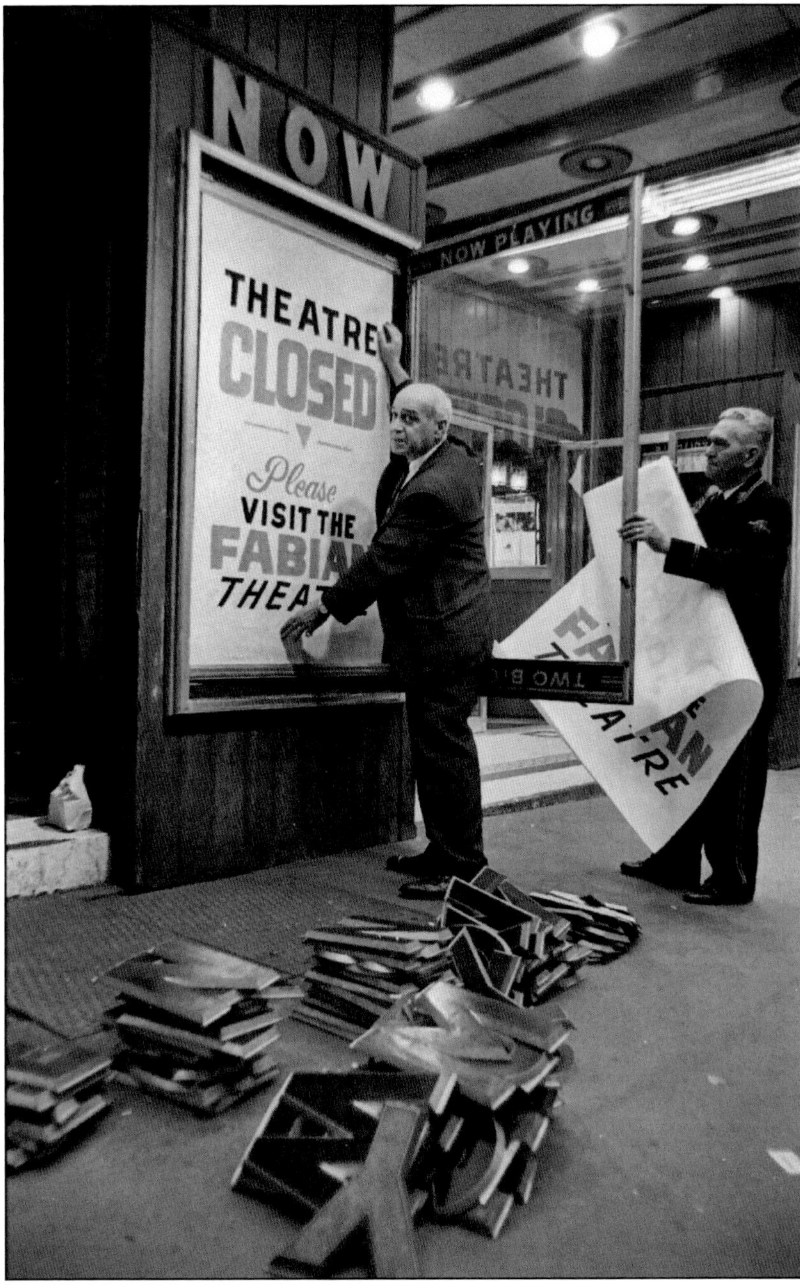

The U.S. Theatre at 284 Main Street in Paterson ended its 101-year reign in September 1967, with the Stanley Warner chain announcing its closing along with the shutdown of the Capital Theatre on Passaic's Monroe Street. The chain purchased the U.S. Theatre in 1959 from Peter Adams, who had operated the venue since 1916, according to a September 8, 1967, article in the *Paterson News*. Once known as the Paterson Opera House, its stage at one time featured J. Gourley, who played the part of Mary Trenchard at Ford's Theatre in Washington, DC, the night President Lincoln was assassinated. She later took up residence in Paterson, the article stated. At the U.S. Theatre's 1967 closing, patrons were directed to another Stanley Warner venue, namely the Fabian on Paterson's Church Street. (Courtesy of the Paterson Museum/Paterson News Collection.)

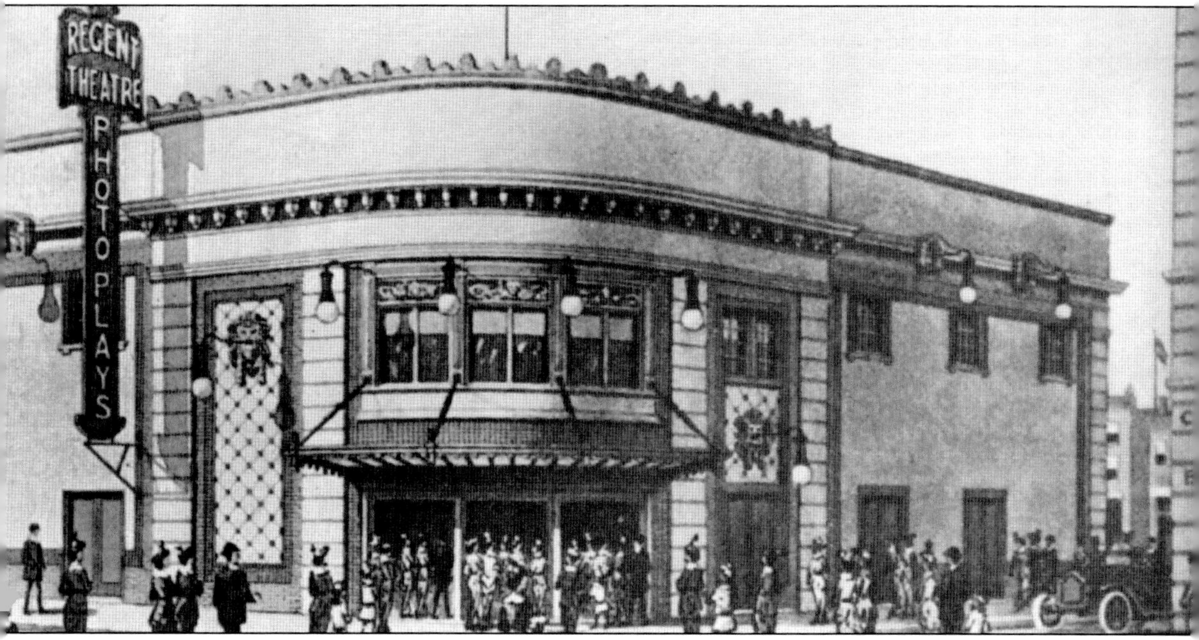

The Regent in Paterson was so expensive to build, it was known as "Fabian's Folly" after Jacob Fabian, who officially opened Passaic County's first theater dedicated to motion pictures on September 14, 1914. Paterson's own Fred Wentworth was the architect of the 2,400-seat picture palace at old Union (now Veterans Place) and Hamilton Streets. The Regent's influence was contagious. The next year, Max Gold built the Garden Theatre, soon selling it to Fabian. In 1923, Fabian leased H.B. Kitay's Rivoli Theatre. Then, just two years later, with talkies about to debut, he erected the Fabian on Church Street. The Regent fell victim to the wrecking ball in favor of a parking lot in 1956, but not before seeing the likes of Bob Hope, Jack Benny, Milton Berle, and, in his first performance in the East, Cab Calloway. Passaic County historian E.A. Smyk said in a 1992 "Tales of Our Heritage" column, "Memories still persist of organist Warren Yates, as well as machines attached to back seats which dispensed candy for pennies." (Courtesy of Richard Walter.)

An Army tank and a crew came out in June 1963 amid the epic retelling of the D-Day invasion of Normandy in *The Longest Day*, starring John Wayne and, as the Paterson marquee states, 41 other stars. The cast included Richard Burton, Eddie Albert, Red Buttons, and Sean Connery of James Bond spy-flick fame. The Garden was built in 1915 by Max Gold, who later sold it to Jacob Fabian, who eventually sold it to the Stanley chain. (Courtesy of the Paterson Museum/Paterson News Collection.)

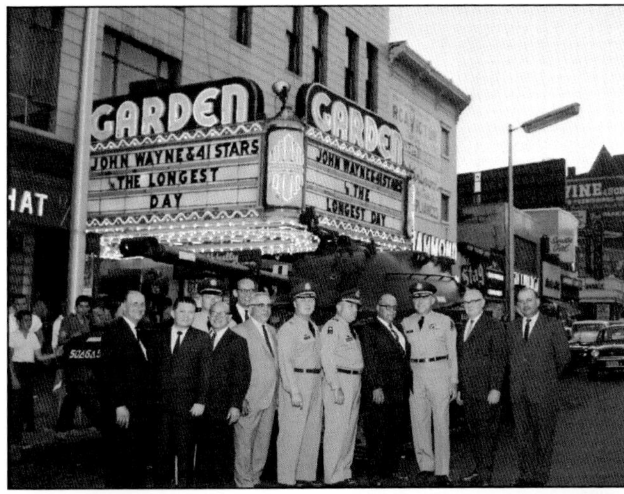

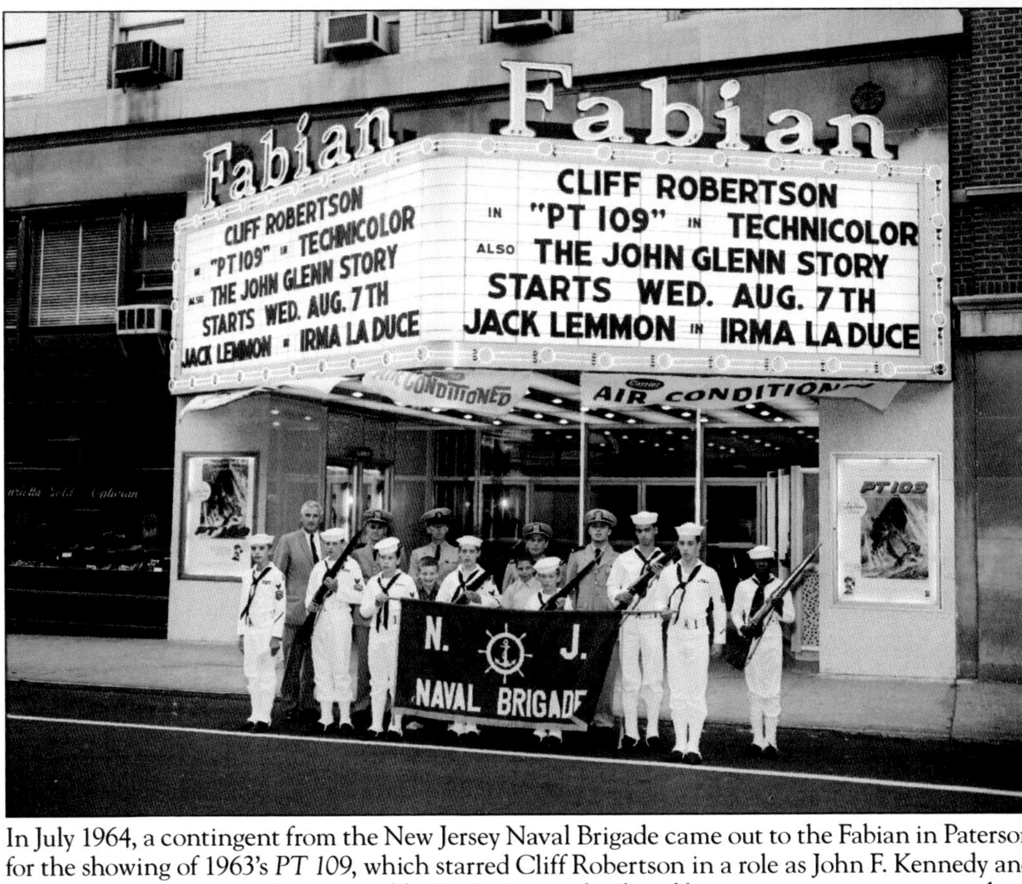

In July 1964, a contingent from the New Jersey Naval Brigade came out to the Fabian in Paterson for the showing of 1963's *PT 109*, which starred Cliff Robertson in a role as John F. Kennedy and his patrol torpedo boat during World War II. It was the first film to portray a sitting president. The marquee also announced the film *The John Glenn Story*, the tale of the first man to orbit Earth; it was nominated for best documentary short in 1962. Paterson sent quite a few of its own to filmdom. Besides comedian Lou Costello, its ranks included Alice White, a flapper in such films as the 1930s *Showgirl in Hollywood*, and curly-haired Bert Wheeler of the comedy duo Wheeler & Woolsey. (Courtesy of the Paterson Museum/Paterson News Collection.)

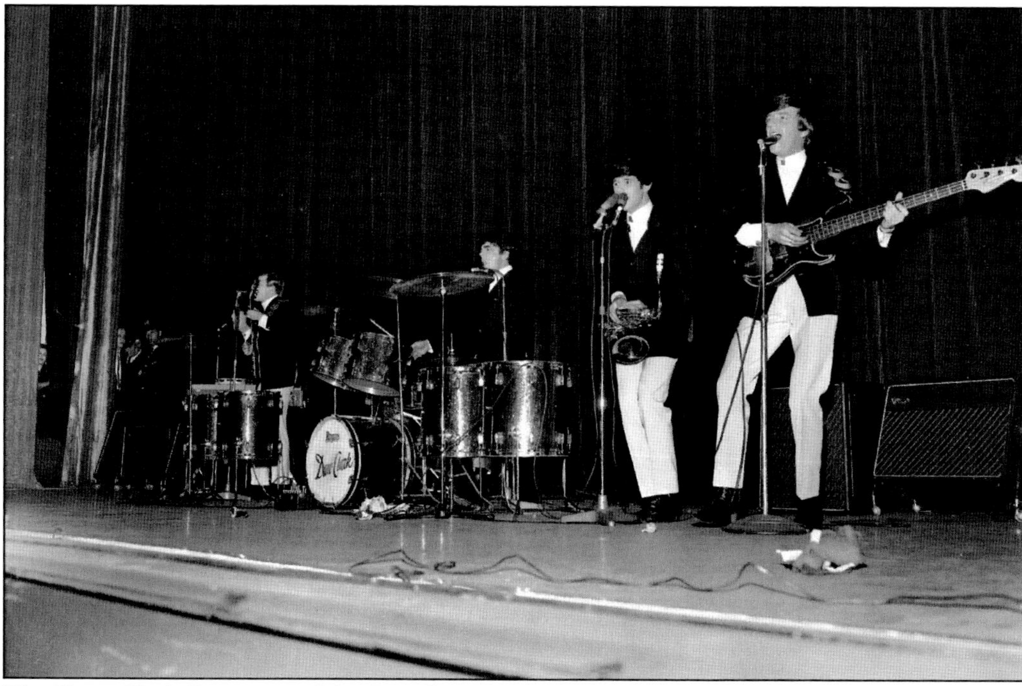

The Dave Clark Five, part of the British music invasion, was promoting its new film *Having a Wild Weekend* and its catchy "Catch Us If You Can" track in August 1965, appearing on stages in Paterson (U.S. Theatre, above) and in Passaic. The group attracted hordes of fans, eventually pumped up by its record-breaking 18 appearances on *The Ed Sullivan Show* at CBS Studios in Manhattan. "Here they come again, hmm-hmm," they sang. "Catch us if you can, hmm-hmm / Time to get a move on, hmm-hmm / We will yell with all of our might / Catch us if you can / Catch us if you can." (Courtesy of the Paterson Museum/Paterson News Collection.)

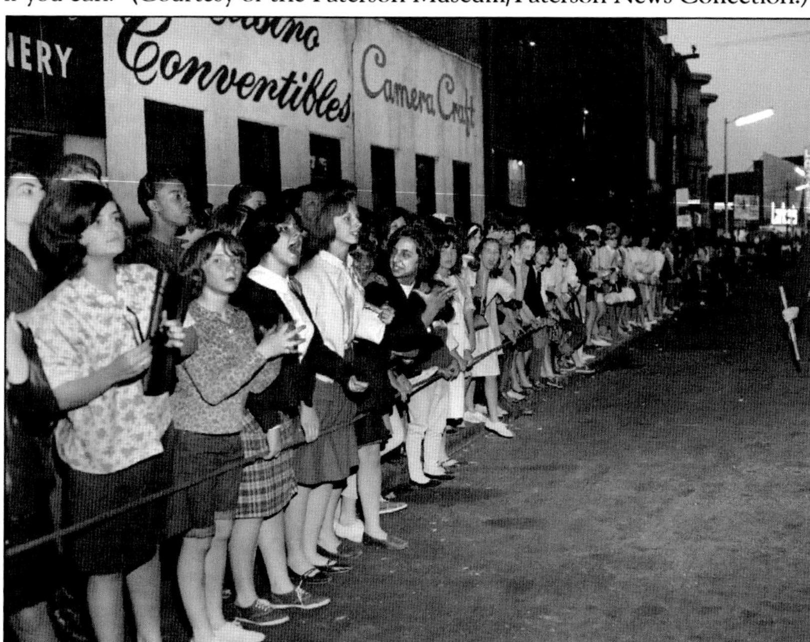

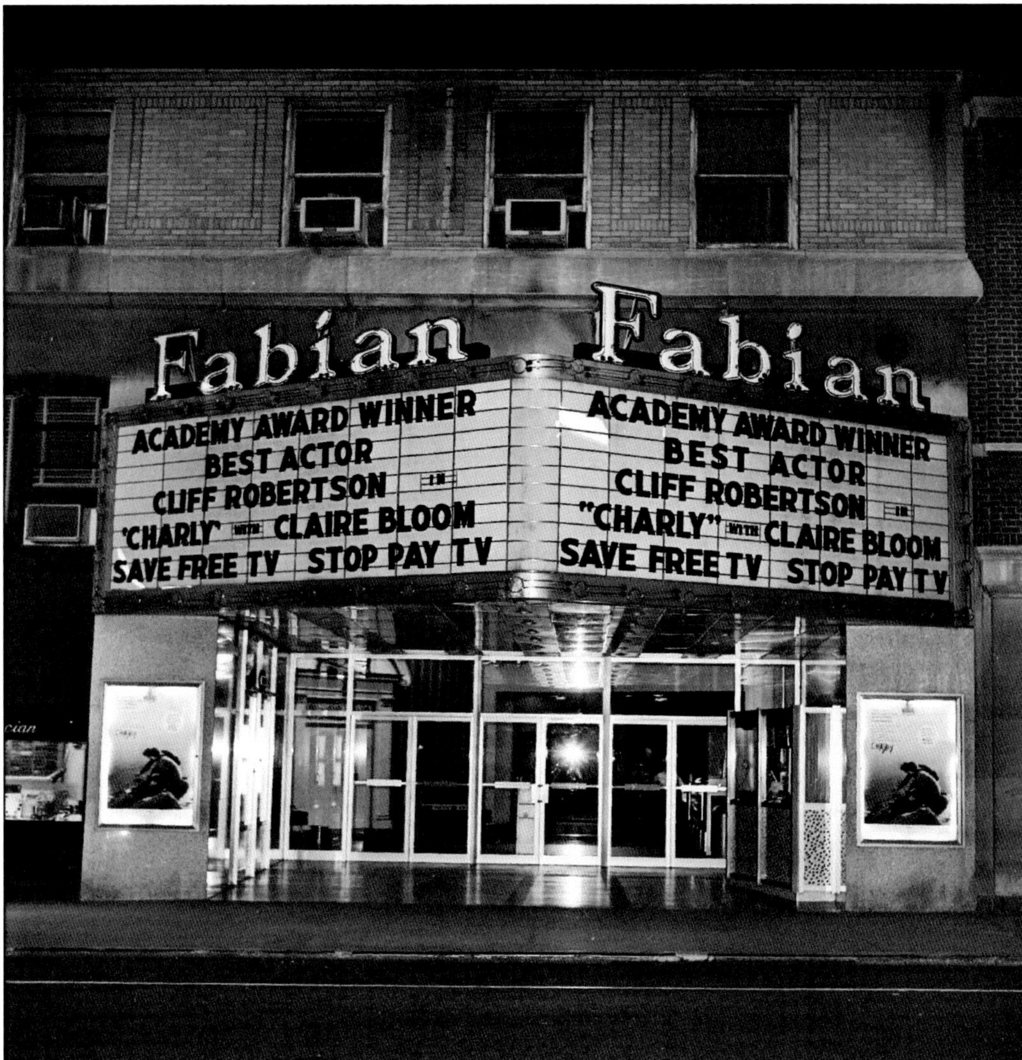

Back in 1969, Cliff Robertson got top billing as best actor for his role in 1968's *Charly*, the story of a mentally challenged man who undergoes an experiment that turns him into a genius. But there was another message on the marquee: "SAVE FREE TV. STOP PAY TV." On Friday evening, April 25, 1969, marquees in Passaic County went dark for two hours to let theatergoers know the perceived perils of pay television. "We want to save free TV," said Howard Herman, owner of the Hawthorne Theatre and head of the New Jersey branch of the National Association of Theater Owners, in a *Paterson News* article. "There is a strong likelihood that many of the better programs now offered on television would find it more profitable to move to the pay-TV channels." That, he said, would deplete the content of broadcasting when people were already complaining of the "vast wasteland" of television programming. What's more, he said the cost of a decoder and charges for each show would rival the cost of a movie theater ticket. "It will affect most those who can afford it least." (Courtesy of the Paterson Museum/Paterson News Collection.)

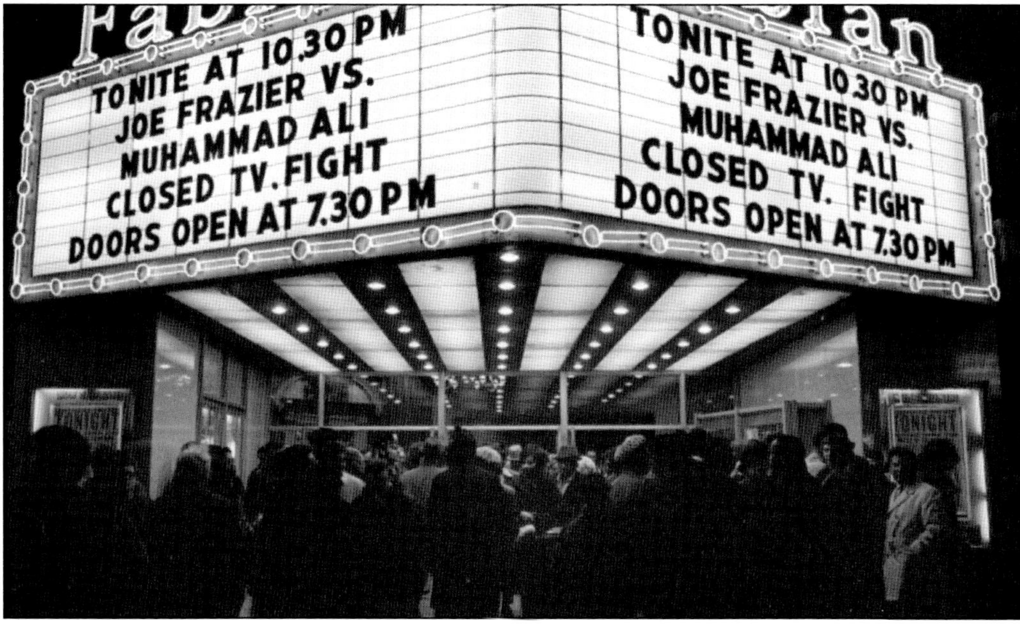

Muhammad Ali and "Smokin' Joe" Frazier—both previously undefeated—met in a Madison Square Garden showdown on March 8, 1971, in a 15-round fight that would live forever in the minds of the 3,000 theatergoers who paid $15 a head to see the brawl on closed-circuit television at the Fabian in Paterson. "At Fabian: Price Was Worth It," read the headline from a story by Walt Keogh. The theater crowd, he reported, appeared to be in Ali's camp, but he would end up losing in a decision. There were some unusual winners though. Fabian's management threw open the doors at the end of the 15th round, letting a crowd of youngsters in gratis to hear the decision. "Yes, they got their money's worth," the reporter wrote. Of course, there was some pre-fight film reels, too: *Number One*, starring Charlton Heston; a travelogue film titled *Gone Fishin'*; and a fight short called *The Champion*. (Courtesy of the Paterson Museum/Paterson News Collection.)

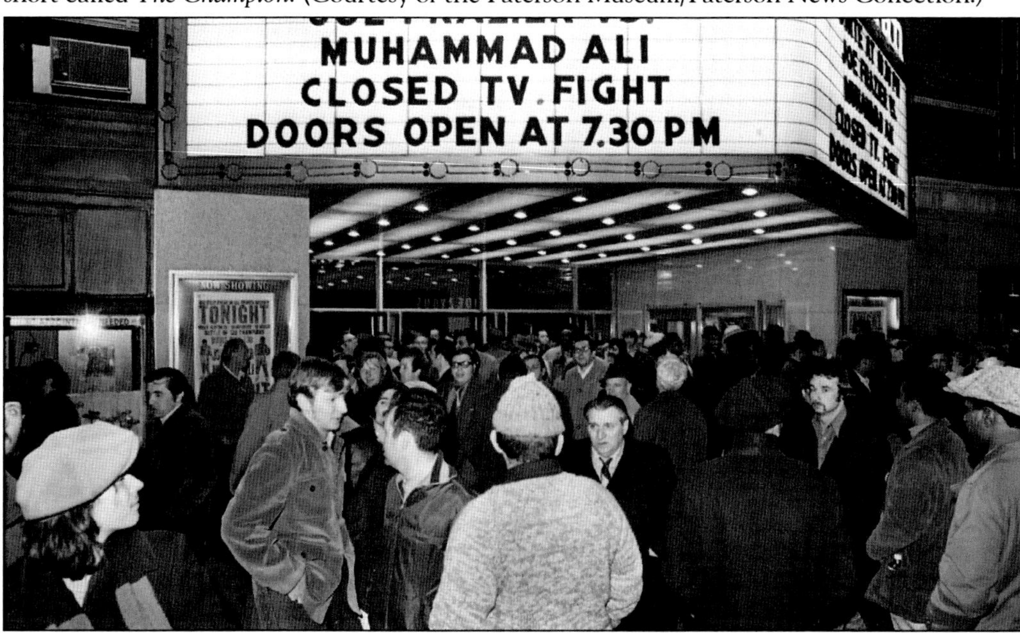

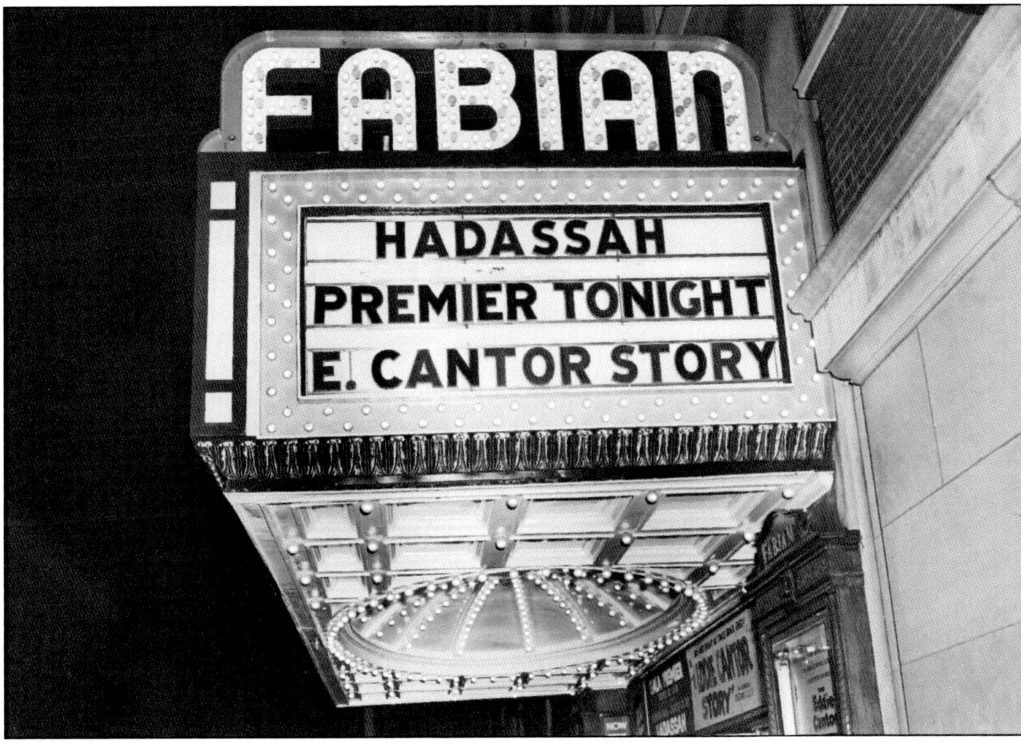

The Eddie Cantor Story, a 1953 Warner Bros. film, was the draw at a Fabian gala sponsored by Hadassah, a women's Zionist organization in the United States. The banjo-eyed vaudevillian's dancing feet and double takes brought him stardom in movies according to his 1964 obituary by United Press International. The show's classic Cantor songs included "If You Knew Susie," "Ida," and "How Ya Gonna Keep 'Em Down on the Farm (After They've Seen Paree?)." (Courtesy of the Paterson Museum/Paterson News Collection.)

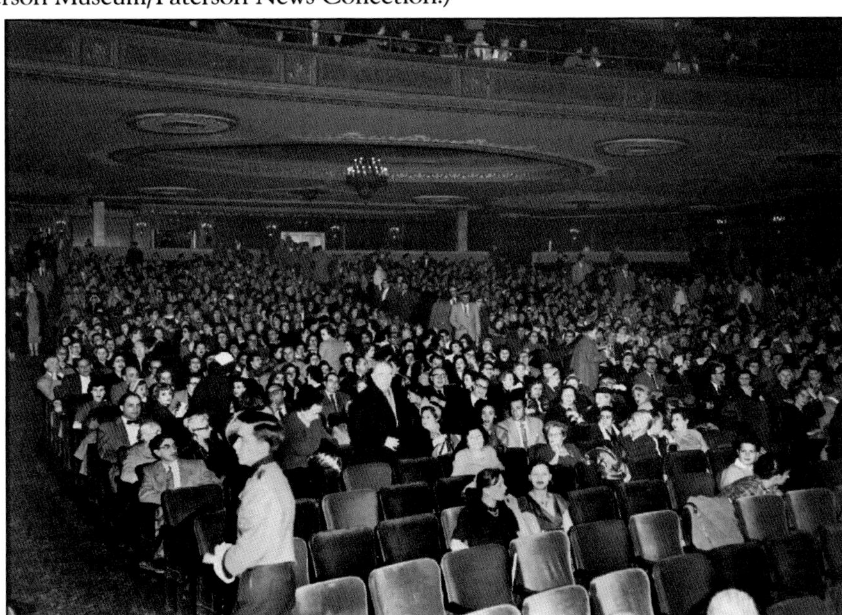

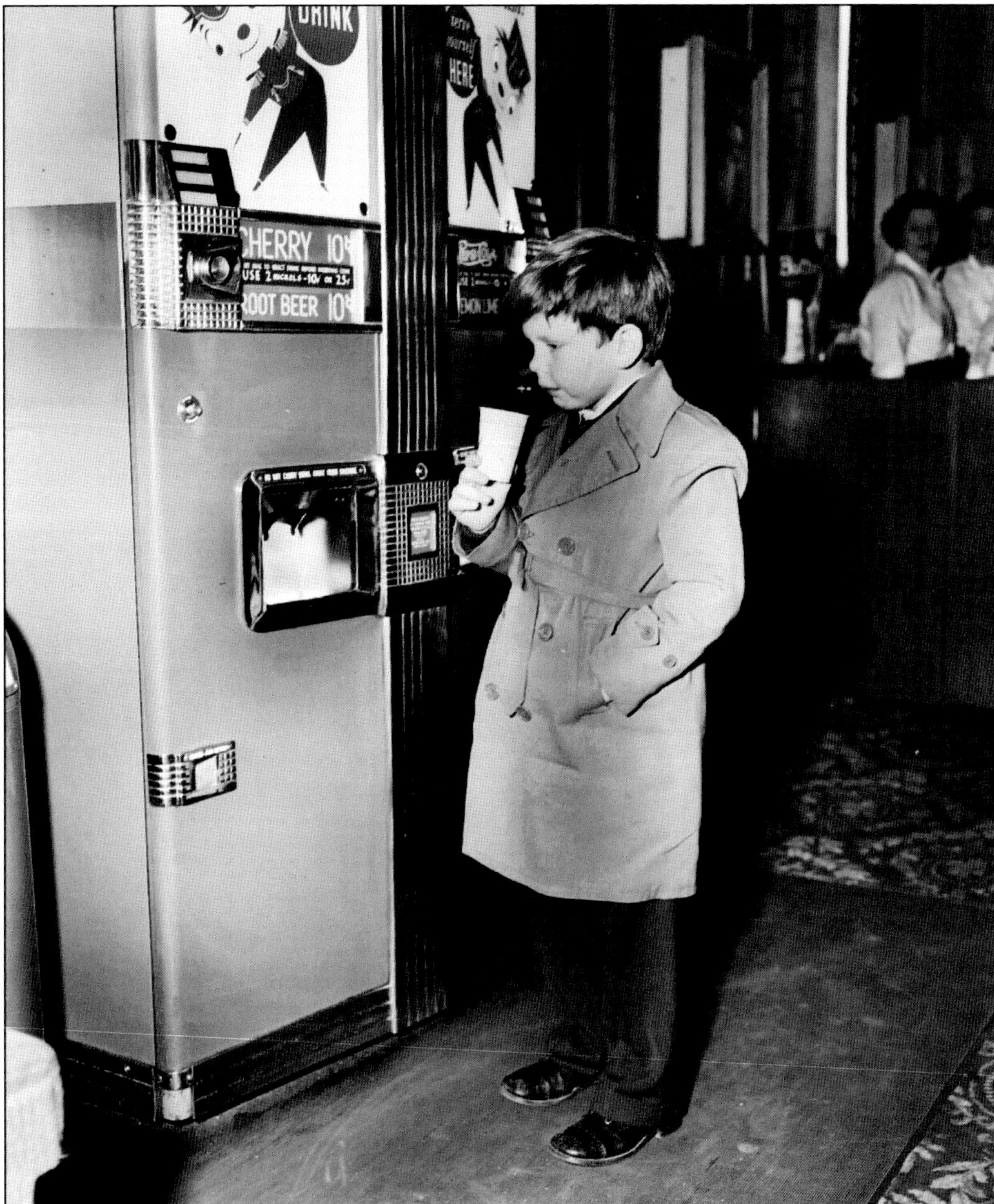

A young theatergoer eyes a Fabian vending machine with a "Serve Yourself HERE" invitation. A cherry soda or root beer could be had for a dime, and if one needed help with the math, it was willing to oblige: "2 nickels = 10¢." The ladies at the snack counter do not seem to mind. (Courtesy of the Paterson Museum/Paterson News Collection.)

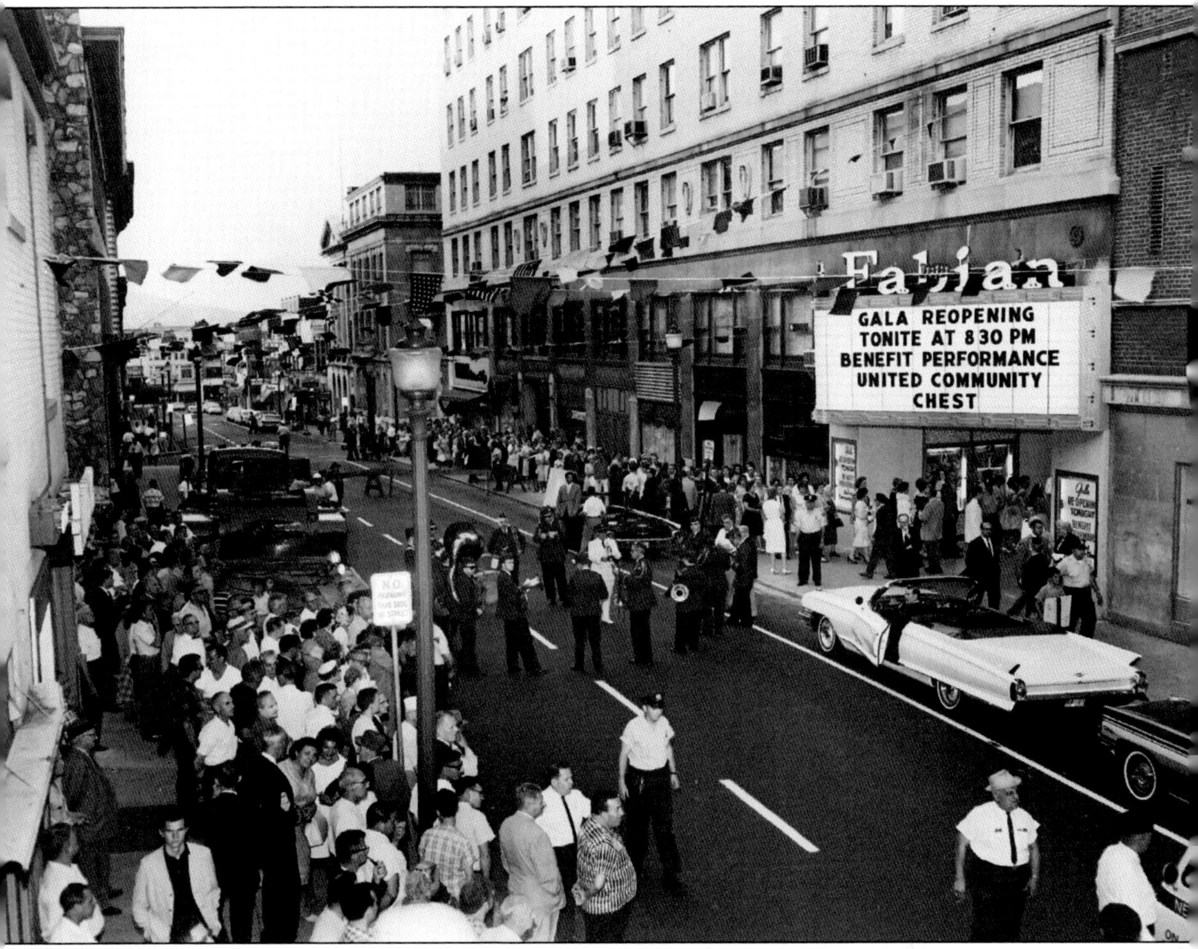

The date June 27, 1962, went down in Paterson's history as the day "a hometown boy," Simon H. Fabian, made good on a promise to spend a $500,000 to refurbish the c. 1925 Fabian. "I have always had a deep personal interest in the welfare of Paterson," said the then president of the Stanley Warner Corp., "and I hope that what our company is doing to update the Fabian properties will play a significant part in the revival of downtown Paterson." The remodeling introduced more legroom while cutting the number of seats from 3,500 to 2,900. "No longer will patrons have to rise to allow latecomers to make their way to mid-aisle seats but may relax undisturbed," read an account in the *Paterson News*. A banner advertisement in the newspaper declared the new theater "THE LAST WORD IN ELEGANCE AND COMFORT!" The movie premiere was none other than *Road to Hong Kong*, starring Bing Crosby and Bob Hope. (Courtesy of the Paterson Museum/Paterson News Collection.)

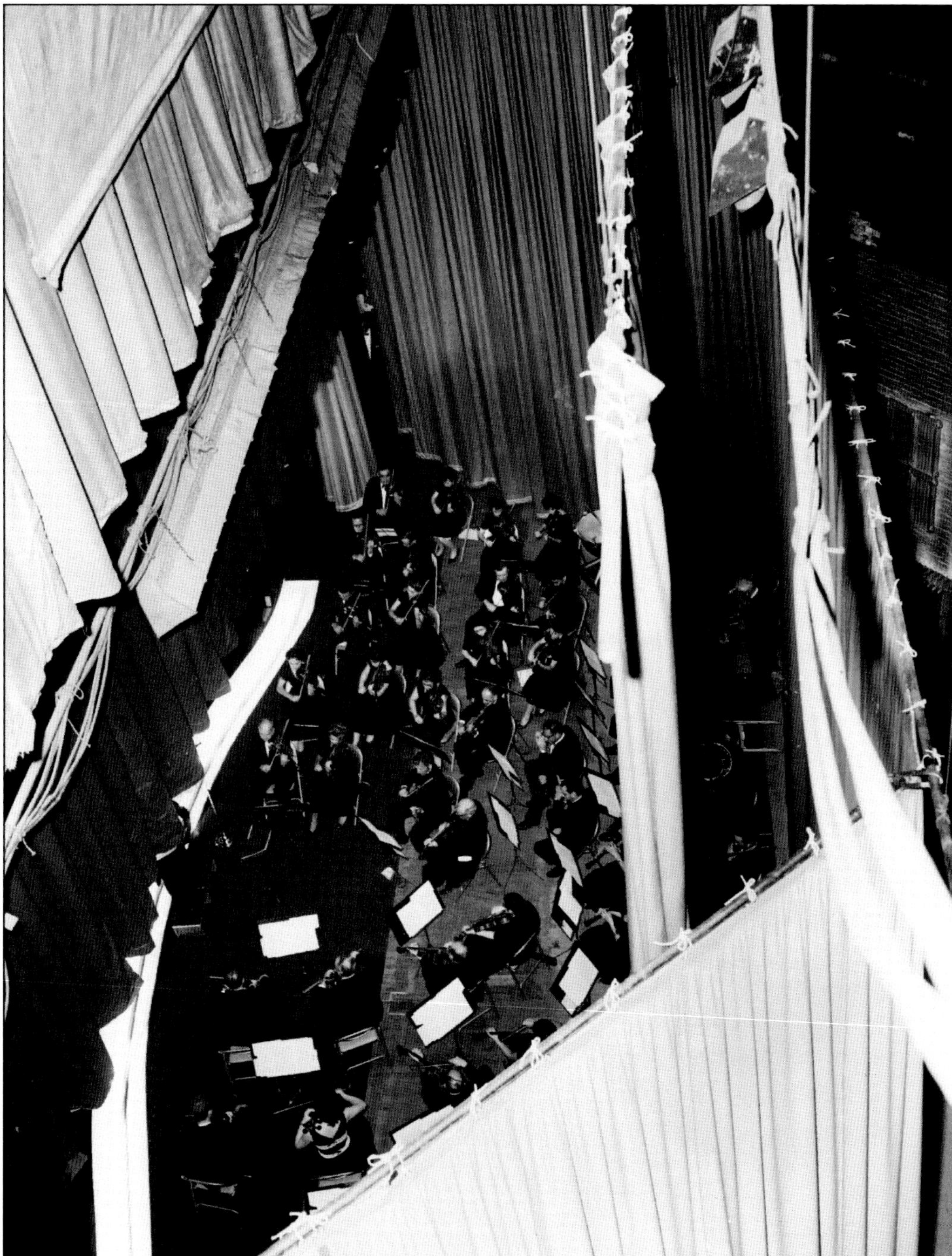

The music for the gala reopening came from the North Jersey Philharmonic, led by Walter W. Schoeder, a music teacher who founded the North Jersey Philharmonic in 1947; he was its conductor for almost 50 years. In this image, Schoeder can be seen on stage (left center, largely hidden by the curtain) among his musicians, who began the evening with the overture from Johann Strauss's *Die Fledermaus* and concluded with the finale from Tchaikovsky's Fourth Symphony. (Courtesy of the Paterson Museum/Paterson News Collection.)

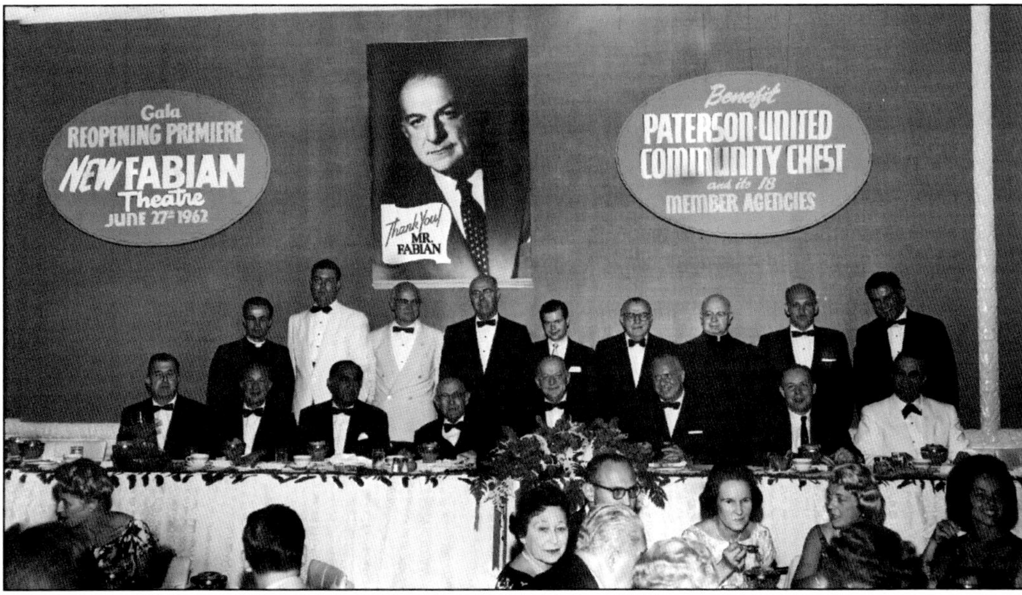

Among the dignitaries at the evening's pre-show, black-tie gala at the Alexander Hamilton Hotel were Harry Haines (seated, fourth from left), publisher of the *Paterson News*, with (to the right of Haines, respectively) Simon Fabian, *News* associate editor and the night's master of ceremonies Abe Greene, and Mayor Frank Graves. Greene, as toastmaster, said of Fabian, "Here is a man who has been out of Paterson for many years but whose heart has never left the city of his birth." (Courtesy of the Paterson Museum/Paterson News Collection.)

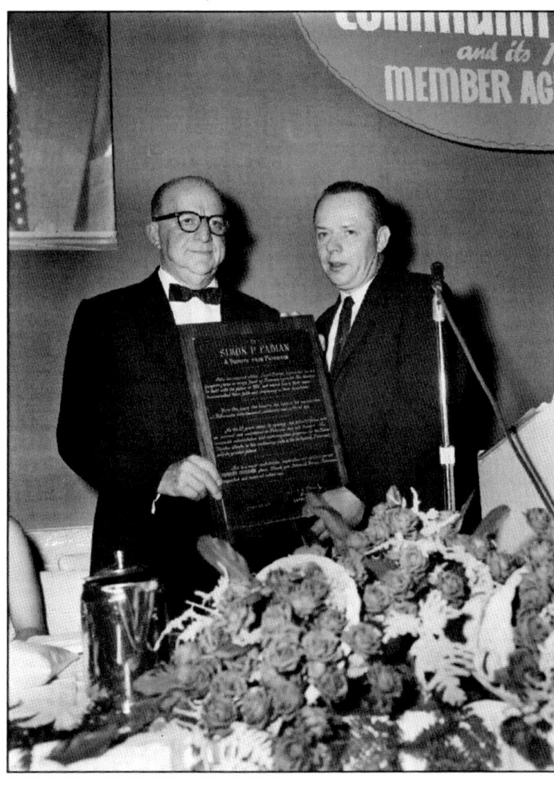

Paterson mayor Frank Graves presents a tribute to Simon Fabian, who summed up his company's investment in Paterson this way: "We cannot sit wistfully by and hope that a good fairy godmother from one of the governments will pull us out of our troubles." (Courtesy of the Paterson Museum/Paterson News Collection.)

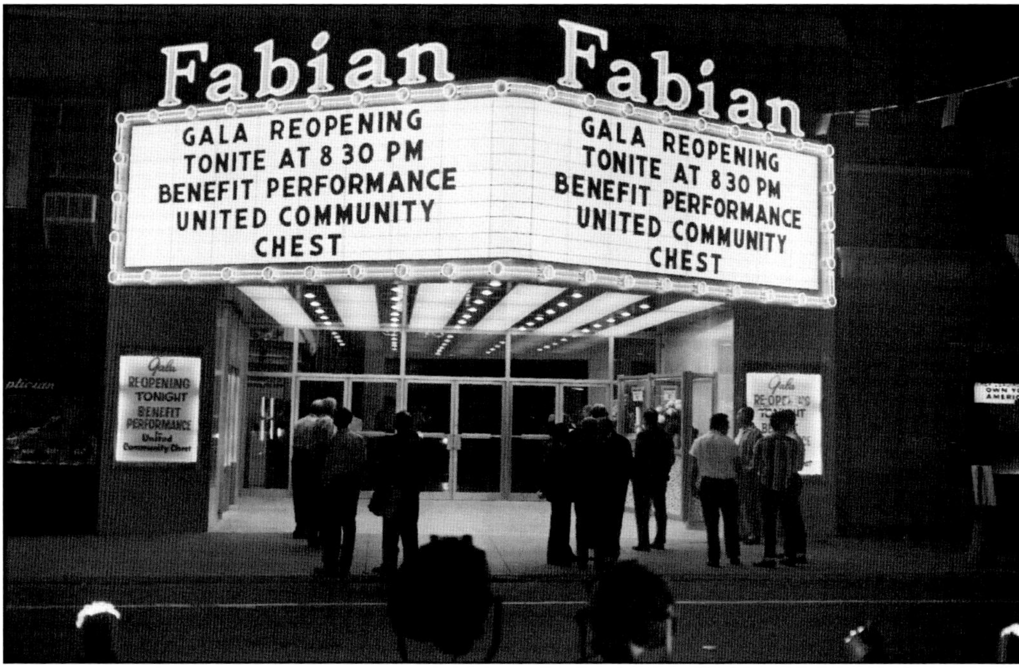

The evening's gala reopening was captured on film for a featurette to be shown in the coming weeks during the Fabian Theatre's regular movie lineup. The narrators were Ed Fraim and Don Fortune, the comedy team behind the *Fraim and Fortune Show* on WJRZ Radio. (Courtesy of the Paterson Museum/Paterson News Collection.)

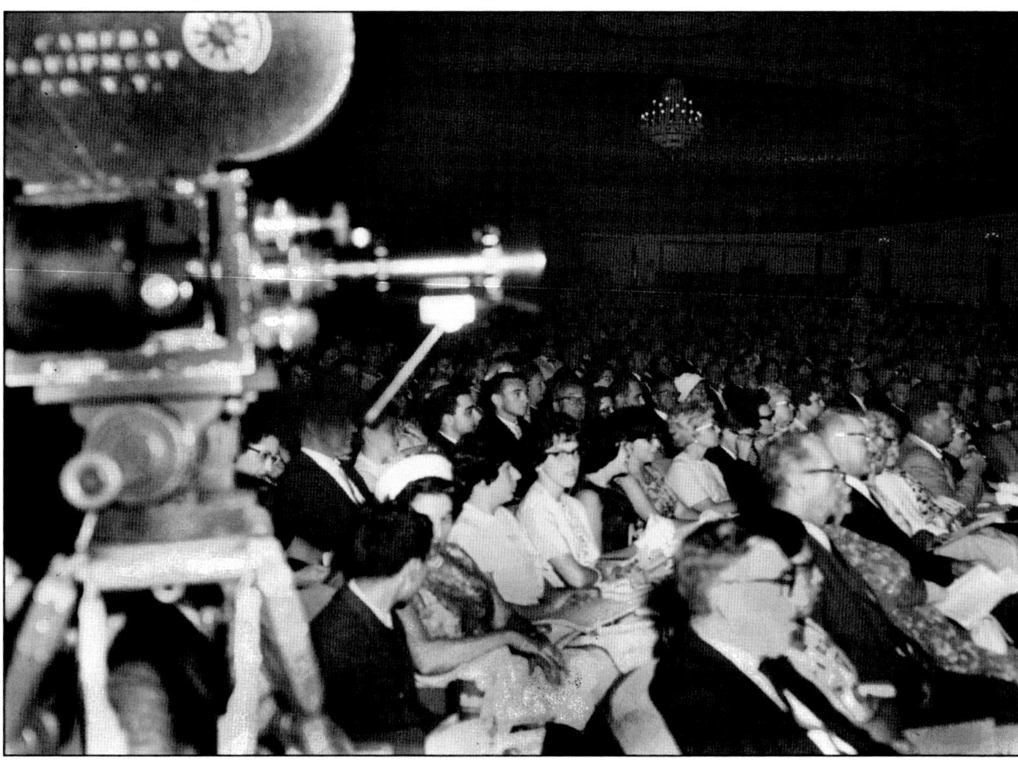

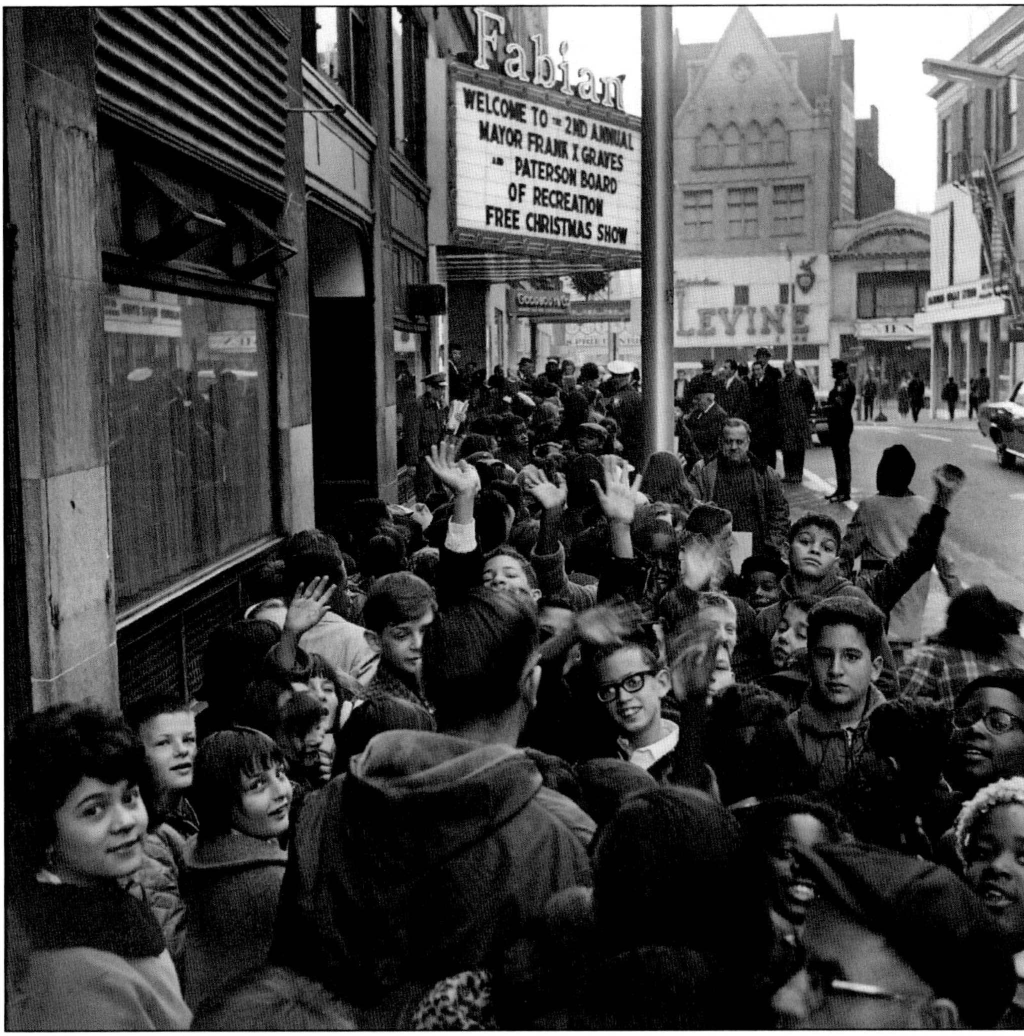

There were lots of cheerful waves as the youthful crowd gathered in December 1965 for the second-annual Christmas show hosted by Frank X. Graves, then Paterson's mayor. A couple of weeks earlier, Graves was on hand for the annual tree lighting in front of city hall, a news story carried on the same page as a report on actress Brigitte Bardot's arrival in New York and news of model Mia Farrow's snipping of her waist-long blond hair. (Courtesy of the Paterson Museum/Paterson News Collection.)

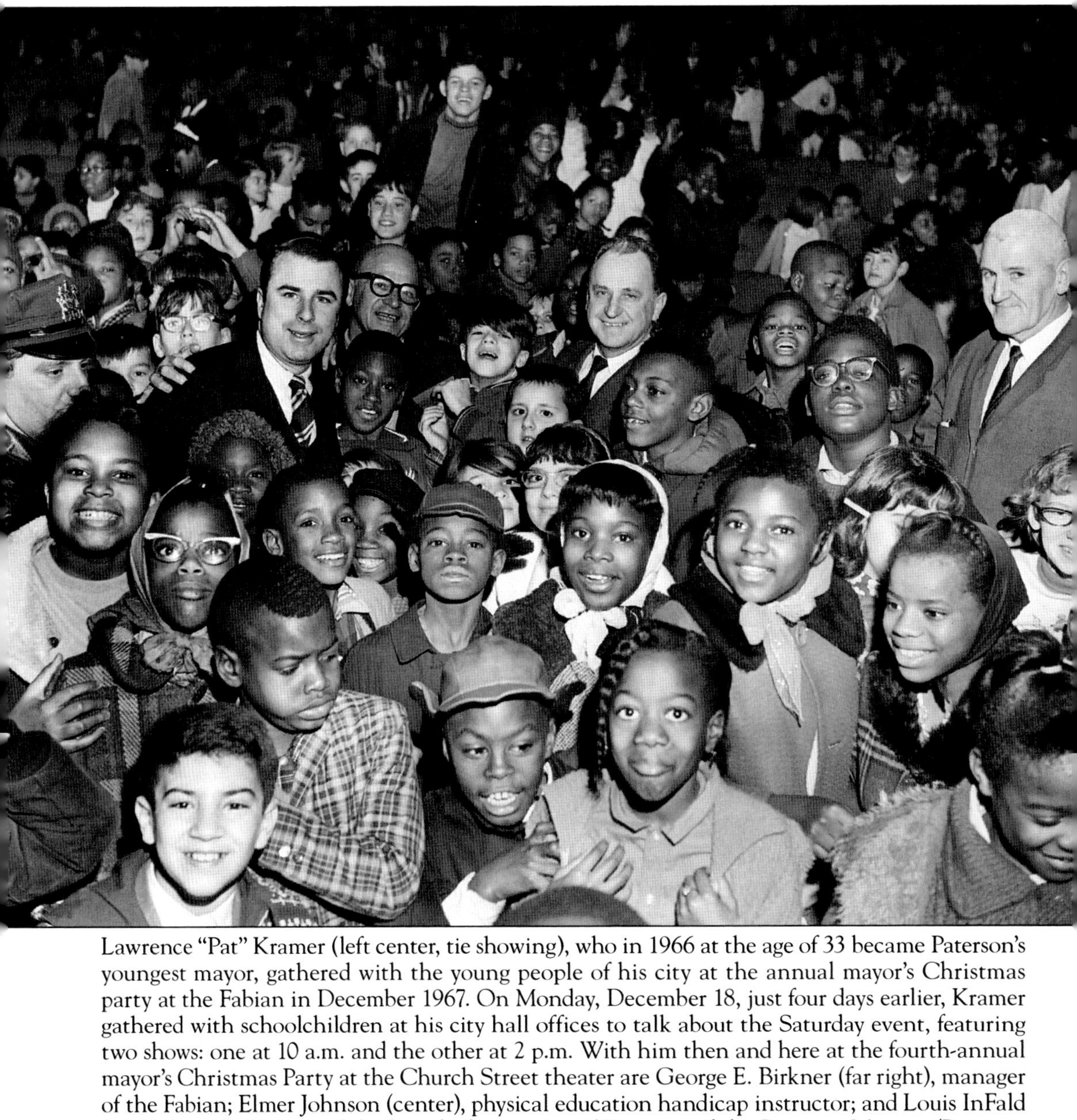

Lawrence "Pat" Kramer (left center, tie showing), who in 1966 at the age of 33 became Paterson's youngest mayor, gathered with the young people of his city at the annual mayor's Christmas party at the Fabian in December 1967. On Monday, December 18, just four days earlier, Kramer gathered with schoolchildren at his city hall offices to talk about the Saturday event, featuring two shows: one at 10 a.m. and the other at 2 p.m. With him then and here at the fourth-annual mayor's Christmas Party at the Church Street theater are George E. Birkner (far right), manager of the Fabian; Elmer Johnson (center), physical education handicap instructor; and Louis InFald (with glasses), director of the board of recreation. (Courtesy of the Paterson Museum/Paterson News Collection.)

Four

Passaic

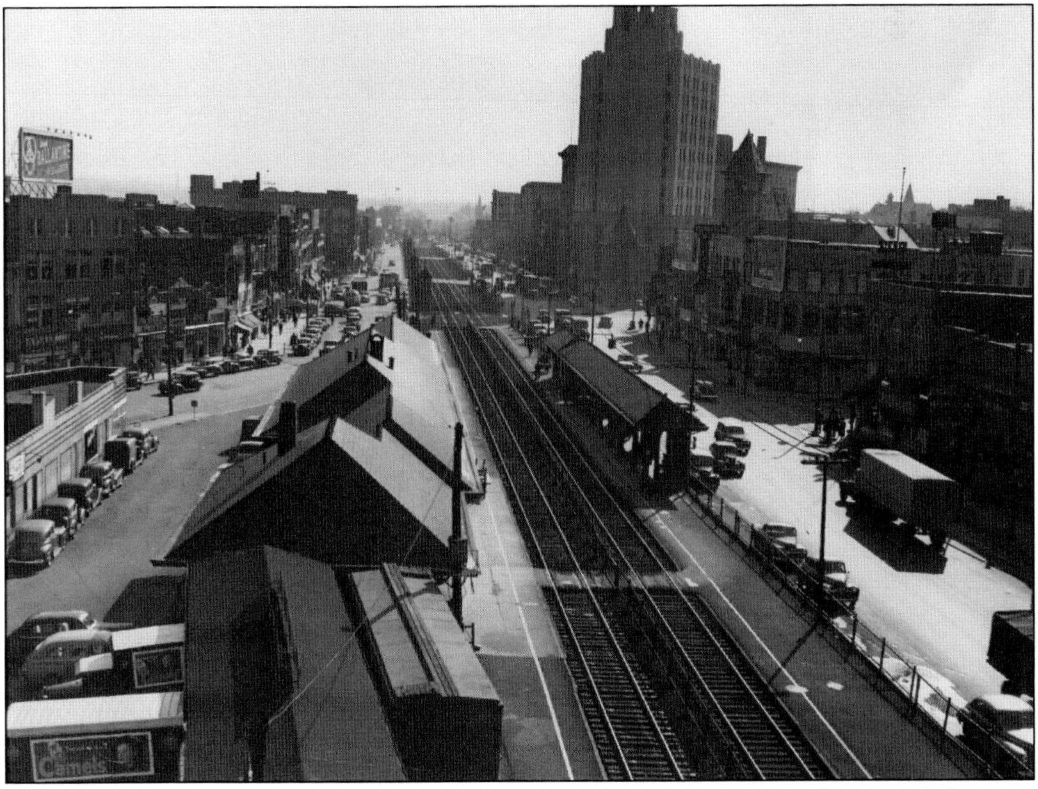

Downtown Passaic, along with the Montauk Theatre (far right), is captured in this 1947 image. The movie house's marquee announces the showing of *The Man I Love*, a romantic melodrama starring Ida Lupino, Robert Alda, and Andrea King. Among the downtown merchants seen here are Pulaski Furniture, Adam Hats, and the Montauk Dress Shop. (Courtesy of the Newark Public Library.)

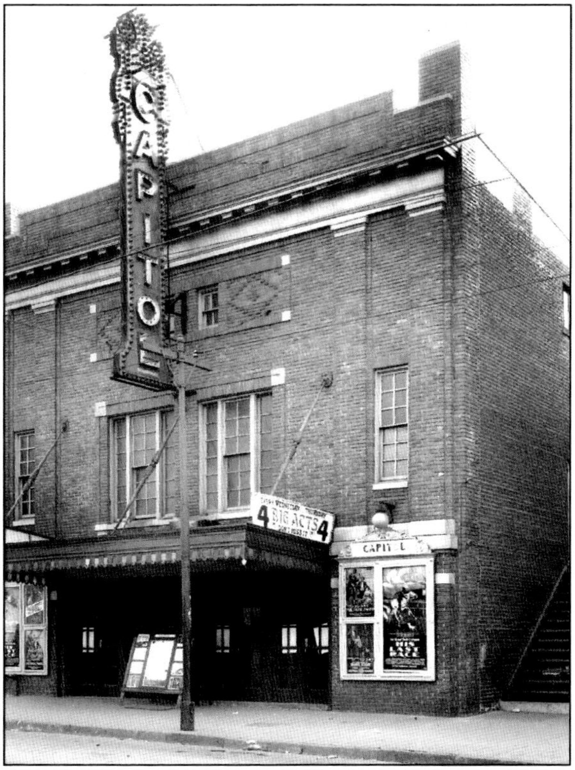

The Capitol, in its early days, featured vaudeville and silent films, such as 1923's *His Last Race*, starring Australian athlete Rex "Snowy" Baker, who was later credited with teaching a young Elizabeth Taylor how to ride and perform stunts in 1944's *National Velvet*. In July 1925, the Capitol's program featured *Cobra*, starring Rudolph Valentino. But the theater's greatest claim to fame came in 1971, when John Scher, a young concert promoter, brought rock and roll to the Capitol. "I don't think there's another theater in the world that has had so many big names in rock consistently playing there," Scher said in a 1981 interview in the *New York Times*. "Ten years ago, I had no idea whether it would last. But every time I got an itinerary from a major group and it said, " 'Boston, Washington, New York City, Passaic,' I got a big kick out of it. And I still do." The concerts would last until 1989, when the theater was demolished. (Courtesy of Mark S. Auerbach.)

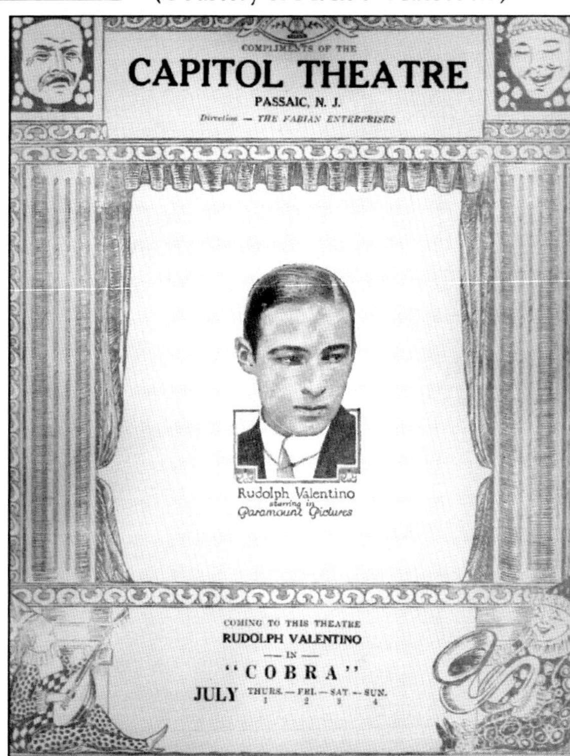

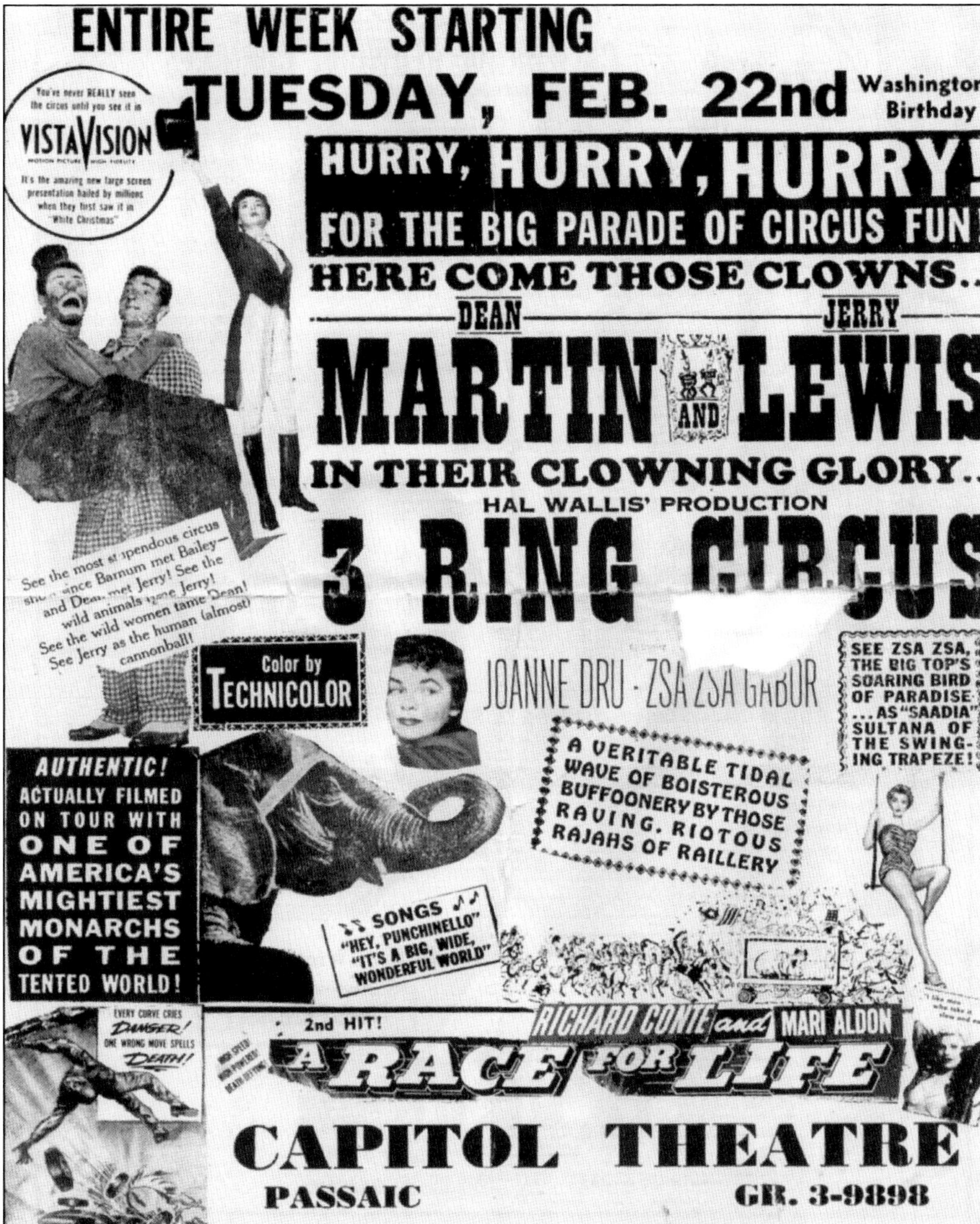

The Capitol Theatre opened in the 1920s with a sizable 3,200 seats. In 1954, it was showing the Jerry Lewis/Dean Martin comedy *Three Ring Circus*. By 1964, the double feature was an Italian "sword-and-sandal" duet, namely *Samson and the Slave Queen* and *Goliath and the Sins of Babylon*. (Courtesy of Mark S. Auerbach.)

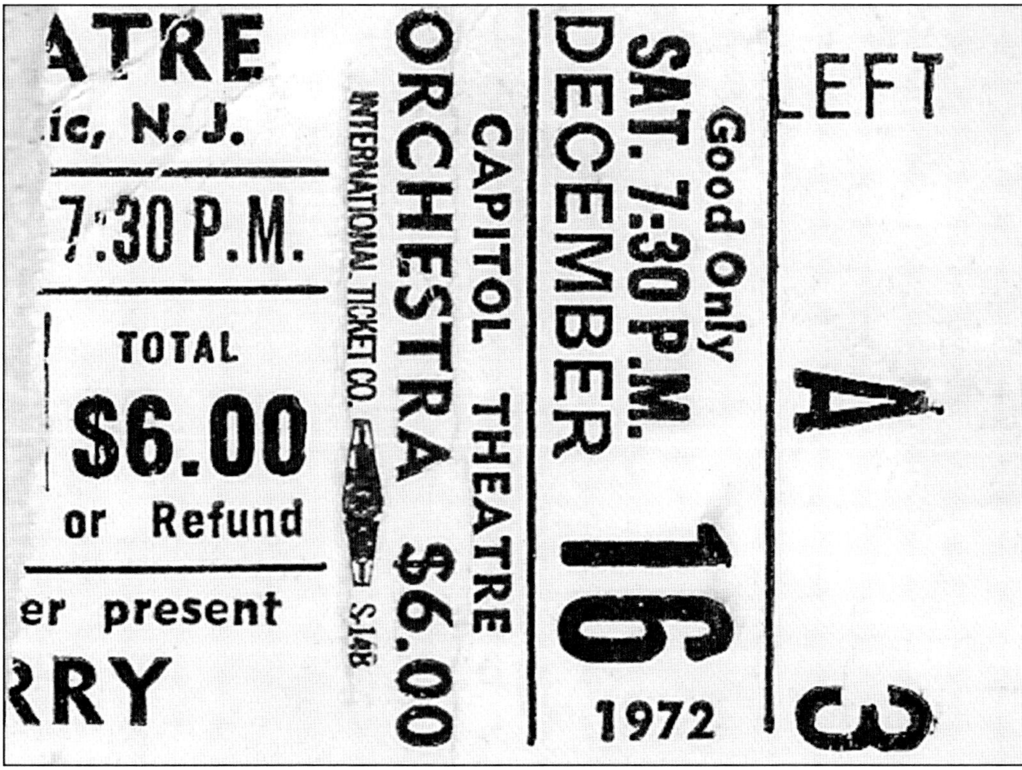

John Scher's Capitol Theatre, within months of its transformation as a concert venue, was a must-stop for the top names in rock and roll from the early 1970s to the 1980s. Among the big names in those early years was Chuck Berry, who took the stage on December 16, 1972, doing one of his signature numbers, "Johnny B. Good," but not before the opening act of the Phlorescent Leech & Eddie, the Turtles alum who would shorten their name the next year to Flo & Eddie. In this case, the young concertgoer who used this ticket on December 16, 1972, sat in A-3, front row on the left, for a mere $6. The other stub, from March 17, 1973, was a mezzanine seat, purchased for $4, for the J. Geils Band with the Edgar Winter Group, whose big hit that year was "Frankenstein." (Author's collection.)

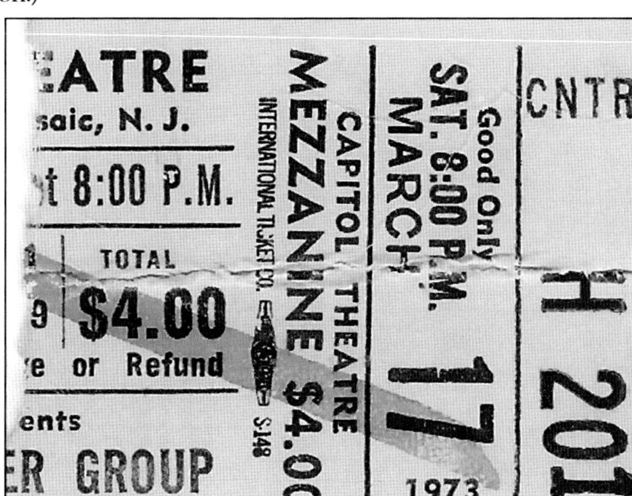

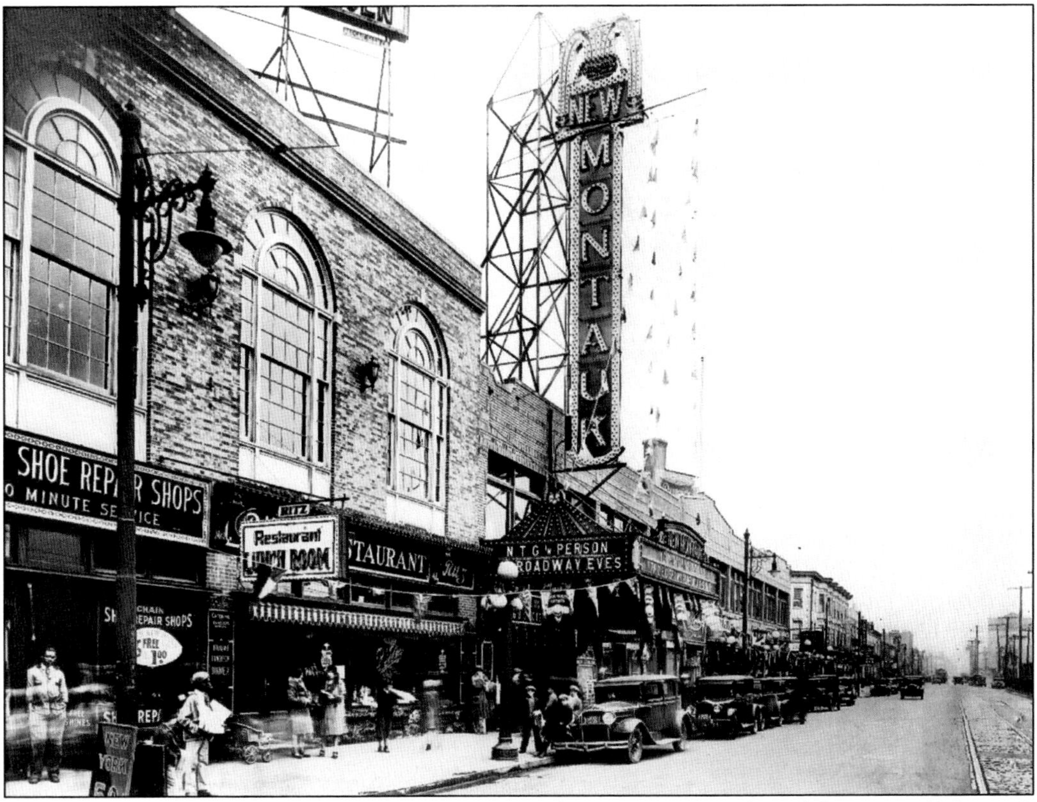

In 1919, Harry Stein, one of Passaic's most prominent businessmen, purchased the original Montauk Theatre, marking the beginning of a Fabian-Stein partnership that spread throughout northern New Jersey when the movie industry was in its infancy, according to Stein's 1952 obituary in the *New York Times*. His company tore down the old Montauk and erected the new one, seen here, in its stead. Later, in 1926, Stein sold many of his holdings to the Stanley-Fabian interests. (Courtesy of Mark S. Auerbach.)

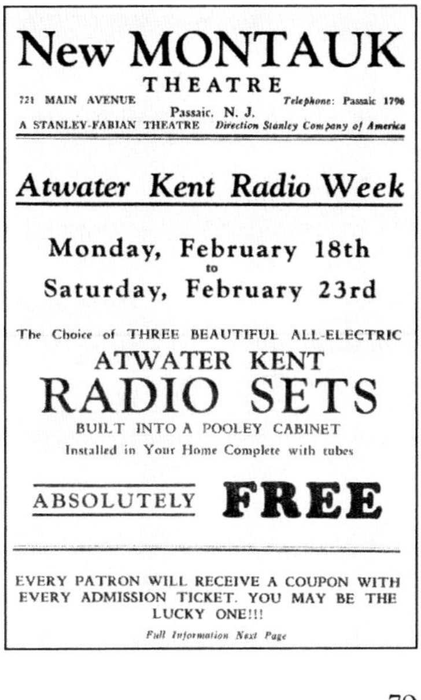

The New Montauk was devoted to standard Hollywood issues through the 1940s through 1960s, showing such movies as *Brute Force*, a 1947 film noir starring Burt Lancaster. In that era, the theater once toted a radio giveaway for Atwater Kent radios, which at one time was the largest radio manufacturer in the nation with a plant covering 32 acres in Philadelphia. By the 1970s, however, the theater was the scene of police raids for the showing of X-rated films after the US Supreme Court ruled that municipalities could, in effect, determine standards of obscenity. On July 4, 1973, police seized such films as *The Devil in Miss Jones* and its star Georgina Spelvin, who was there for a personal appearance, according to the *New York Times*. "She was arrested while holding a dozen roses and talking with newsmen in the lobby," the *Times* reported. "Theatergoers in the lobby booed the police as they seized her." (Courtesy of Mark S. Auerbach.)

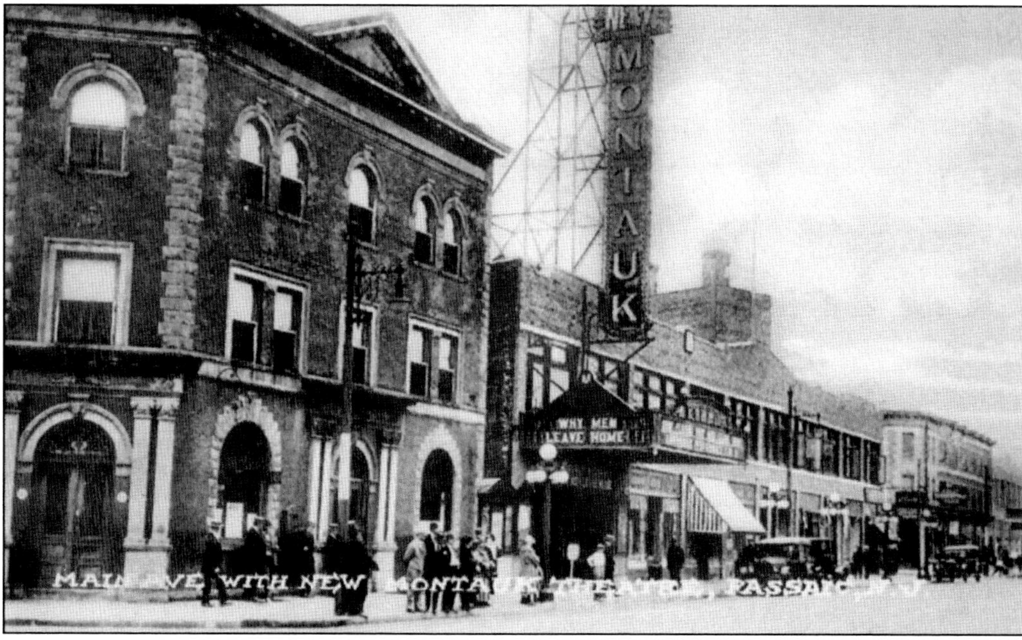

The New Montauk opened on Passaic's Main Avenue in 1924, topped by the famed Ritz Ballroom, the site of many wedding receptions in its day. One of the early films hawked on the marquee was *Why Men Leave Home*, a comedy about divorce. Director John M. Stahl spoke of his film this way: "Most marital difficulties have a very small beginning. In this picture, I have tried to point out these things without delivering a sermon on celluloid." (Courtesy of the Julius Forstmann/ Passaic Public Library Collections and Mark S. Auerbach.)

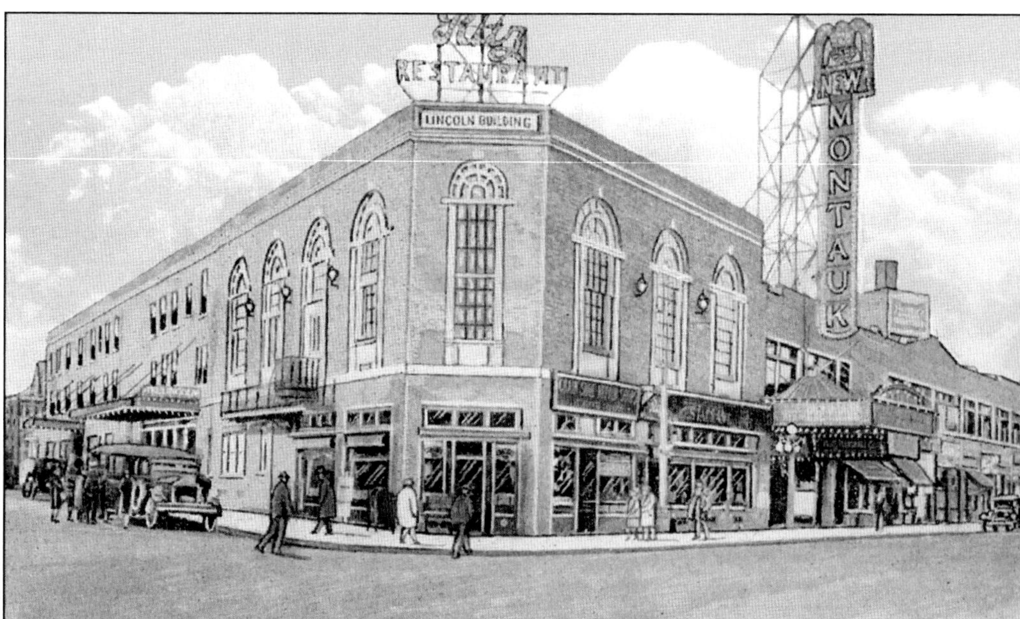

The Playhouse, on Passaic's Main Street, opened in 1914 for stage productions and soon shifted to vaudeville and films. The 1,035-seat movie house lasted until the mid-1950s. One of its productions in 1934 featured Mario Siletti, an acting teacher who helped found the National Shakespeare Conservatory. For 25 years, Mr. Siletti taught acting at the Stella Adler Studio, New York University, and the National Shakespeare Conservatory, according to his 1991 obituary in the *New York Times*. At the age of 4, on the Lower East Side, Siletti began acting in productions by the Italian Theatre, which his father, Mario Sr., had founded. The play *Beati Paoli*, published early in the 20th century, is a portrait of a secret society that was said to have challenged the authority of church and state alike. (Courtesy of Mark S. Auerbach.)

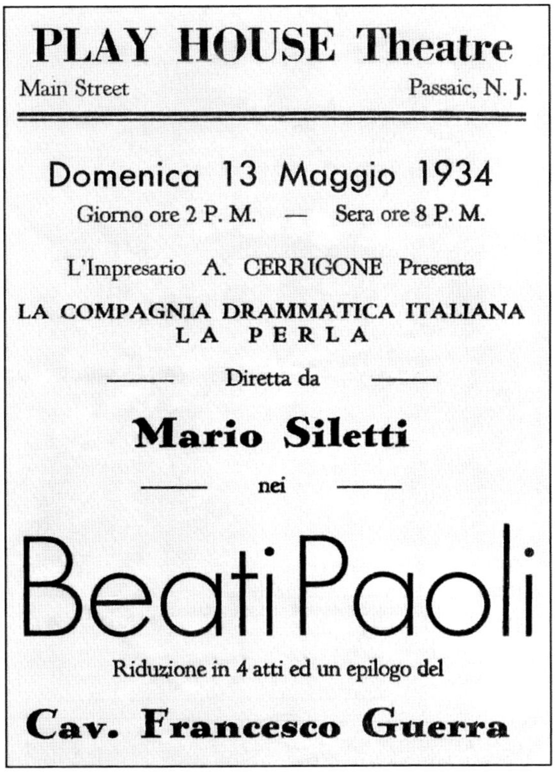

PLAY HOUSE Theatre

Main Street — Passaic, N. J.

Domenica 13 Maggio 1934

Giorno ore 2 P. M. — Sera ore 8 P. M.

L'Impresario A. CERRIGONE Presenta

LA COMPAGNIA DRAMMATICA ITALIANA

LA PERLA

Diretta da

Mario Siletti

nei

Beati Paoli

Riduzione in 4 atti ed un epilogo del

Cav. Francesco Guerra

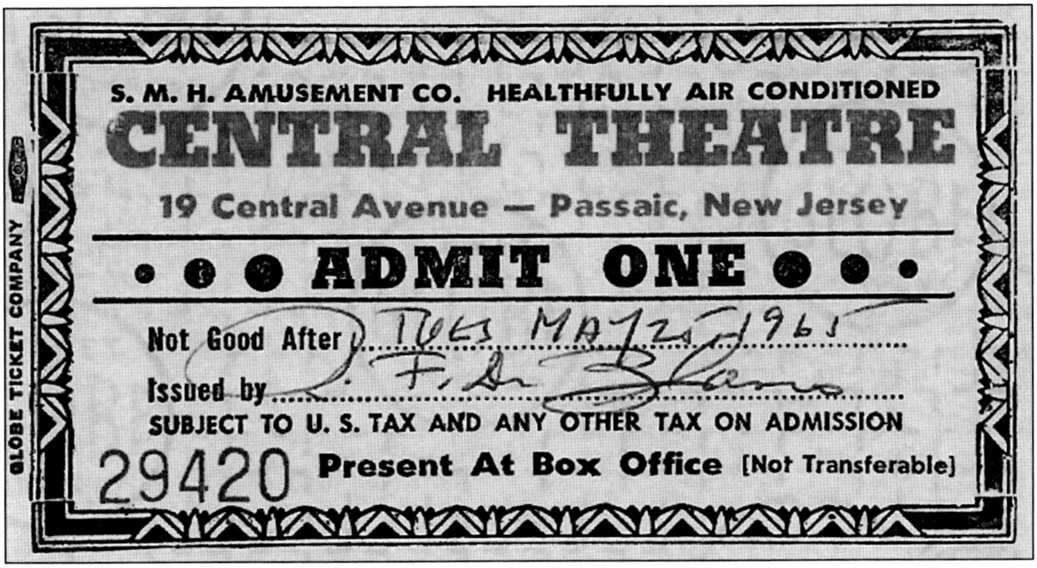

S. M. H. AMUSEMENT CO. HEALTHFULLY AIR CONDITIONED

CENTRAL THEATRE

19 Central Avenue — Passaic, New Jersey

ADMIT ONE

Not Good After ....

Issued by ....

SUBJECT TO U. S. TAX AND ANY OTHER TAX ON ADMISSION

29420 Present At Box Office [Not Transferable]

GLOBE TICKET COMPANY

This "Admit one" ticket provided entry into Passaic's Central Theatre in 1964. Years earlier, in 1955, the Central was the location of the world premiere of *Singing in the Dark*, the story of a concentration camp survivor who suffers from traumatic amnesia. The film's star, Moishe Oysher, made a personal appearance. Fast-forward to the 1974, and one of its features was a showing of all five of the original *Planet of the Apes* movies. Just up the block on Monroe Street, John Scher's Capitol Theatre, embarking on a career as a rock-concert palace, was getting a new marquee as a sign of its newfound success. (Courtesy of Mark S. Auerbach.)

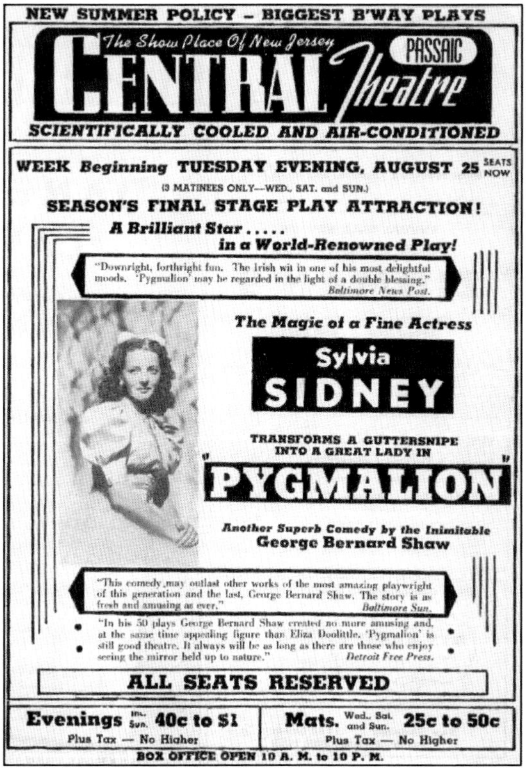

On the stage at the Central, actress Sylvia Sidney once starred in the touring production of *Pygmalion*. According to her 1999 obituary in the *New York Times*, Sidney displayed a "vulnerable but spunky persona" that helped make her "the ultimate heroine of realistic movies of the 1930s." Film historian David Thomson noted, "There are close-ups in *Fury* of Sidney watching Spencer Tracy in a burning jail, as harrowed as any Lillian Gish close-ups" seen in a masterpiece by famed director D.W. Griffith. (Courtesy of Mark S. Auerbach.)

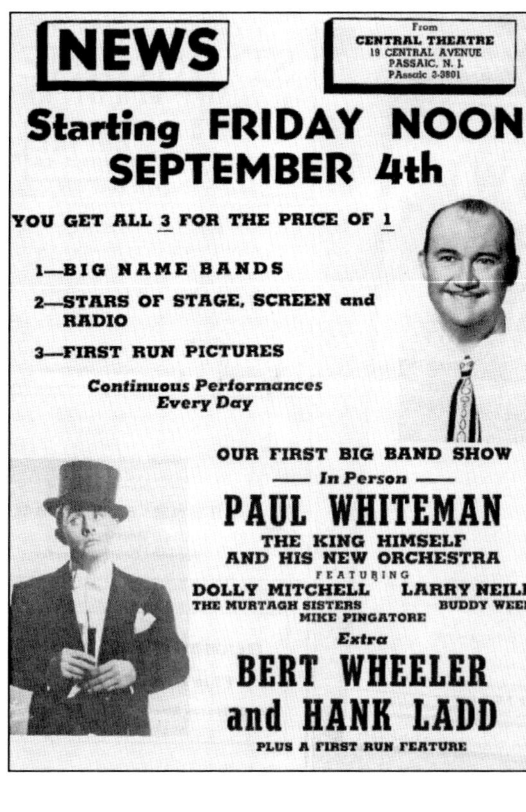

The Central Theatre, which once dwarfed a nearby diner on Passaic's Central Avenue, had an incredible 2,357 seats when it opened in 1940, drawing such acts as the Andrew Sisters, the Three Stooges, and even Pink Floyd in its later years. Most of all, it will be remembered as the last American venue played by Glenn Miller before he departed to entertain the troops in Europe during World War II. Here, the Central features Paul Whiteman and his "new orchestra." The bandleader, who picked up three Grammy Awards in the 1920s, had one of his last big hits with "Smoke Gets in Your Eyes" in 1934. The design of the theater, built by Harry K. Hecht, is attributed to John and Drew Eberson. It was eventually demolished and replaced by a McDonald's restaurant. (Courtesy of Mark S. Auerbach.)

Five

Suburban Passaic

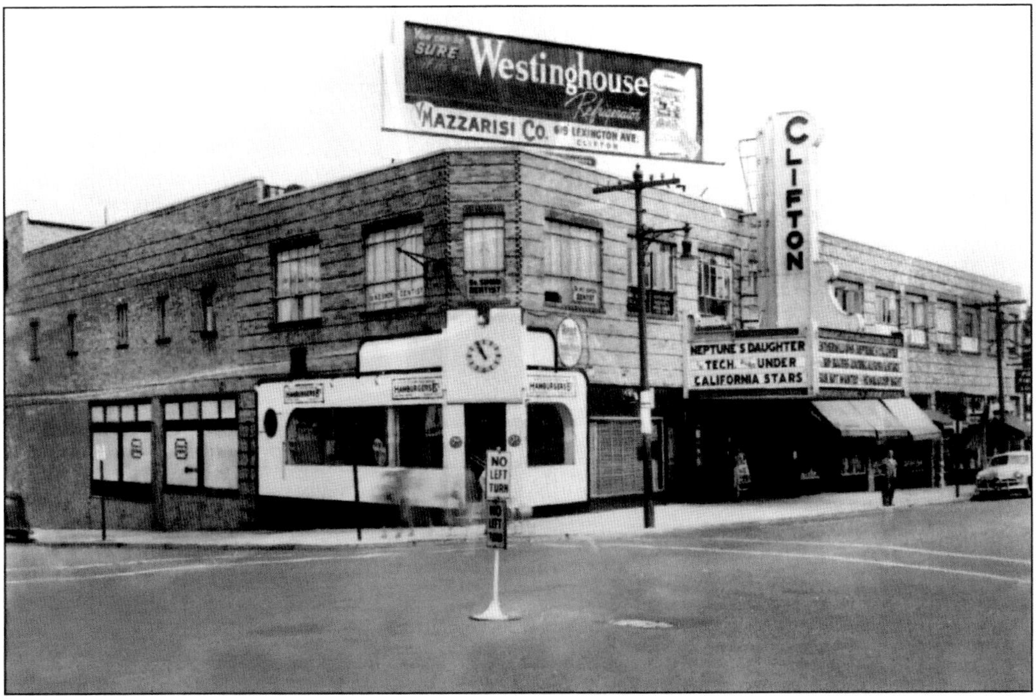

A dozen years after its Main Avenue opening, the Clifton Theatre was showing *Neptune's Daughter*. The 1949 musical starred Esther Williams and Red Skelton in the tale of a romantically cynical young woman and the man who changes her point of view. The Oscar-winning score included the song "Baby It's Cold Outside." At the theater's opening in 1937, *Emile Zola*, starring Paul Muni, and *Double or Nothing*, starring Bing Crosby, was the double feature, with a trailer about the sinking of the US gunboat *Panay* by the Japanese. (Courtesy of the Mark S. Auerbach and Van Dillen Collections.)

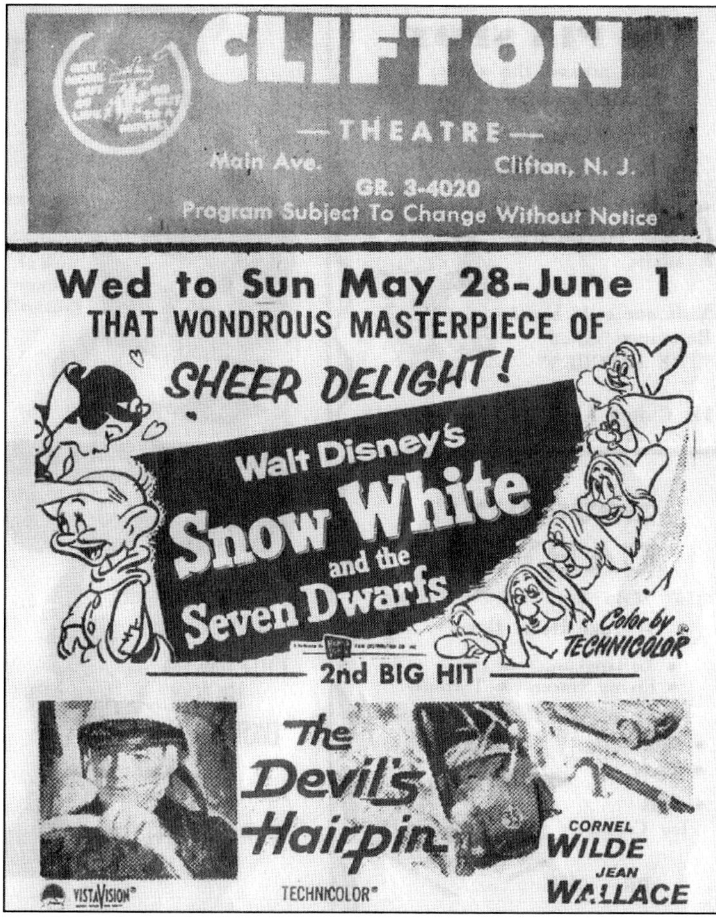

At its opening, the Clifton Theatre was led by manager Joseph Lefkowitz, who had spent many years running the Montauk and Capitol Theatres in neighboring Passaic. Fast-forward to the 1950s, and the movie house was a Main Avenue fixture, showing such films as 1953's *Dream Wife* with Cary Grant and, a few years later, *Snow White and the Seven Dwarfs.* (Courtesy of Mark S. Auerbach.)

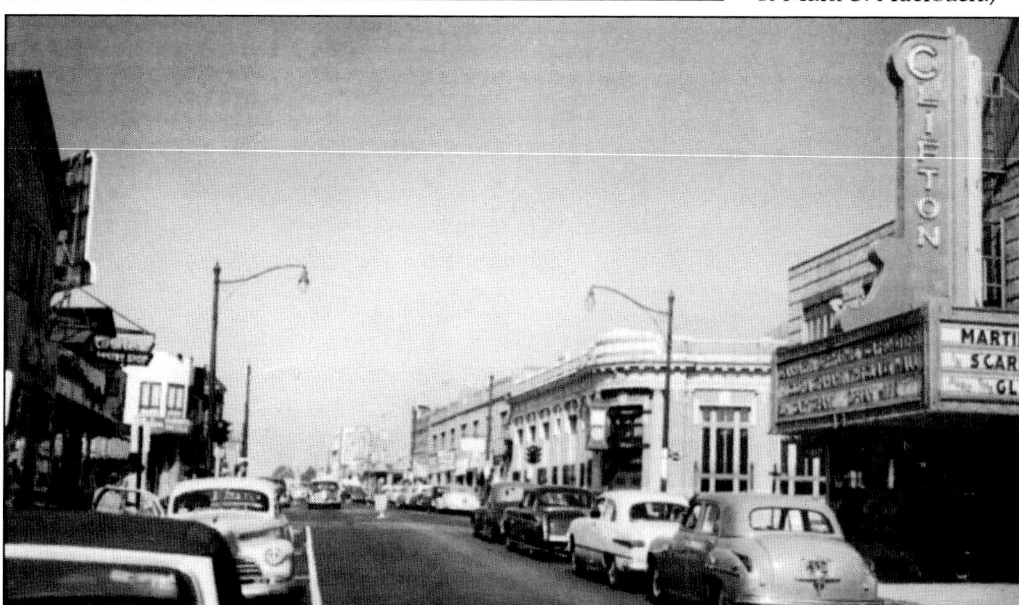

The 1,050-seat Clifton Theatre, declaring itself a "crowning achievement of theater elegance," ran this newspaper advertisement for its New Year's Eve 1937 opening on the city's Main Avenue. (Author's collection.)

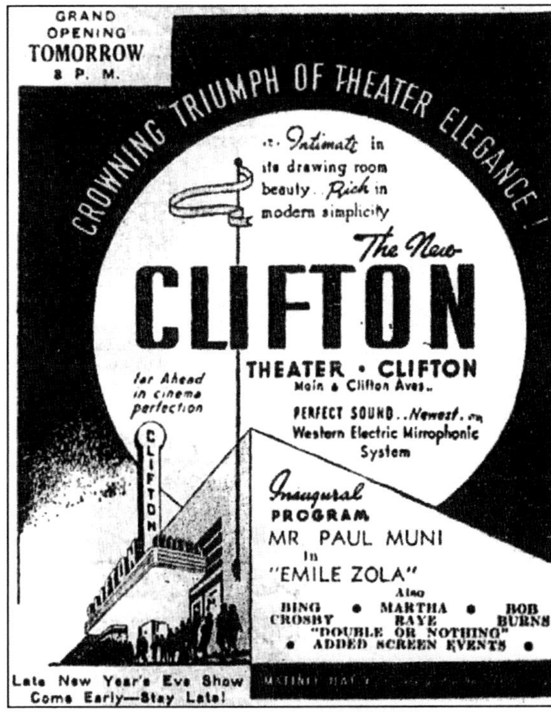

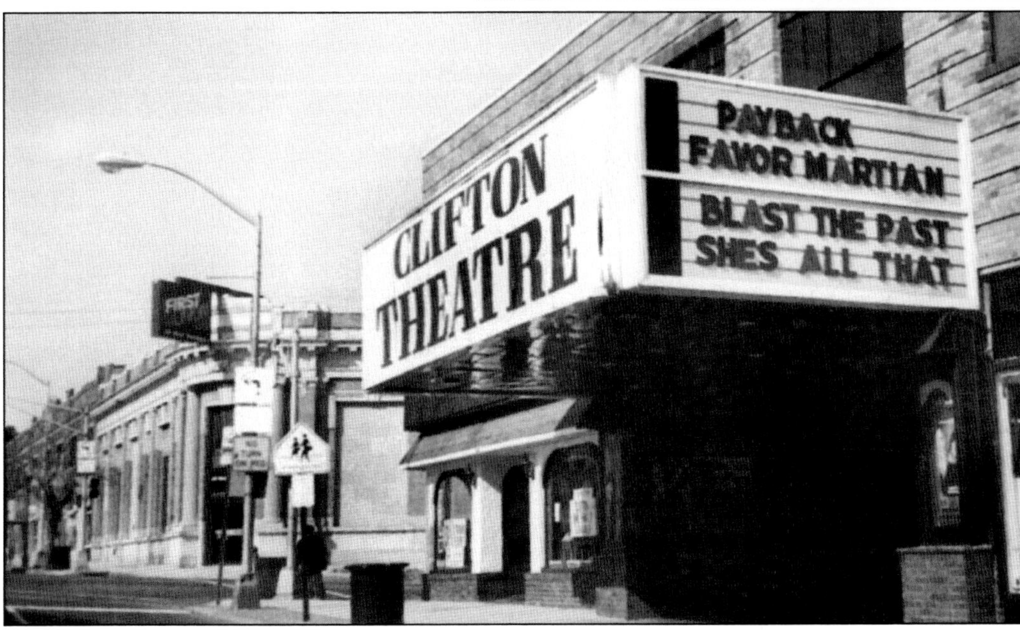

The Clifton Theatre, shown here in 1999, closed in April 2000, destined to be replaced in a redevelopment plan that soon bought a Walgreen's pharmacy to Main and Clifton Avenues. "I can remember going with friends to Saturday matinees," Mayor James Anzaldi said in an article by reporter Justo Bautista of Hackensack's *The Record*. "And once a year, the PTA would have movie day. . . . It was good while it lasted, but the theater business is so different today. Everything is plex, 16-plex." A year earlier, a 16-plex did indeed open at the new Clifton Commons shopping complex along Route 3. (Courtesy of Mark S. Auerbach.)

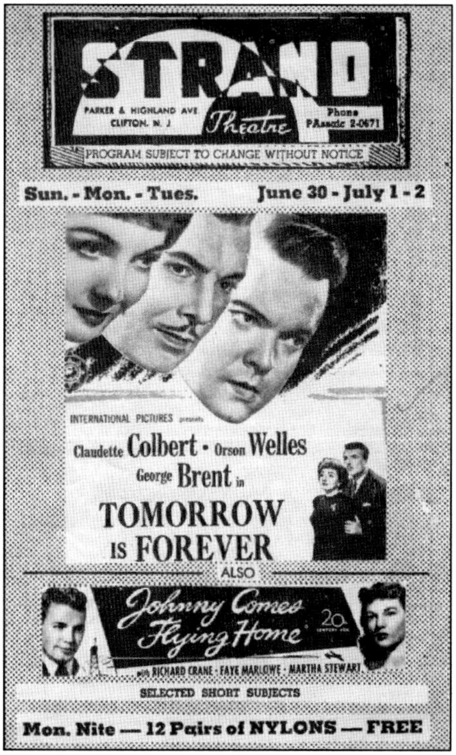

The Strand Theatre, a small venue with just 665 seats in Clifton's Botany section, drew crowds into the 1950s. The top billing in July 1946 was *Tomorrow Is Forever*, a love story that took theatergoers "through a deep emotional bath" in the words of a film reviewer at *Variety* magazine in late 1945. (Author's collection.)

In 1952, a mailer for the Allwood Theatre in Clifton carried advertisements for such nearby businesses as the Treasure Nook gift shop and the Rain Barrel Launderette, both neighbors on Market Street. Later, the theater was converted to a six-screen movie house. (Author's collection.)

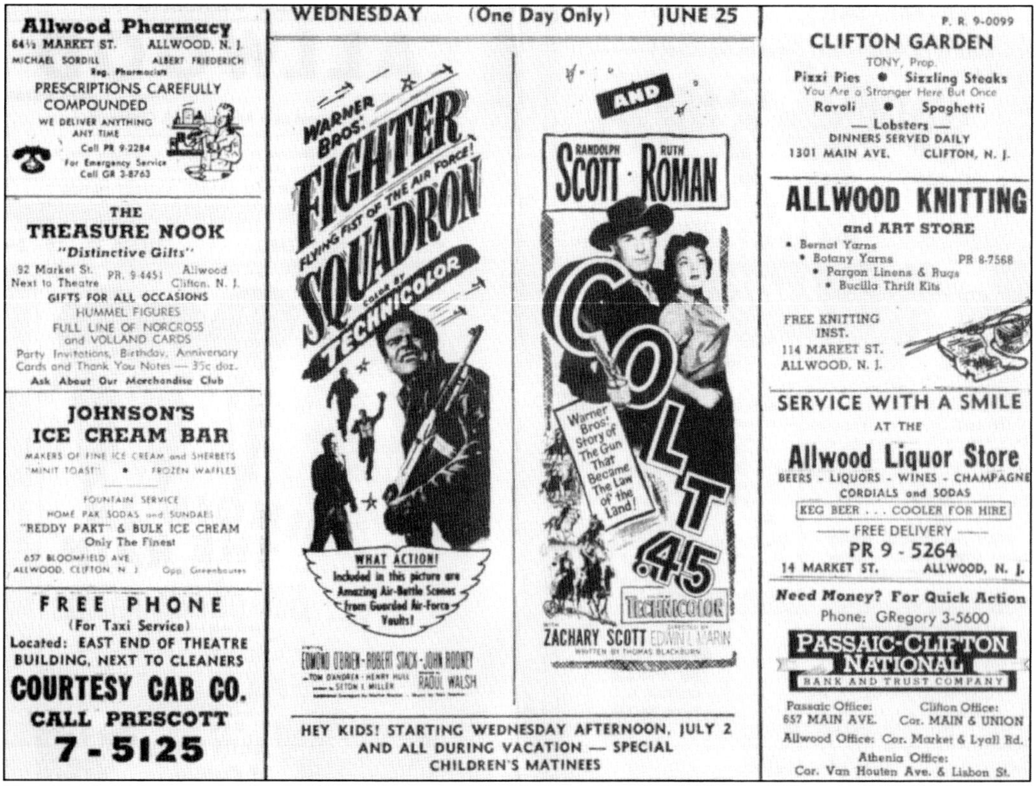

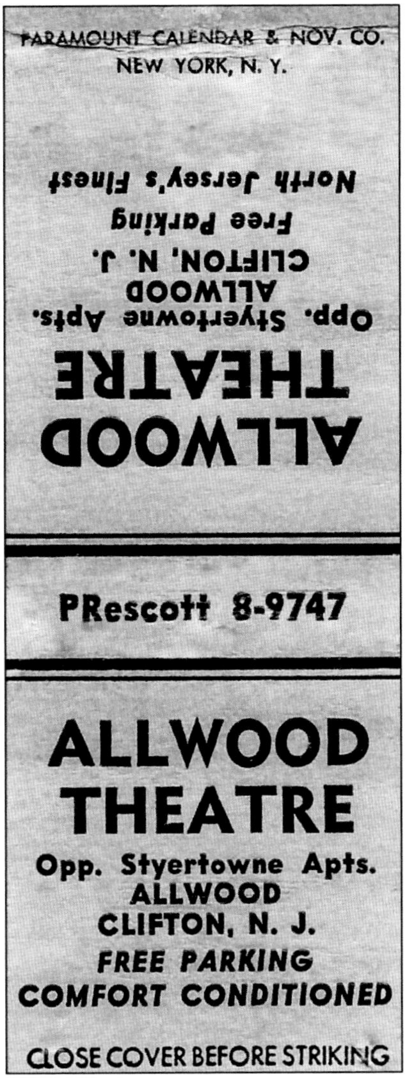

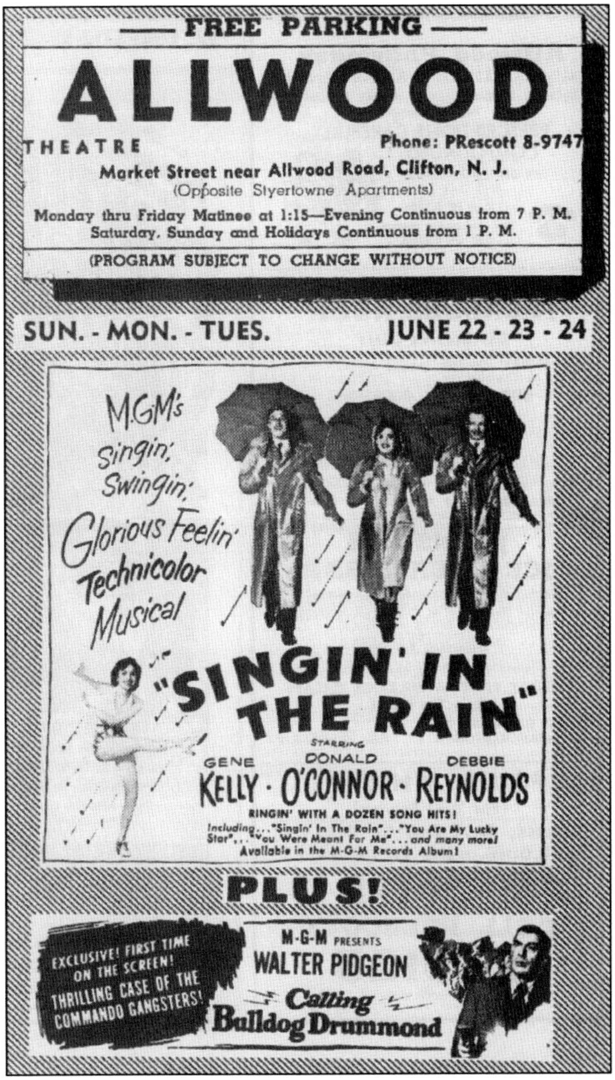

Hollywood came to Clifton's Allwood section on July 26, 1950, when more than 1,000 people gathered under floodlights for the opening of the Allwood Theatre. The celebrity on hand was Tom Ewell, who starred with Katharine Hepburn and Spencer Tracy in 1949's *Adam's Rib*. Ewell, according to an article by Daniel Duffield of the *Herald-News*, told visitors to the Allwood about his experience working with Tyrone Power in the 1950 war drama *American Guerrilla in the Philippines*. He would later star opposite Marilyn Monroe in 1955's *The Seven Year Itch*. Also on hand at the Allwood opening were Harry Hecht, the theater executive from Clifton's Rosemawr section, and Simon H. Fabian, president of Fabian Theaters, Inc. In a full-page newspaper advertisement toting the theater's opening, the design of the movie house is credited to architect Sidney Schenker of Paterson. A premiere of *Broken Arrow*, starring Jimmy Stewart, was the first to flash on the screen, ahead of the feature *Night and the City* with Richard Widmark. (Author's collection.)

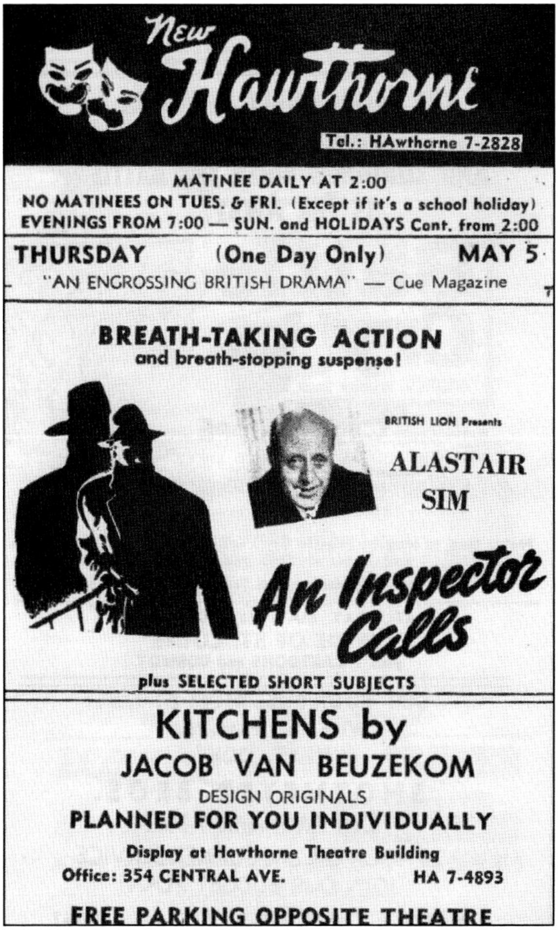

The Hawthorne Theatre opened on January 14, 1928, stating in its first brochure that it would be screening such films as *Ben Hur* and *Beau Geste*, the first film version of Percival Christopher Wren's classic adventure novel about three brothers who join the French Foreign Legion to shield their family's honor. Here, its mailer advertises the showing of 1954's *An Inspector Calls*. The Hawthorne Theatre was designed in the Moorish-Spanish style by Henry Barrett Crosby according to a story on the theater's opening in the *Hawthorne News*, a weekly. Other works attributed to Crosby are the George L. Pease Memorial Library (1923) in Ridgewood, Clifton Public School No. 15, and the old Clifton High, now a middle school. (Author's collection.)

The Oxford Theatre on Stevens Avenue near Main Street in Little Falls was dubbed "one of the foremost theaters of Spanish design in the East" when it opened. (Author's collection.)

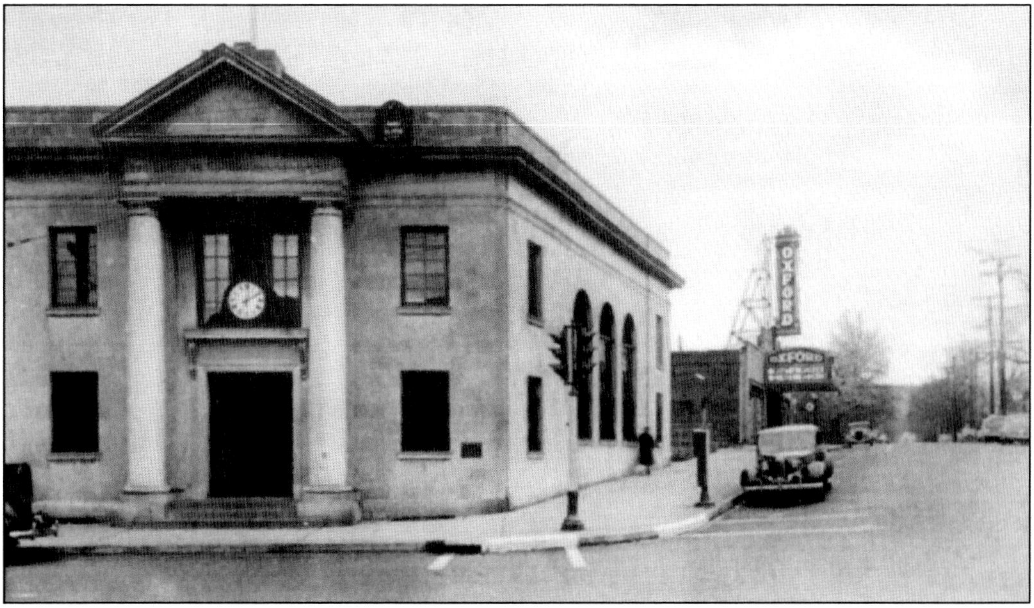

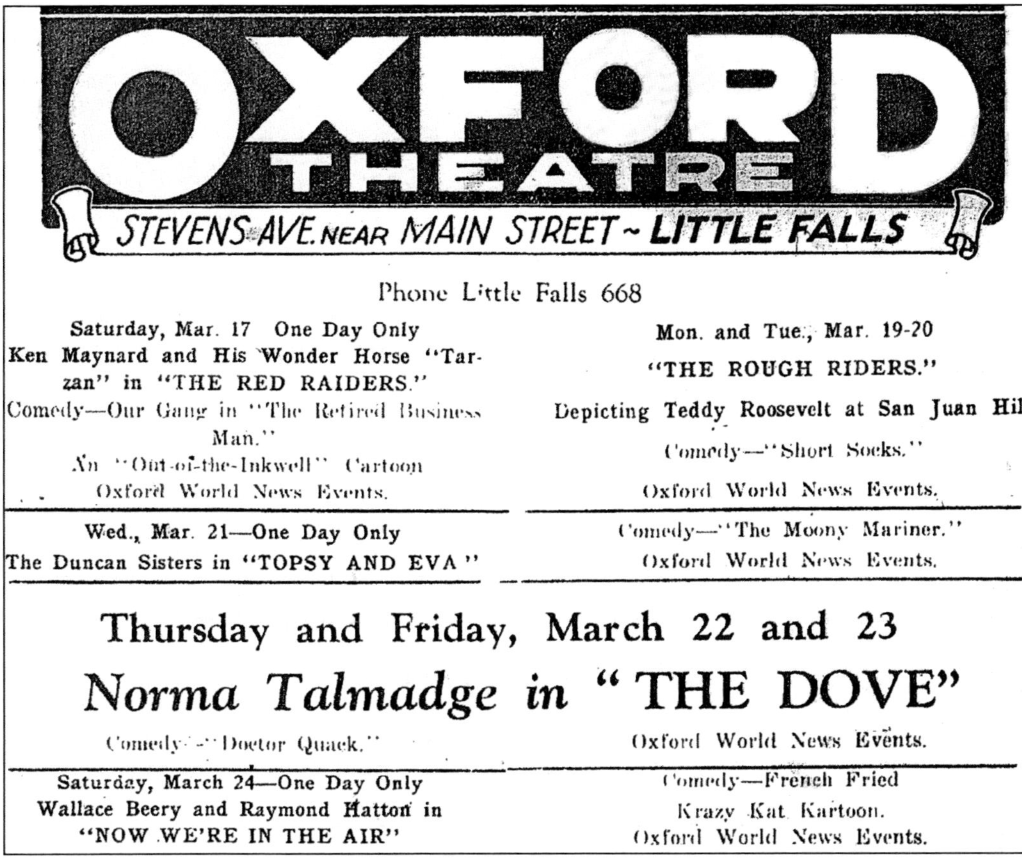

"Theater Opening in Little Falls a Gala Affair" read the headline in the March 1, 1928, edition of the *Little Falls Herald*. Some 1,200 to 1,300 gained entry to the 1,200-seat theater, with an additional 500 left outside on opening night, February 24. The theater staff even had the honor of getting their names mentioned in print: Lillian Jundoso and Theresa Freund, ushers; Eleanor Romaine, cashier; and Edward Bissier, "at the door." The theater building, meanwhile, already had a new occupant: Albert Sietsema opened a new music store, selling Victrolas, pianos, and sheet music. Just days later, the Oxford was running advertisements in the newspaper. (Courtesy of the Little Falls Public Library.)

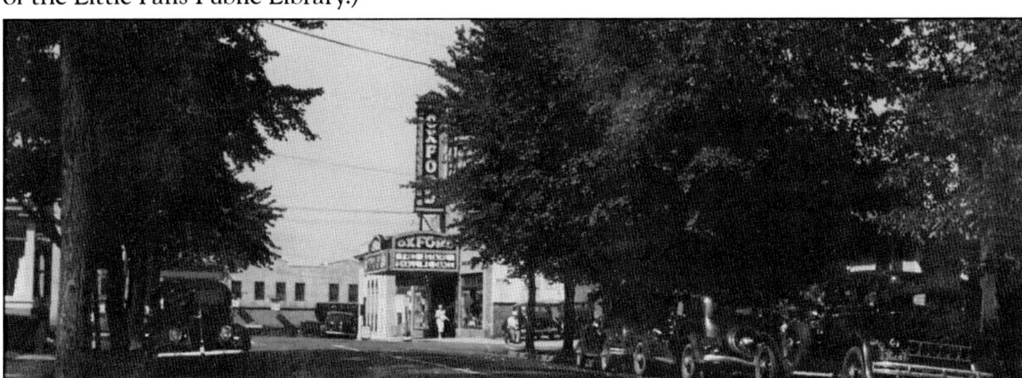

In 1937, the Oxford in Little Falls was showing *Shall We Dance*, with Fred Astaire and Ginger Rogers. (Courtesy of the Little Falls Public Library.)

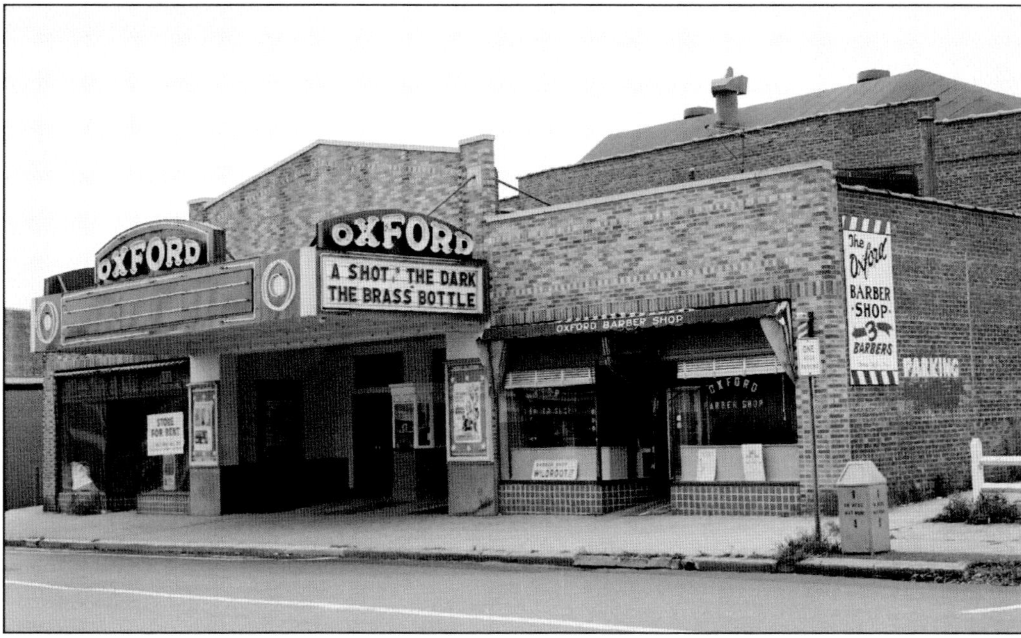

In August 1964, the comedy *A Shot in the Dark*, starring Peter Sellers, was the fare at the Oxford Theatre. The movie house soon closed and was demolished. (Courtesy of the Paterson Museum/Paterson News Collection.)

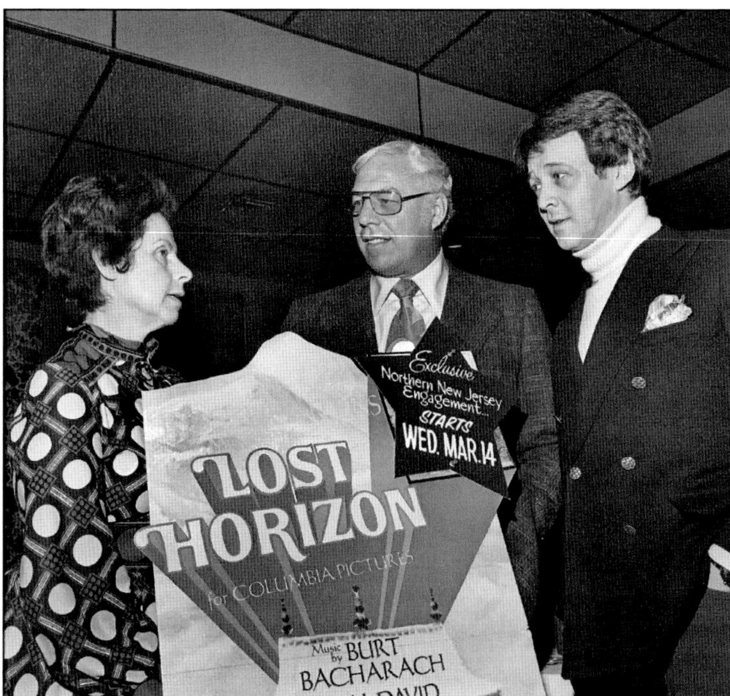

The world premiere of *Lost Horizon* brought out George Kennedy (center) and Bobby Van (right), two of its stars, to one of the four New York metropolitan-area debuts on March 13, 1973; this one was at the Totowa Cinema. The event was a benefit for the Passaic County Heart Association. The film was a retelling of the classic tale of James Hilton's utopian lost world, something that played out in a score featuring the pop music of Burt Bacharach. (Courtesy of the Paterson Museum/Paterson News Collection.)

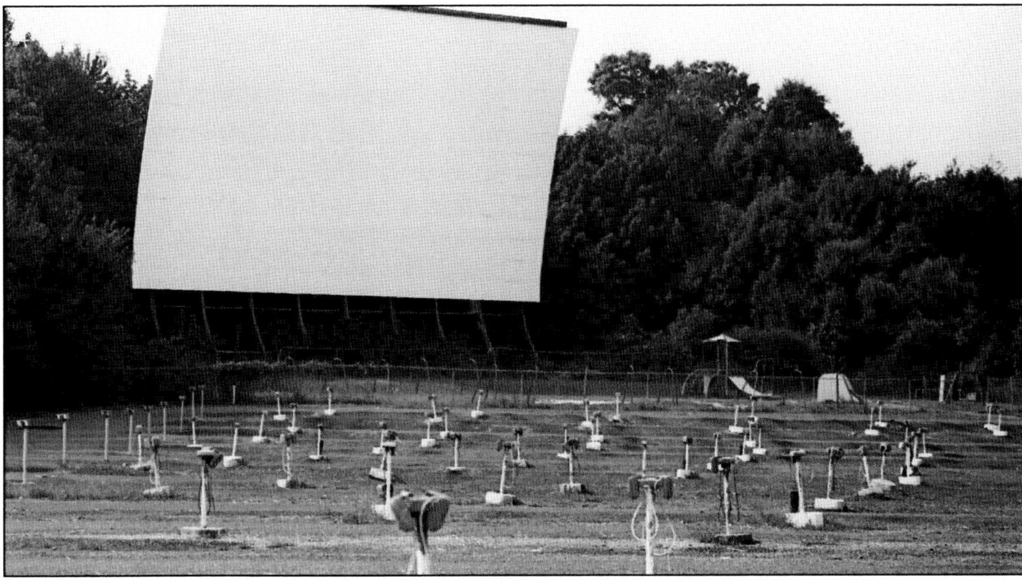

The Totowa Drive-in, on Route 46 and Union Boulevard, ended its 20-year stint in September 1974, the victim of rising real-estate values, and, in this case, making way for a new $9-million Hoffmann LaRoche, Inc., warehouse, according to a September 12, 1974, article in the *Paterson News*. Until the end, business was said to be booming at the General Cinema drive-in, then one of 10 it operated in New Jersey. "We recently showed *The Exorcist*, and we had cars backed up for almost a quarter-mile," the manager told reporter Dean Bender. In Totowa, the drive-in could hold about 1,200 cars. (Courtesy of the Paterson Museum/Paterson News Collection.)

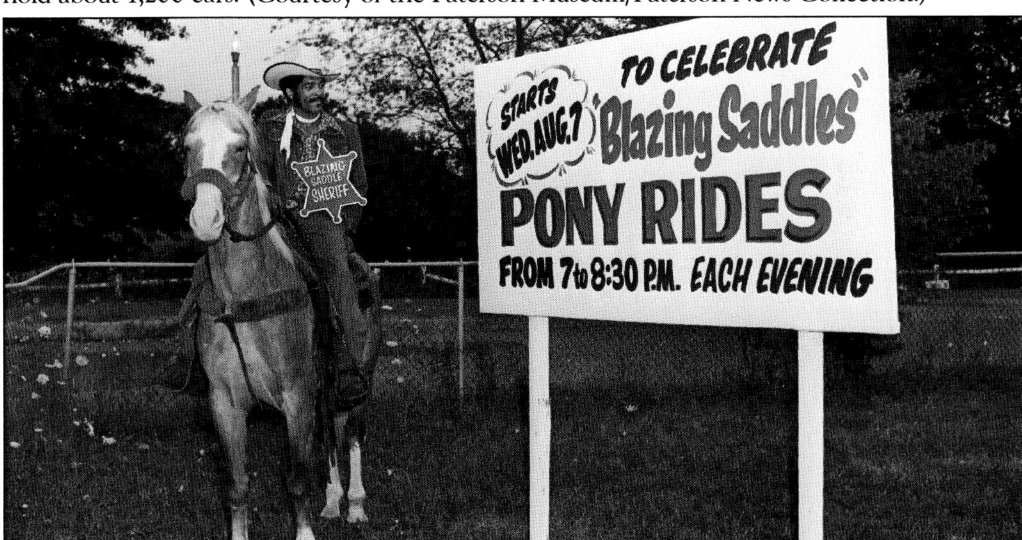

Mel Brooks's bad-taste spoof of Westerns, *Blazing Saddles*, arrived at the Anthony Wayne Drive-in on August 7, 1974, making for an outdoor theater experience off Route 23 in Wayne. The drive-in kicked in pony rides for the debut, starting at 7 p.m. each show night. Admission was just $3 per carload. The double feature also brought actress Jane Fonda to the big screen in the crime comedy *Steelyard Blues*. That week, the fare at other Wayne theaters was more subdued, namely with the showing of Walt Disney's *Herbie Rides Again* at the United Artists Wayne at the Preakness Shopping Center. (Courtesy of the Paterson Museum/Paterson News Collection.)

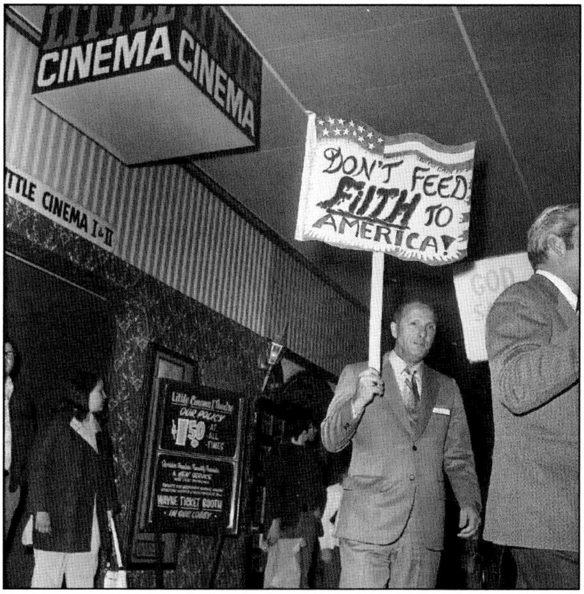

In 1973, pressure was on in Wayne against pornographic films, with the town's governing body even considering a ban on X-rated movies. At the Little Cinema at Willowbrook Mall, seen here, a group called Operation Groundswell picketed the showing of *It Happened in Hollywood*. Just days before, pickets did the same at the Wayne Theatre at Preakness over the showing of *Bed Career*. Read one placard: "Obscene Films Debase Womanhood and the Family Unit." (Courtesy of the Paterson Museum/Paterson News Collection.)

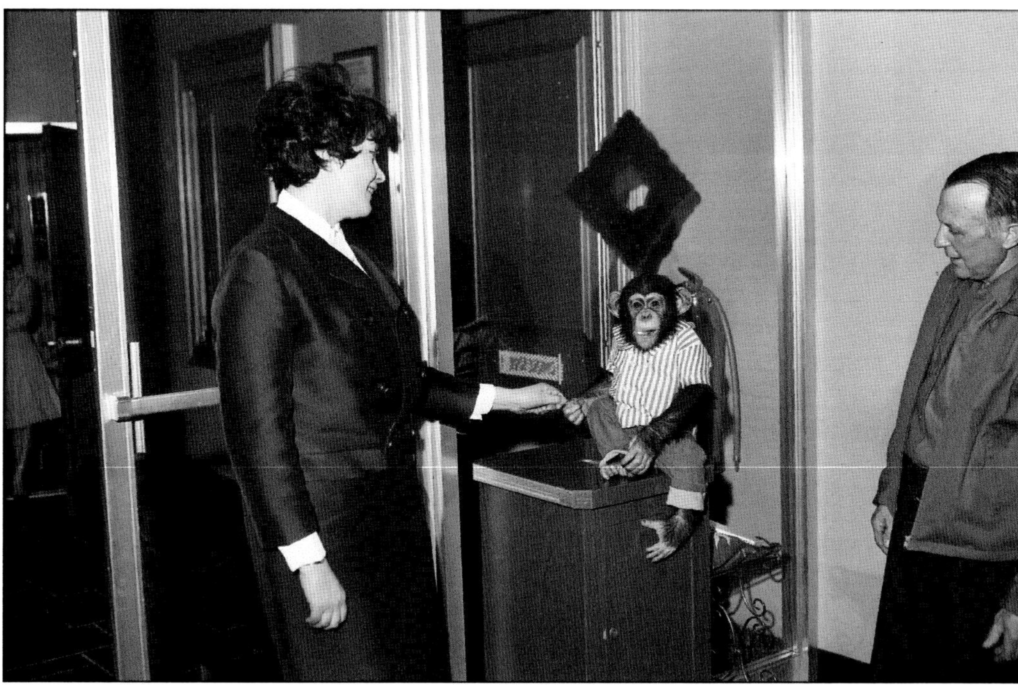

"Twiggy the Chimp" checks the theater stub for Patti Kilmurray, manager of the Wayne Theatre at the Preakness Shopping Center in Wayne, when *Planet of the Apes*, starring Charlton Heston and Kim Hunter, made its debut in April 1968. By 1973, the ape saga had generated four sequels: *Beneath the Planet of the Apes*, *Escape from the Planet of the Apes*, *Conquest of the Planet of the Apes*, and *Battle for the Planet of the Apes*. Yet, it was the closing scene in the original that is likely to best live on in the memory of filmgoers: the image of Heston, playing astronaut Taylor, falling to his knees on a beach as he recognizes the half-buried *Statue of Liberty* and laments the world's end with the words, "You blew it up! Damn you! God damn you all to hell!" (Courtesy of the Paterson Museum/Paterson News Collection.)

Six

HUDSON

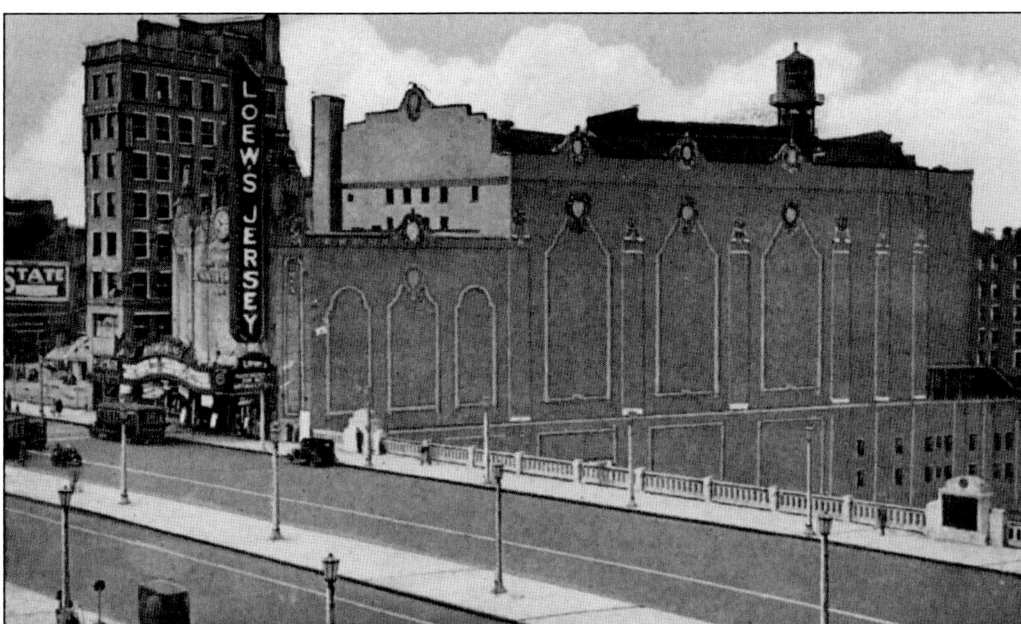

Loew's Jersey, attributed to designers Rapp & Rapp, opened in 1929 as one of Loew's five "Wonder Theaters." The 3,200-seat theater, overlooking Journal Square in Jersey City, featured an Italian baroque auditorium and was equipped with four identical Robert Morgan pipe organs, according to *Great American Movie Theaters*, by David Naylor. The restored Landmark Loew's Jersey is a performing-arts center today. (Author's collection.)

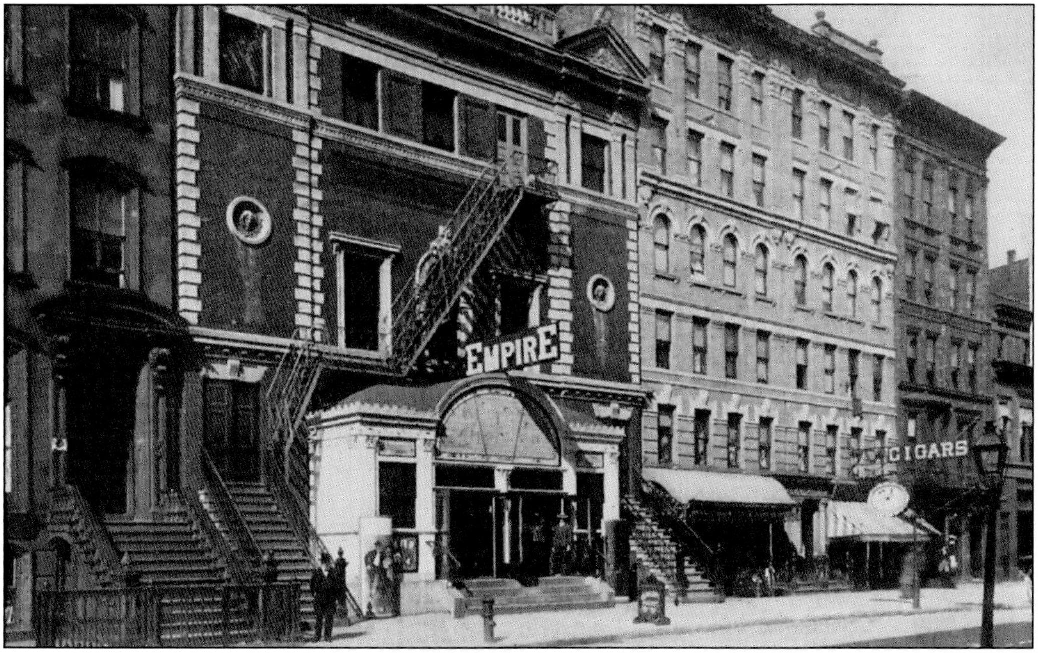

The Empire (above), a vaudeville house at 118 Hudson Street in Hoboken, was later known as the Rialto, which in December 1948 was the scene of a *Tribute to Frank Sinatra* (below), one of Hoboken's own. In the pit that night was John Marotta and his orchestra, as well as a future Hoboken mayor Steven Cappiello, seen on the stage in the fourth row. Looking down from the center of the balcony is Natalie "Dolly" Sinatra, the crooner's mother. (Courtesy of the Hoboken Historical Museum.)

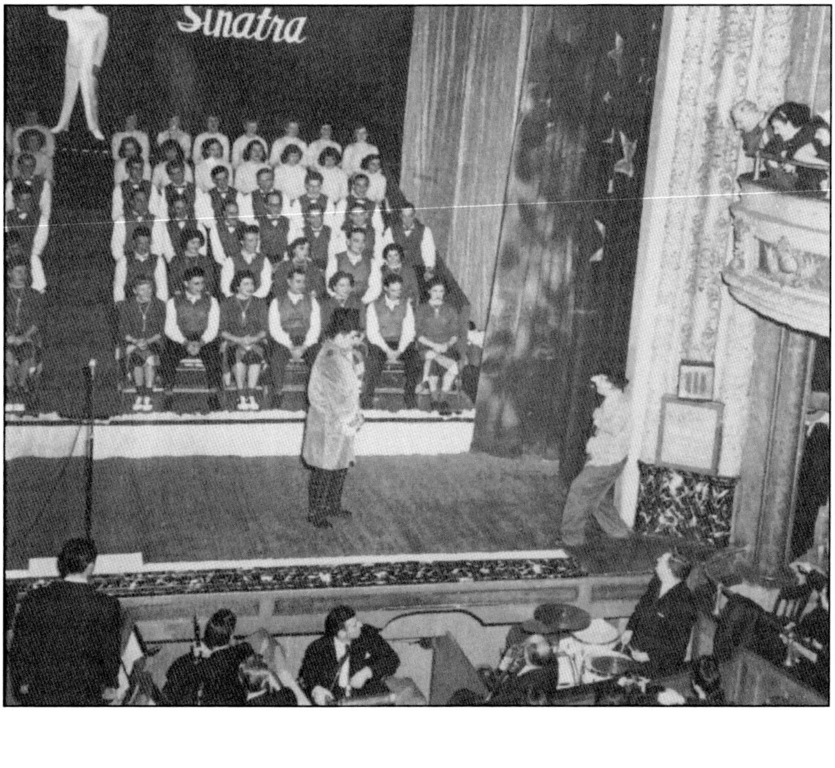

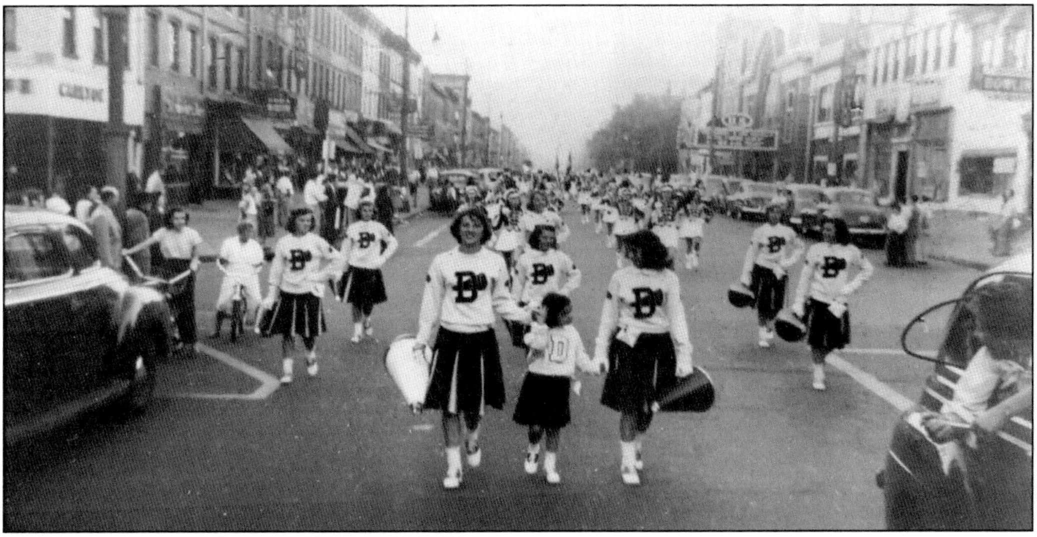

Demarest High School cheerleaders and marching band members make their way down Hoboken's Washington Street and past the U.S. Theatre marquee (right) after winning a football game in 1950. (Courtesy of the Hoboken Historical Museum.)

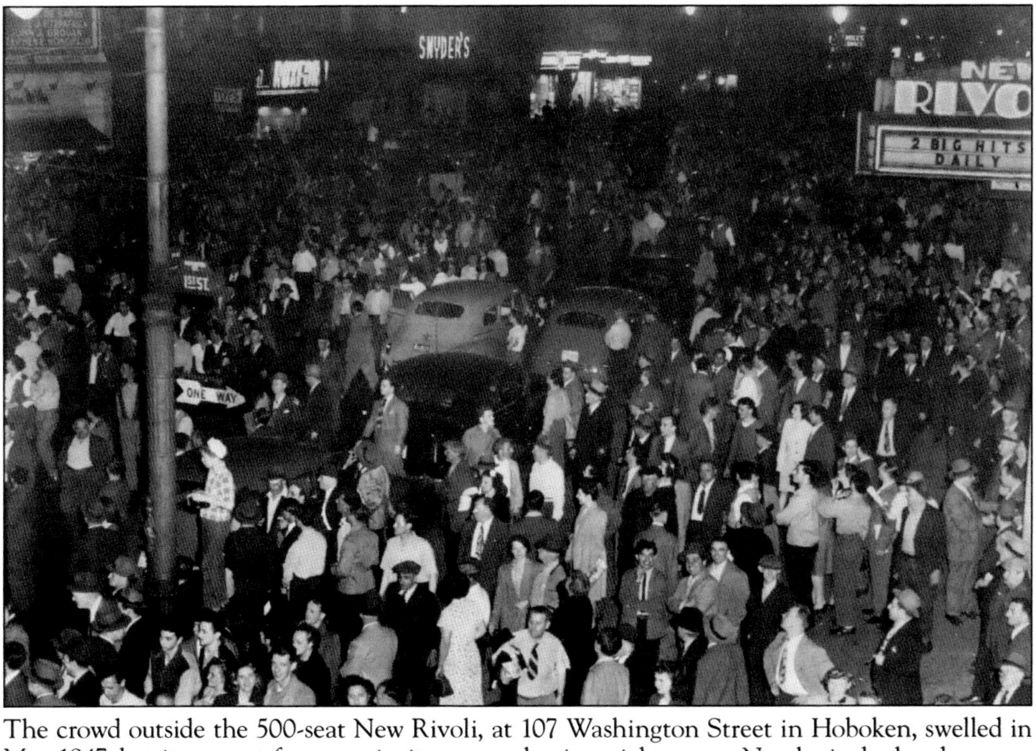

The crowd outside the 500-seat New Rivoli, at 107 Washington Street in Hoboken, swelled in May 1947, but it was not for a movie; it was an election night event. Nearby is the headquarters of the Good Government candidate slate. (Courtesy of the Hoboken Historical Museum.)

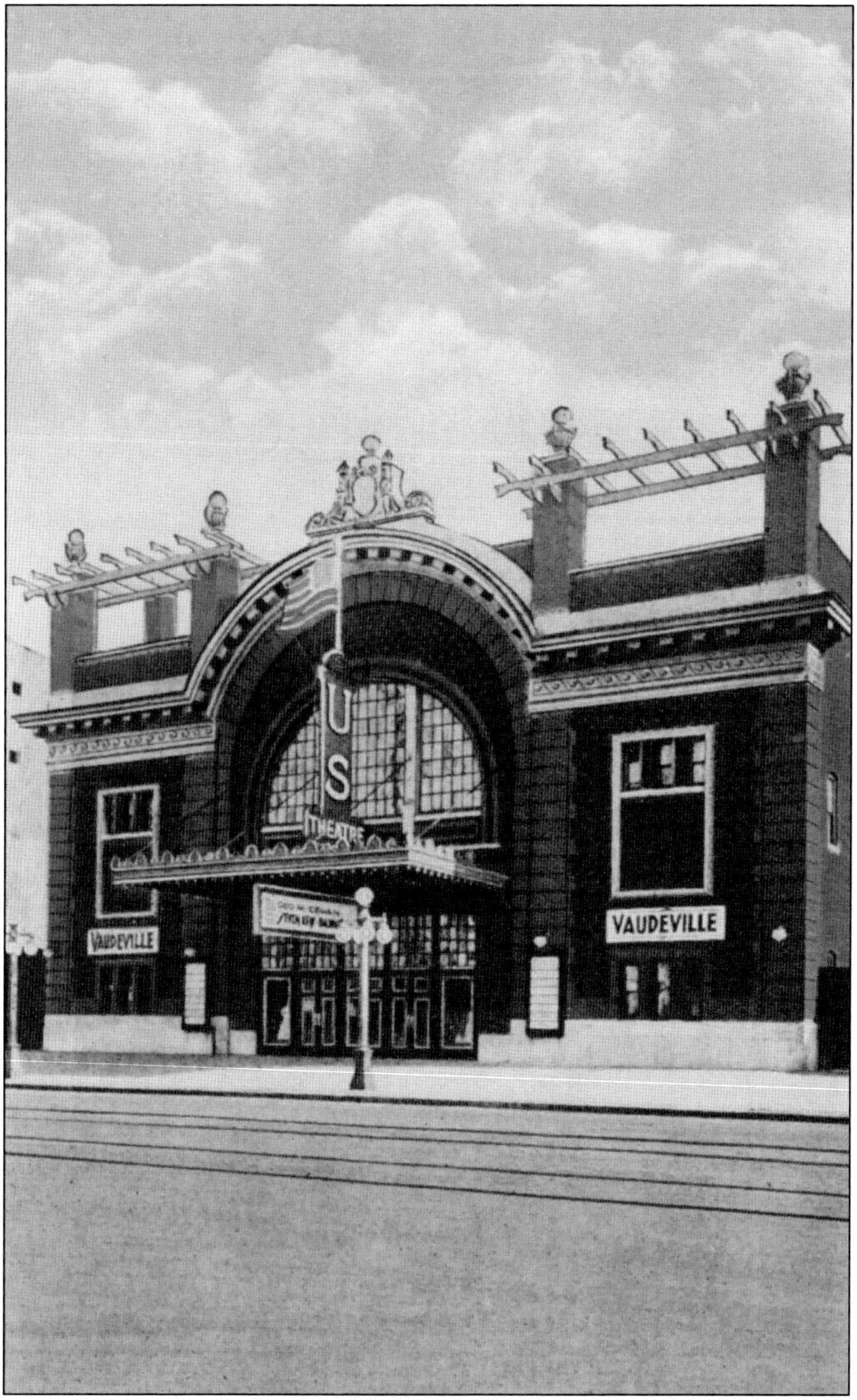

The 1,050-seat U.S. Theatre on Hoboken's Washington Street showed George M. Cohan's silent comedy *Seven Keys to Baldpate* in 1917. The film features a writer, played by Cohan, who arrives at the Baldpate Inn to win a wager to finish a novel in a single day, only to be repeatedly interrupted. In 1942, the same theater showed the film *Yankee Doodle Dandy*, a musical biography of song-and-dance man Cohan. (Courtesy of the Hoboken Historical Museum.)

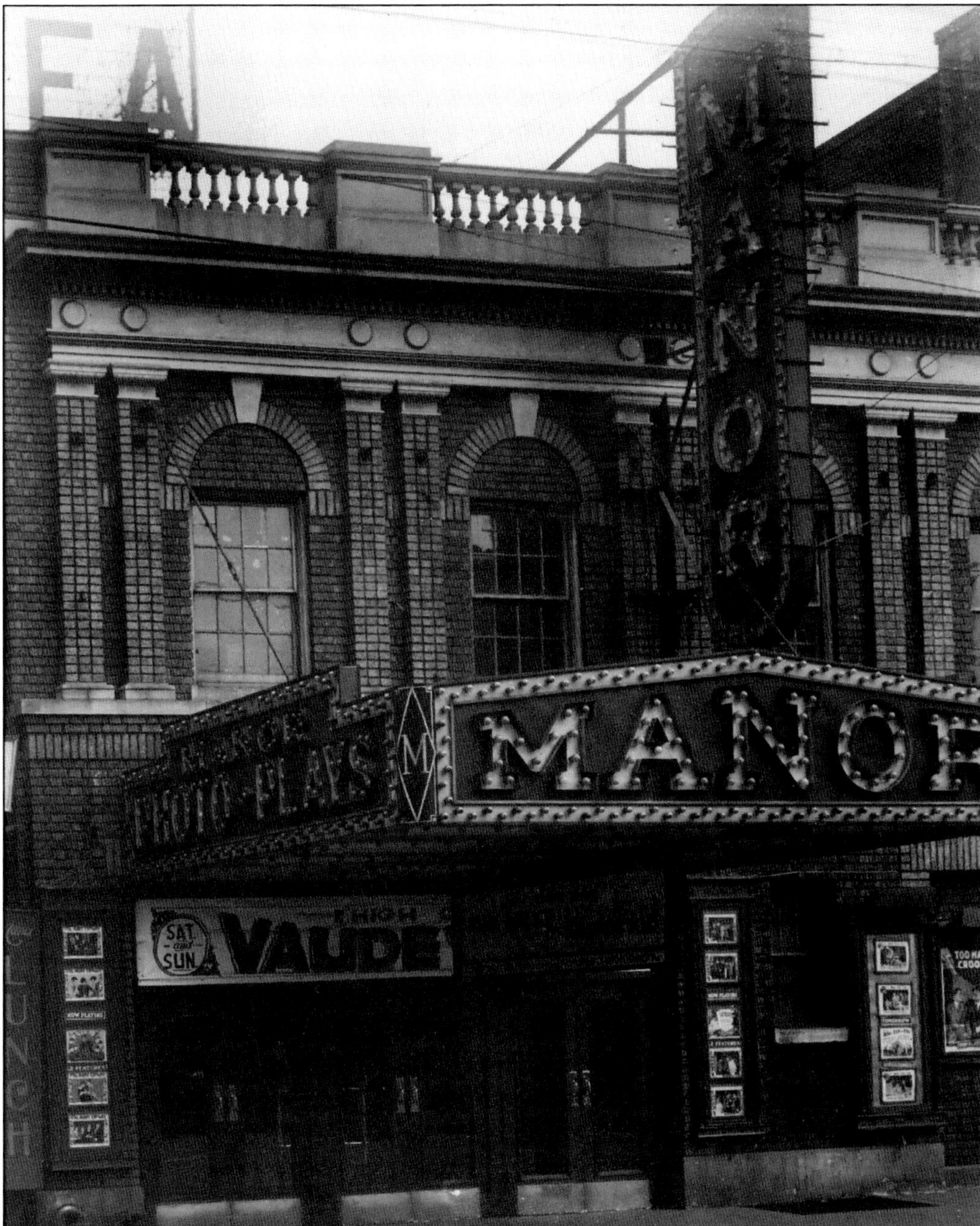

The Manor Theatre, at 58–60 Fourteenth Street in Hoboken, was showing 1927's *Too Many Crooks*, starring Mildred Davis, who was then well known for her roles as the leading lady in Harold Lloyd comedies. The Manor was the successor to the Ideal Theatre. (Courtesy of the Hoboken Historical Museum.)

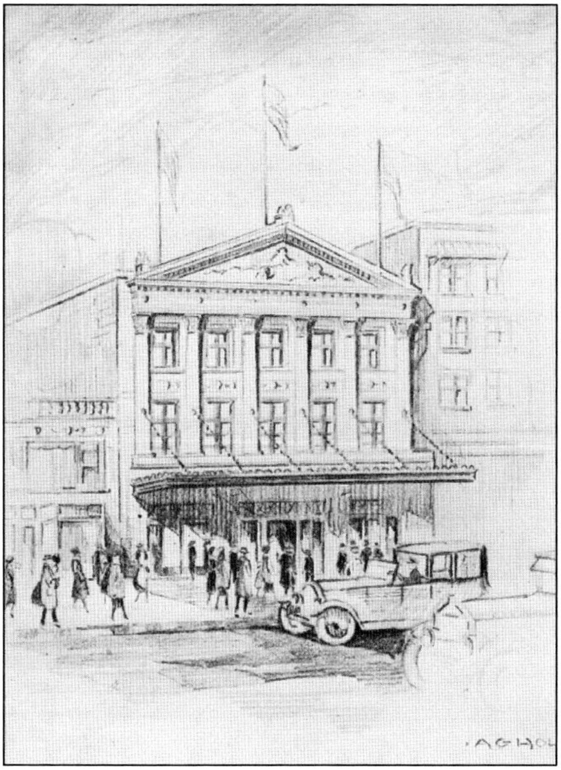

The premier program for the State Theatre in Jersey City featured this illustration of the venue by A.G. Holbrook. The event, on Monday evening, April 24, 1922, began with the State Orchestra led by conductor J.B. Shadduck playing the "The Star-Spangled Banner" and later included selections from *Madam Butterfly*. But there was more. The guests, who included Gov. Edward I. Edwards and Jersey City mayor Frank Hague, also witnessed "Vaudeville's Greatest Sensation," The Boltens, as well as a number of other acts. The evening wrapped up with the showing of D.W. Griffith's *Orphans of the Storm*, starring Lillian and Dorothy Gish, accompanied by an arrangement by Kate Claxton. The president of the State Theaters Corp., Frank G. Hall (below), put it this way: "It has been my one aim to give Jersey City a theater and entertainment worthy of its people, and in doing this I deserve no praise because I deem it an honor and a duty." (Author's collection.)

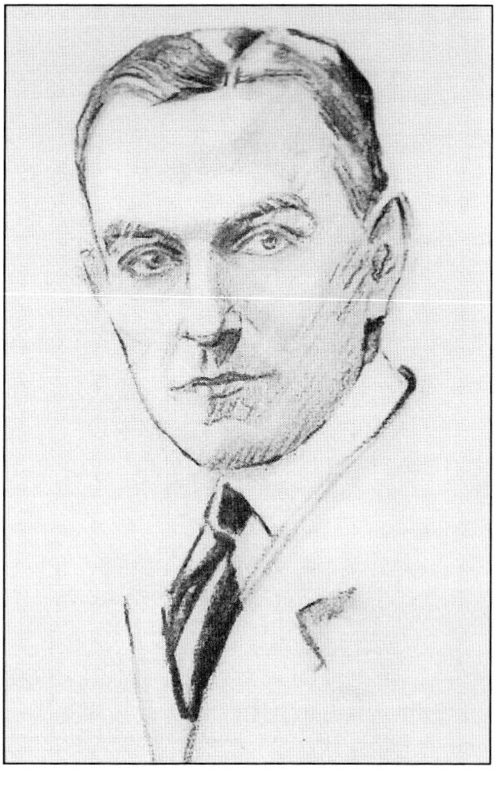

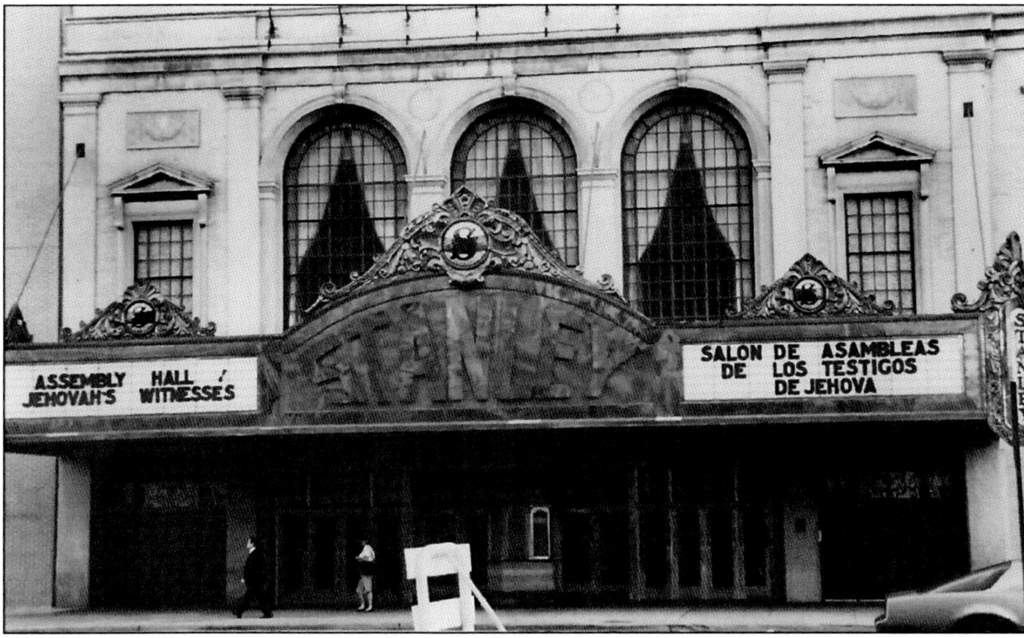

The Stanley Theatre on Jersey City's Kennedy Boulevard represents the apex of the theater-design career of its architect, Fred Wentworth, according to *The Life & Times of Fred Wesley Wentworth* by Richard E. Polton. Built in 1928, its 4,300-seat, Italian-courtyard auditorium had a proscenium arch modeled after the Rialto Bridge in Venice, according to David Naylor's *Great American Movie Houses*. Once acquired in 1983 by the Jehovah's Witnesses, the theater's old orchestra pit was replaced with a baptismal font. (Courtesy of the Hauss/Lewis Collection.)

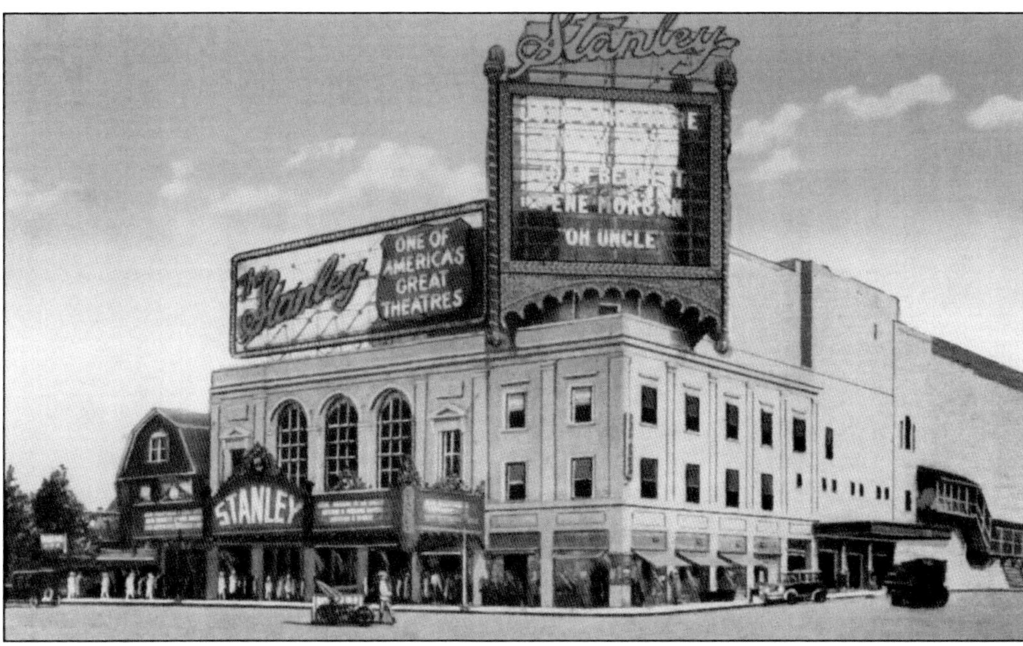

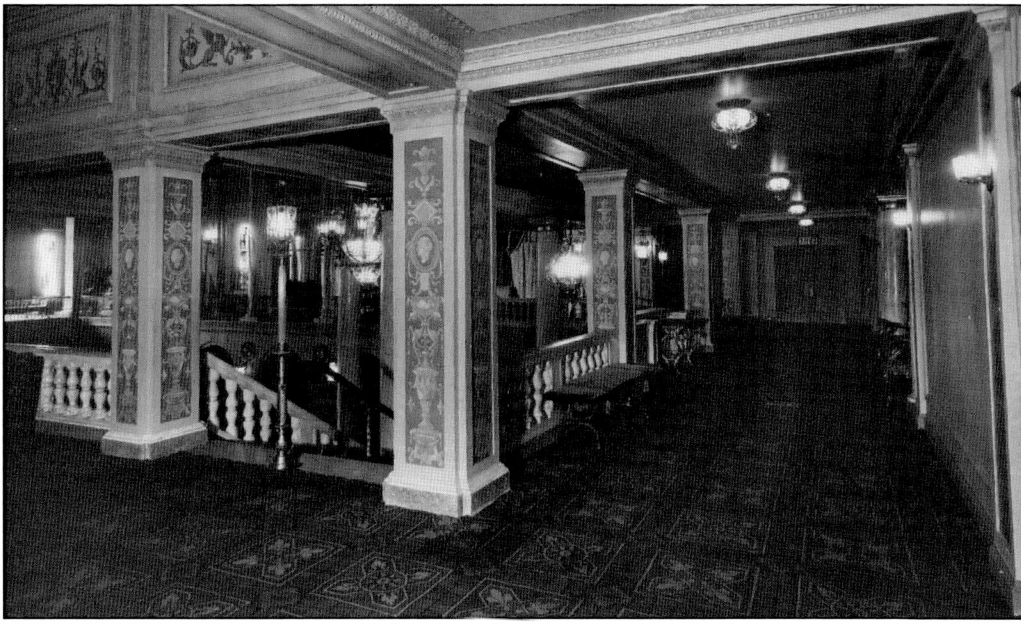

The interior of the Stanley Theatre was something to behold. One of its crystal chandeliers, suspended from the second floor amid decorative columns and a broad center staircase, came from New York's original Waldorf Astoria hotel of the 1880s, according to New Jersey City University. It is said to be 13 feet tall and 10 feet wide, illuminated by 144 bulbs that reflect off 4,500 crystal teardrops. (Courtesy of the Newark Public Library.)

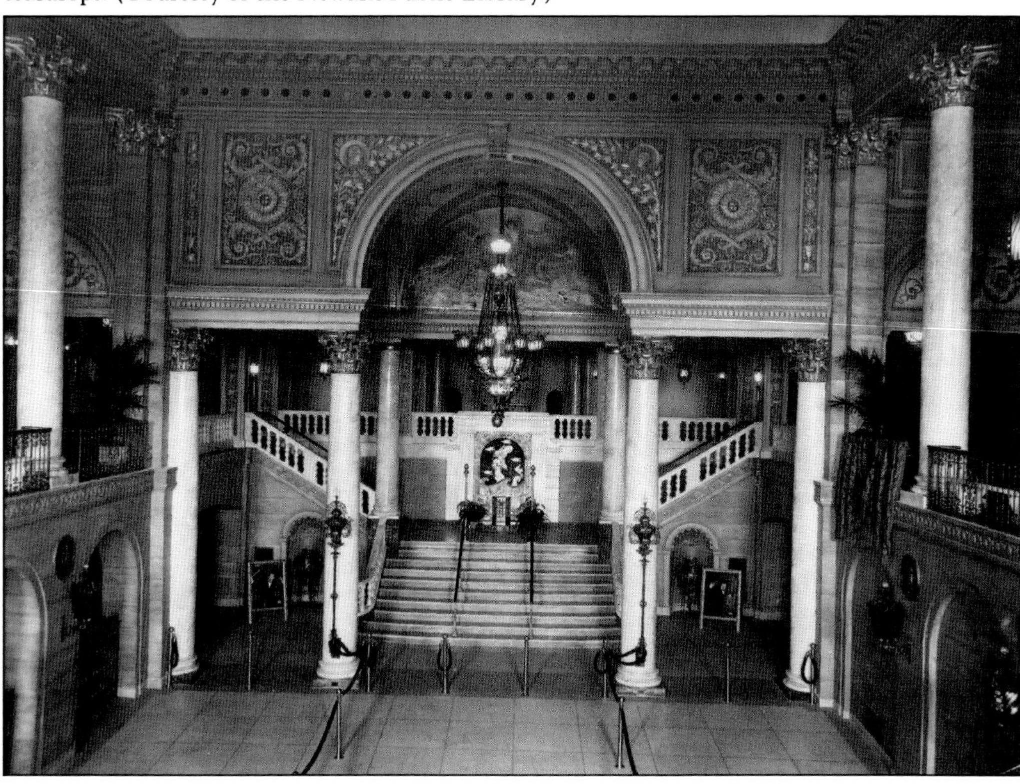

Seven

BERGEN

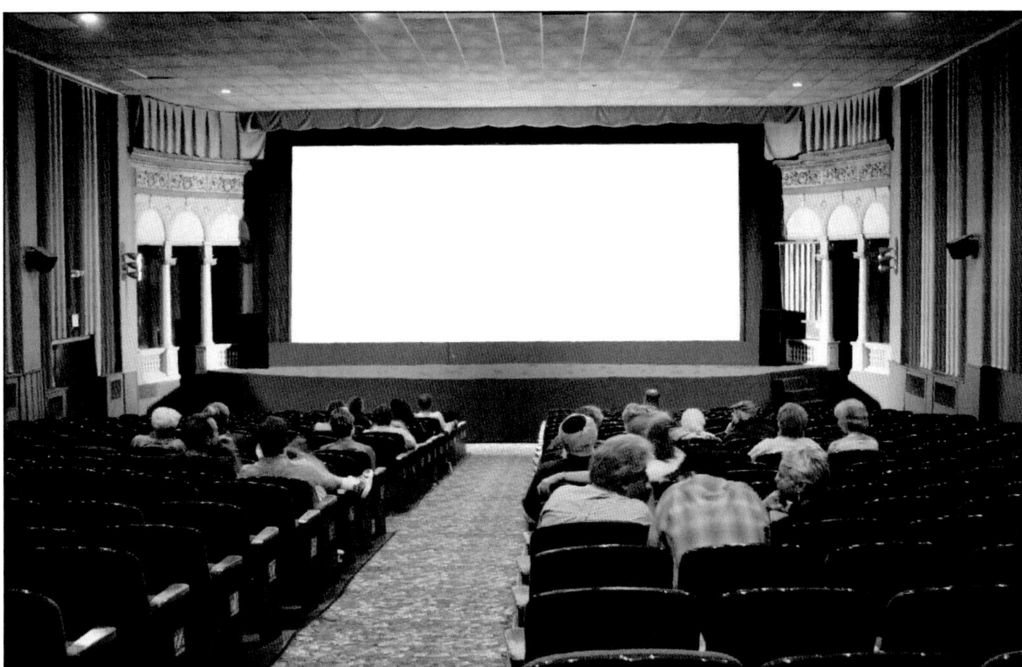

The Rialto was an intimate Ridgefield Park theater, where movies were projected on this screen by a classic Peerless Magnarc lamp house and Simplex E-7 Projector. The suburban town was once home to Ozzie Nelson, who grew up there before starring in the 1952–1966 TV sitcom *The Adventures of Ozzie & Harriet*. The c. 1927 movie house featured 500 seats and remained a single-screen theater on Main Street into 2008. "It was a true classic downtown theater," said Keith Ramer of Montclair in an article on NY1.com. (Courtesy of the Rialto/Sol Lang.)

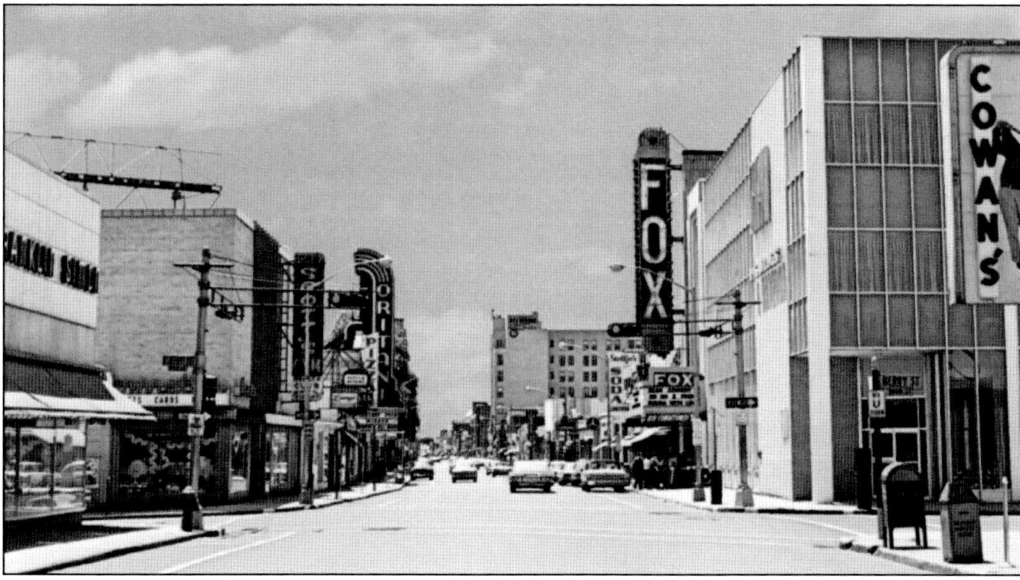

In 1965, competing Hackensack movie houses the Oritani and the Fox had this marquee matchup: The Oritani was showing *Mirage*, a thriller starring Gregory Peck as a New York accountant suffering from amnesia, while the Fox was showing a double feature starring Sean Connery in the James Bond spy flicks *Dr. No* and *From Russia with Love*. By the 1990s, the Art Deco–style Fox was gone, as was the Oritani. Gone were the days when a young William Marsden Read III would trek from neighboring Maywood to work as an usher at the Fox in the days before World War II. (Courtesy of the Johnson Public Library.)

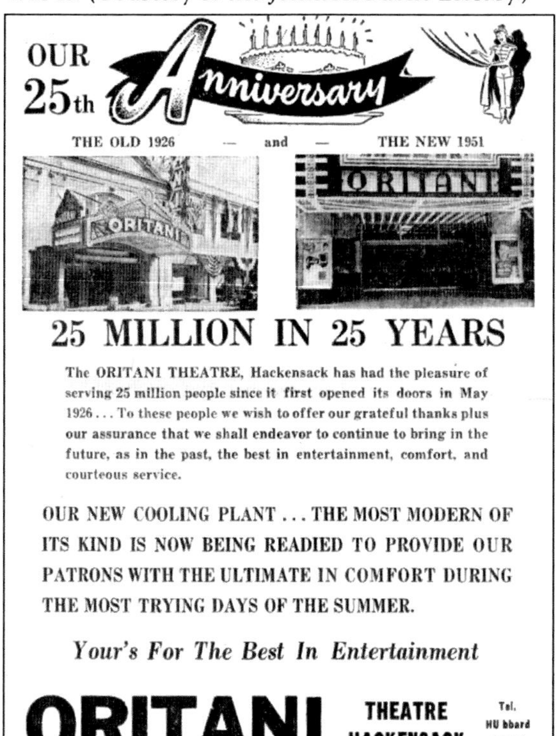

By 1951, Hackensack's Oritani Theatre touted 25 million patrons since it first opened in 1926. Imbedded in the sidewalk outside, according to a May 1951 article in the *Bergen Record*, was a circular plaque bearing the likeness of an Indian and a small turtle-like creature, with the inscription "Chief Oritani and His Mark." The theater, it turns out, was named after an American Indian chief who lived from 1577 to 1667 and led the Hackensack tribe, a branch of the Lenape. It was always kept polished, said George Birkner, a manager, but not by the theater's staff; college sororities had their pledges do the work. (Courtesy of the Johnson Public Library.)

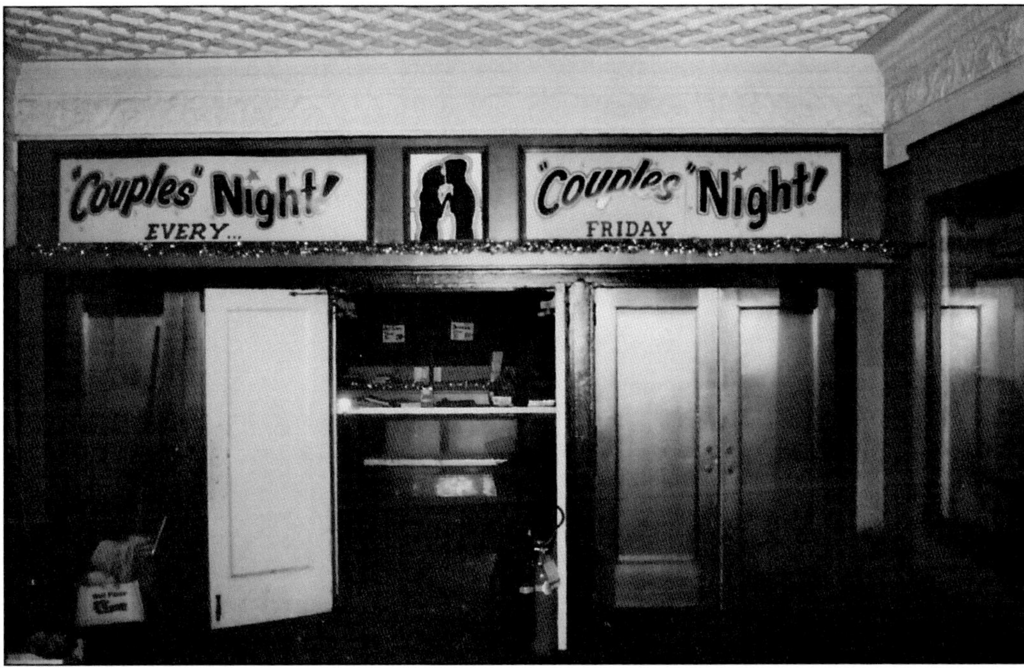

The Queen Anne Theatre, whose imposing facade can still be seen by passing motorists along busy Route 80 in Bogota, had 1,391 seats and in its heyday featured "Couples Night" every Friday. The theater, shown in the 1990s, in recent years housed a laundry. Still, it held memories, including this one captured in *The Ultimate James Bond Fan Book*, by Deborah Lipp. "On one memorable occasion," she wrote, "we saw a triple-feature of *Thunderball*, *You Only Live Twice*, and *Goldfinger* at the Queen Anne Theater in Bogota, New Jersey. We came in part way through *Thunderball*, watched the next two, and then stayed to see the beginning of *Thunderball* again. The influence of this experience on my young mind cannot be understated." (Courtesy of the Hauss/Lewis Collection.)

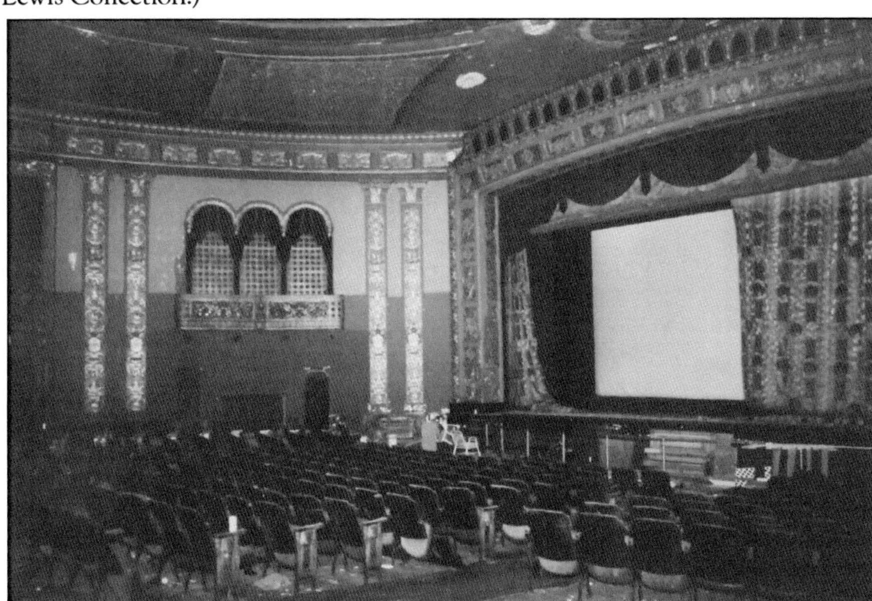

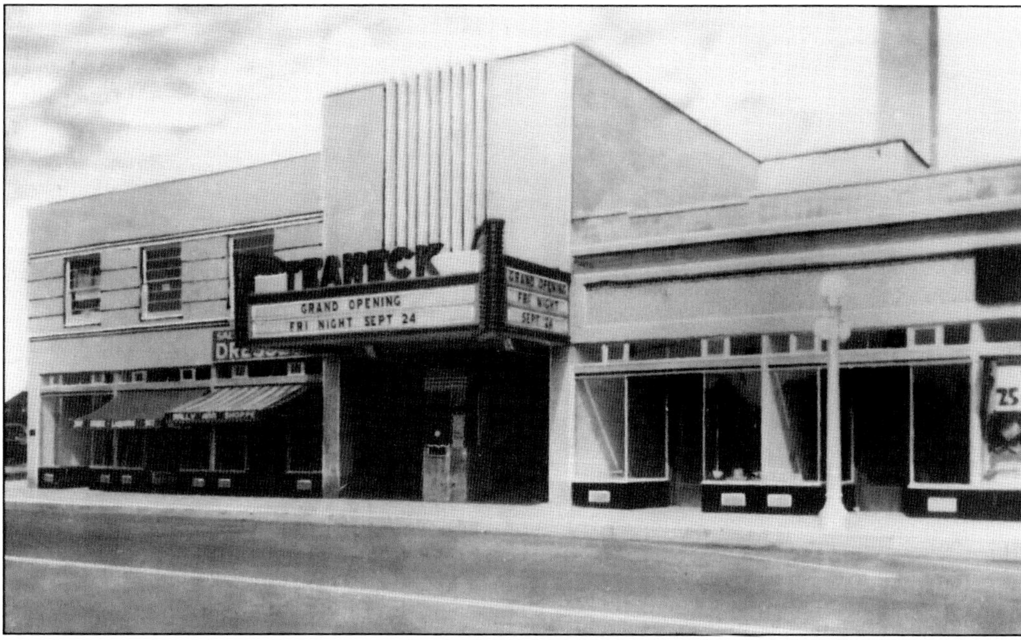

The 1,050-seat Teaneck Theater, later known as Cedar Lane Cinemas, opened in 1937, the handiwork of architect John Eberson. The first films were *Thin Ice* with Tyrone Power and *Wild and Woolly* with Jane Withers. In the audience that night of October 31 was township manager Paul A. Volcker, whose son would grow up to become the chairman of the Federal Reserve under Pres. Jimmy Carter and Pres. Ronald Reagan. Far earlier, in 1923, Eberson designed the Majestic Theatre in Houston, deemed the world's first "atmospheric" theater; it was one in a stable of some 100 theaters he designed in his career. (Courtesy of the Teaneck Public Library.)

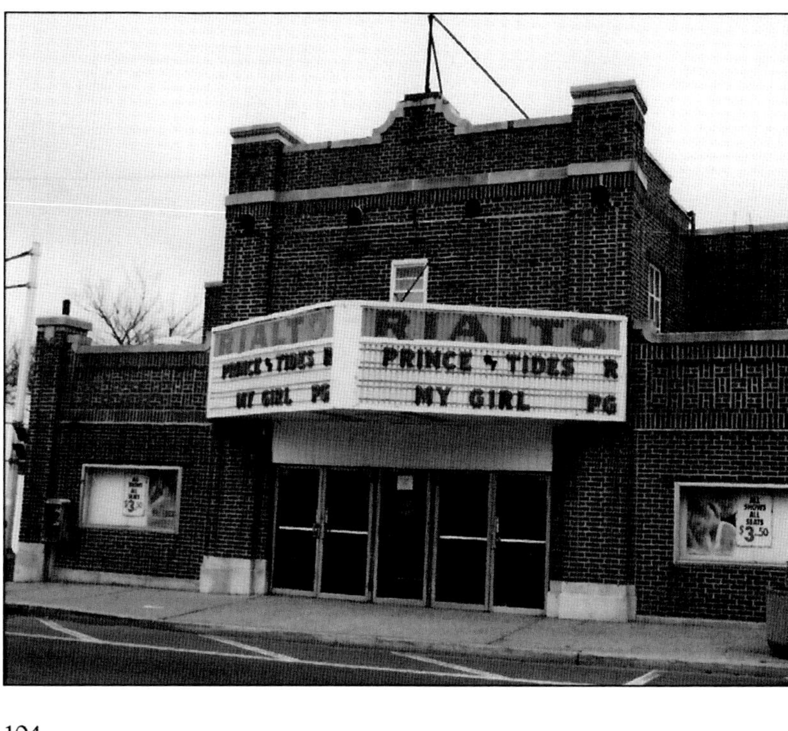

The Rialto was the hometown theater in Ridgefield Park. The c. 1927 movie house, the interior of which is pictured on page 101, featured 500 seats. (Courtesy of the Rialto.)

Eight

UNION

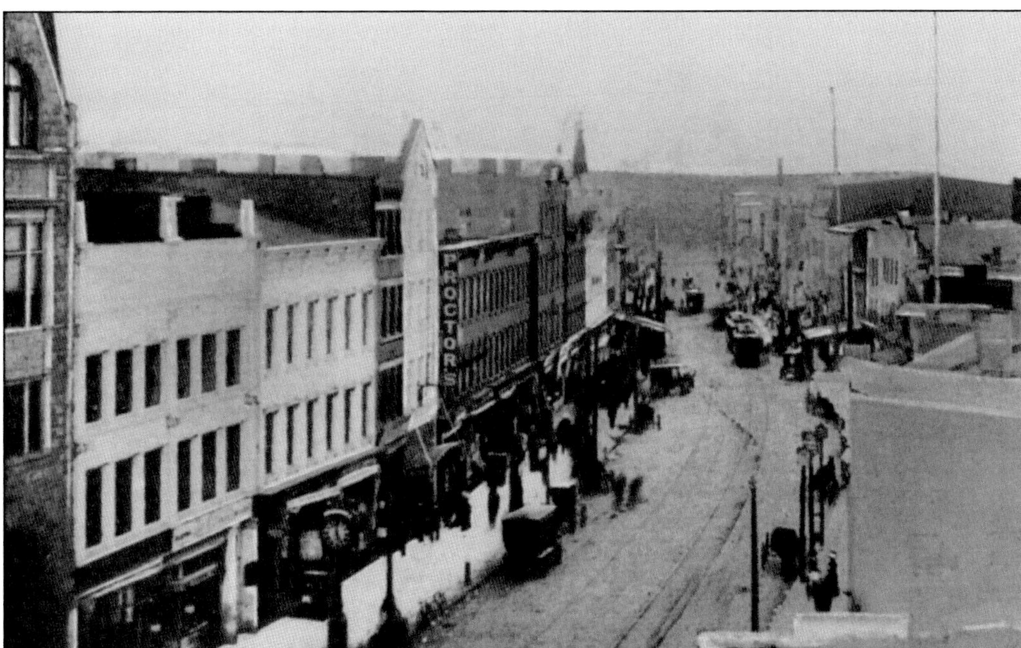

The March 10, 1922, edition of New York's *Evening Telegram* proclaimed, "Reade Acquires N.J. Theatres" when he increased his holdings to 13 in-state theaters with the $300,000 purchase of F.F. Proctor's Theatre, on Plainfield's Front Street, shown in this 1910 postcard scene. The theater, which opened as the Stillman Music Hall in 1884, was purchased from the Stillman estate and joined Reade properties in Asbury Park and New Brunswick, among others. The theater operated as Proctor's until 1922, when it was renamed the Oxford. It was among many Plainfield theaters, including the Astor, the Bijou, the Liberty, and the Strand, another of Reade's movie houses. (Author's collection.)

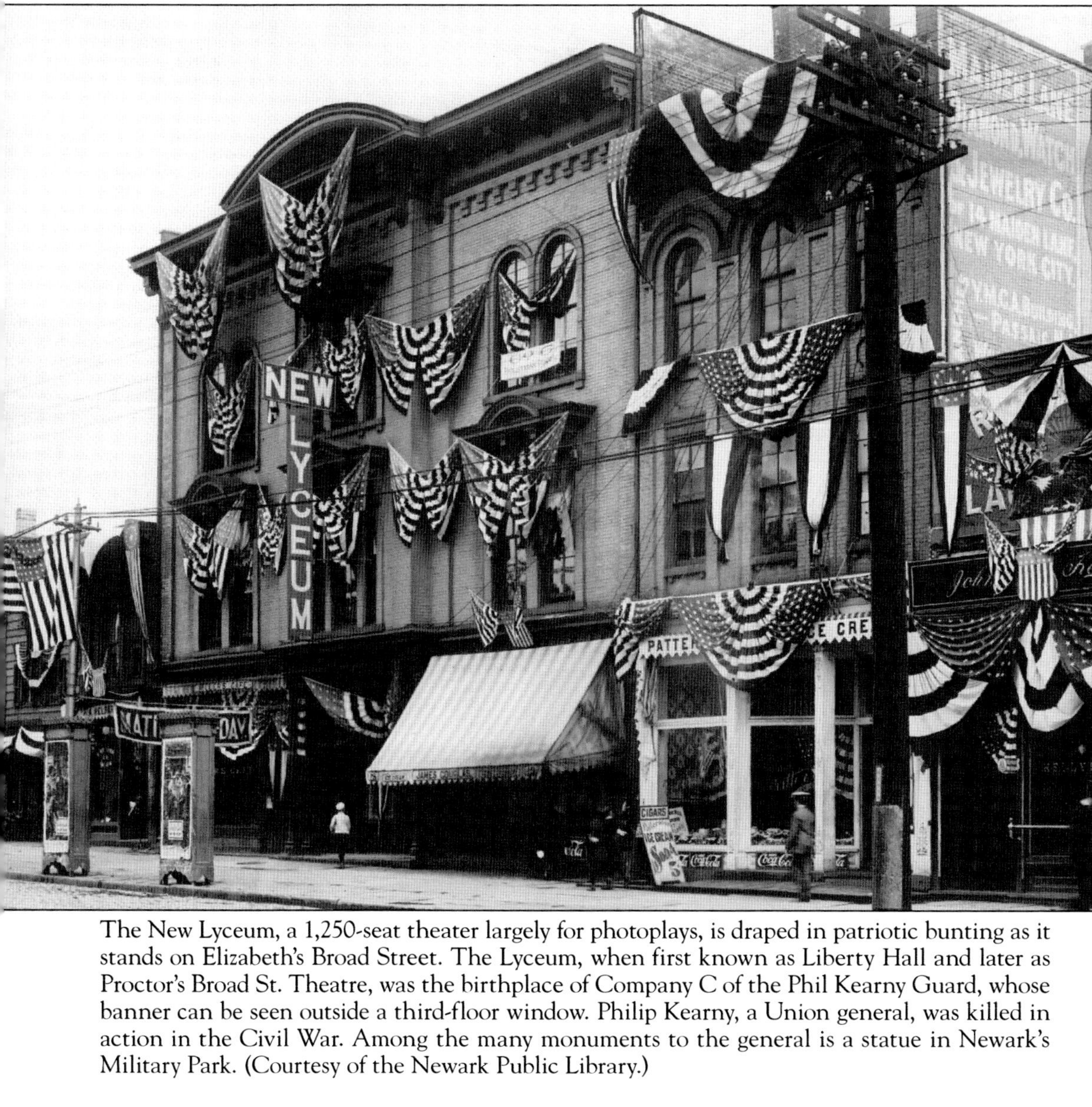

The New Lyceum, a 1,250-seat theater largely for photoplays, is draped in patriotic bunting as it stands on Elizabeth's Broad Street. The Lyceum, when first known as Liberty Hall and later as Proctor's Broad St. Theatre, was the birthplace of Company C of the Phil Kearny Guard, whose banner can be seen outside a third-floor window. Philip Kearny, a Union general, was killed in action in the Civil War. Among the many monuments to the general is a statue in Newark's Military Park. (Courtesy of the Newark Public Library.)

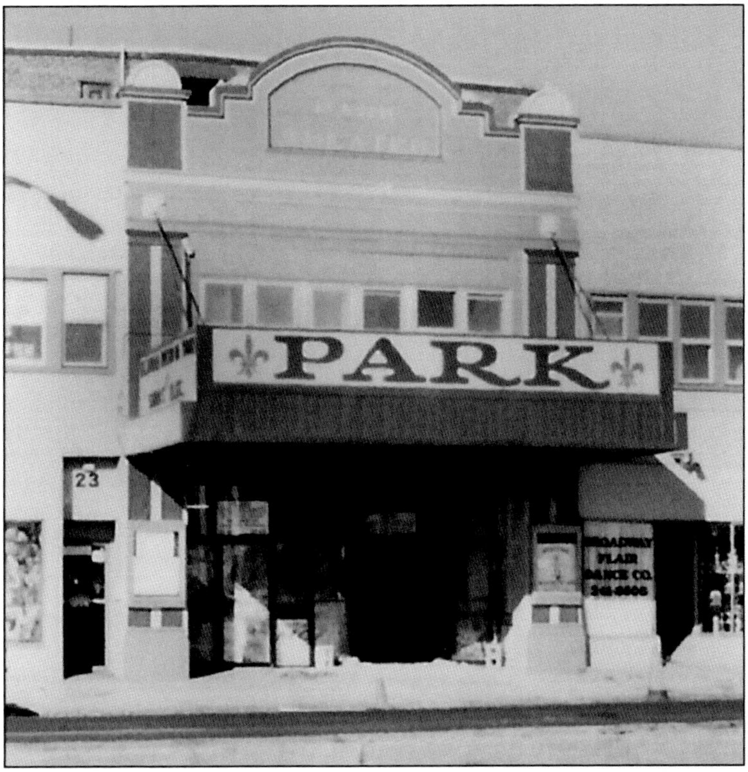

In 1999, the Art Deco Park Theatre in Roselle Park, a 1920s venue with some 1,267 seats, featured the premiere of the romantic comedy *Just the Ticket*, whose cast came to town in 1997 to film scenes with stars Andy Garcia and Andie MacDowell. The theater closed in 2010. (Courtesy of the Hauss/Lewis Collection.)

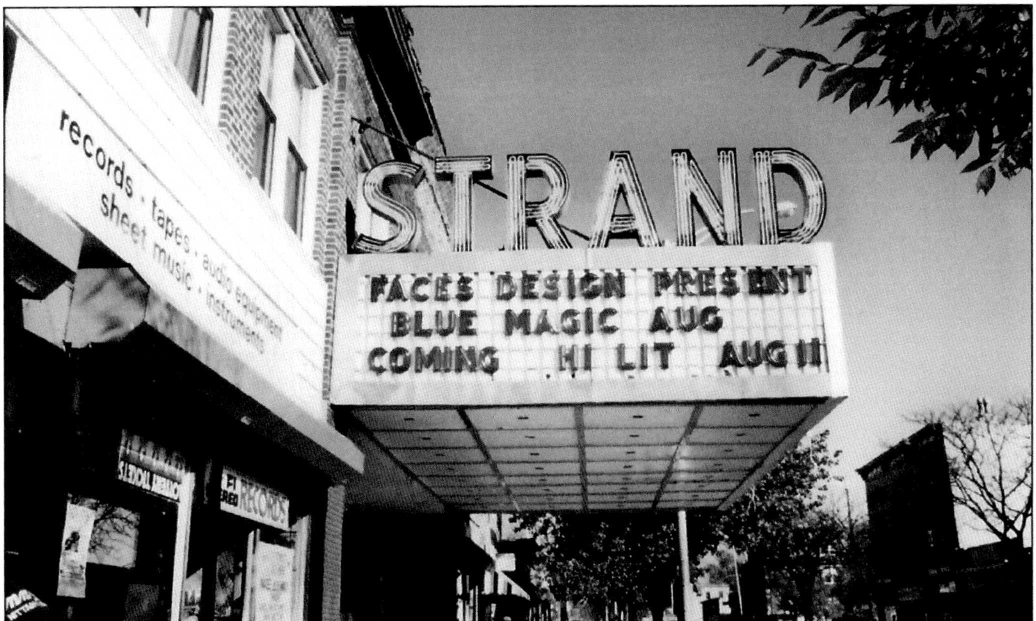

The Strand, on Plainfield East First Street, had some 1,712 seats and was described as a Walter Reade-Sterling theater in a 1960s advertising brochure. On the night of August 11, 1964, it created a special ticket showing the "Fab Four" for the premiere of *A Hard Day's Night*. Admission to the Beatles movie was $1.49. (Courtesy of the Hauss/Lewis Collection.)

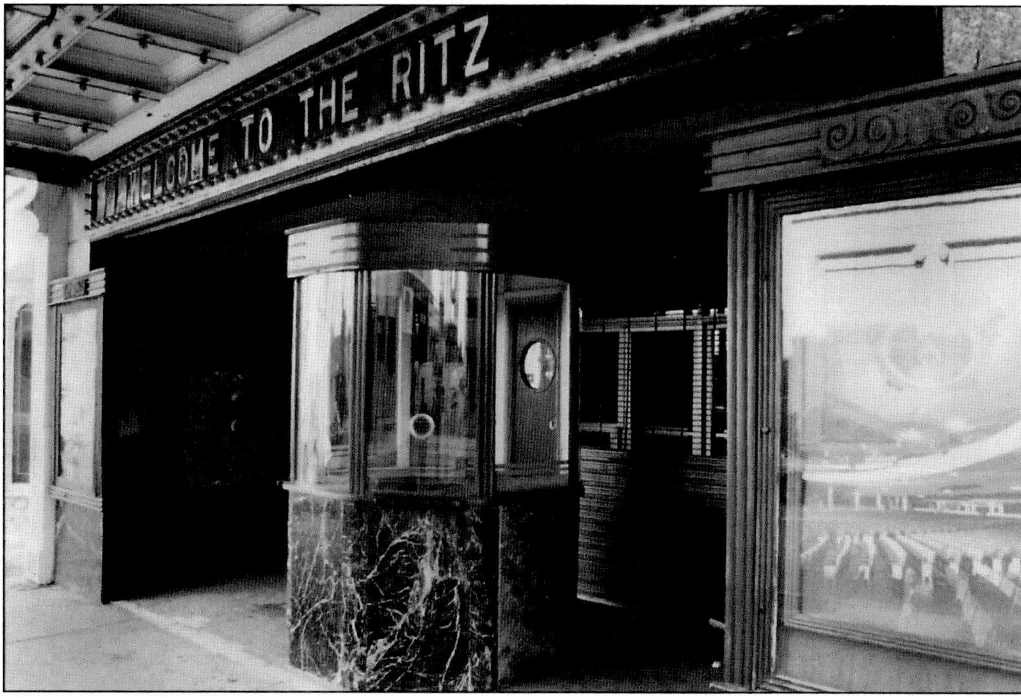

The Ritz Theatre, which remains a mainstay on Elizabeth's E. Jersey Street, dates to 1867 and over the decades featured the likes of comedians Jack Benny and George Burns, as well as Cab Calloway, Sammy Davis Jr., and the Temptations, according to a 1988 article by Heidi Mae Bratt of the *Daily Journal* and illustrated by a photograph taken by the newspaper's longtime chief photographer, Joseph Buscaino. In one of its reincarnations in 1980, a newcomer by the name of Whitney Houston graced the stage as the opening act for singer Ray Charles. Later, its marquee was used as a backdrop for Woody Allen's 1999 film *Sweet and Lowdown*. (Courtesy of the Hauss/Lewis Collection.)

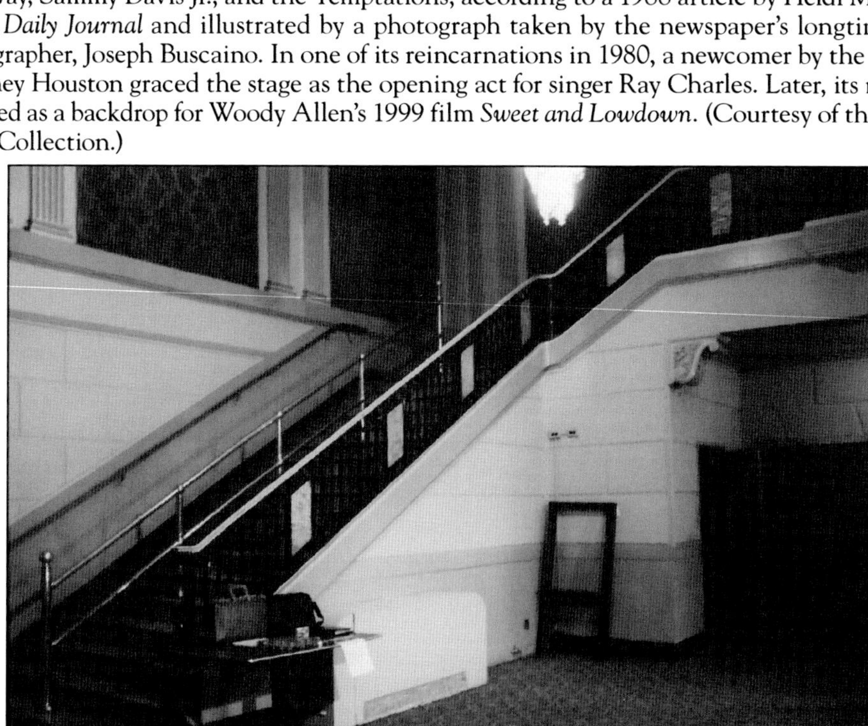

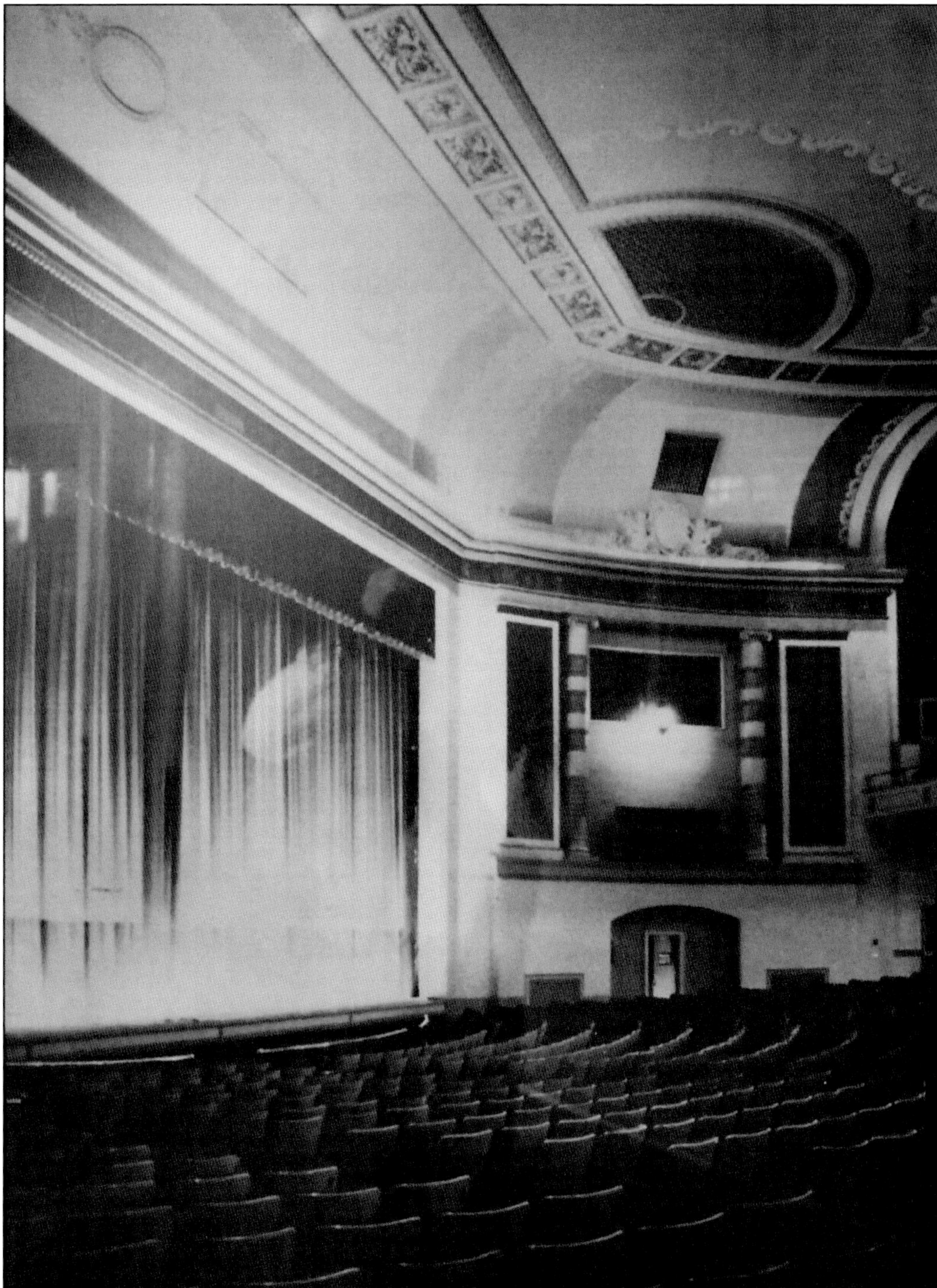

The 2,772-seat theater, which began showing movies in the 1930s, was a palace in its own right. "That Ritz Theatre was just as gorgeous and extravagant as any theater in New York City," Helene Wallack, a teenage usherette in the 1920s, recalled in an article by the *Star-Ledger*'s Jeff Whelan. (Courtesy of the Hauss/Lewis Collection.)

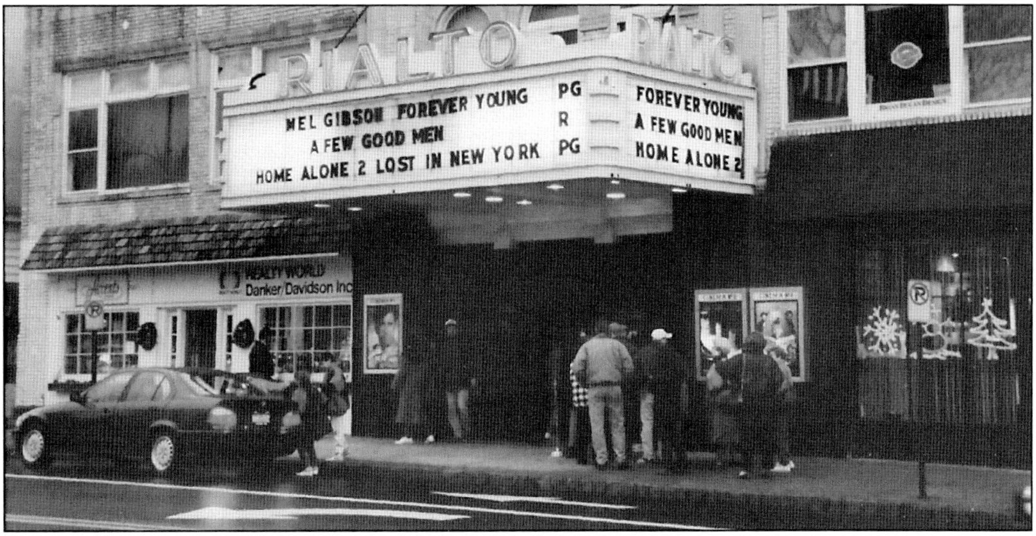

On September 6, 1922, The Rialto, at 250 East Broad Street in Westfield, opened with 1,000 people paying 20¢ for a matinee and 30¢ for an evening's silent picture. A few years later, the epic film *Ben Hur* flickered on its screen. Among the enticements in the 1950s was a Davy Crockett costume contest. In 1996, though, came a transforming experience as a "Save the Rialto" campaign, which was intended to save the movie house from being converted to retail, led to a renovation into six movie theaters with 1,050 seats. Shown above in 1992, the theater became a model for downtown revival now trumpeted by the National Trust for Historic Preservation. (Courtesy of the Hauss/Lewis Collection.)

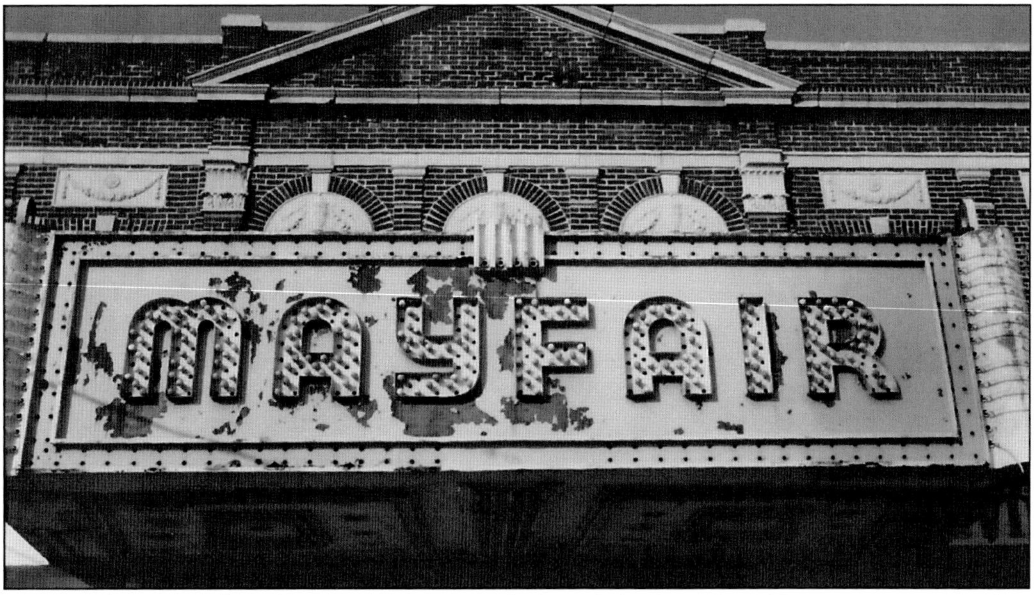

"Beautiful new Mayfair Theatre opening tonight," read the June 8, 1928, newspaper story that unveiled the new photoplay house with 1,258 seats in Hillside. The pitch of the floor, sloping 1.5 inches to the foot, was said to improve the view of the screen. Among other amenities was the women's "cosmetic room," which was decorated with antique furniture and carpeted with a rug made by the famed British weaving concern Milton, and the men's smoking room, which was a replica of an old English drawing room with its own fireplace. (Courtesy of the Hauss/Lewis Collection.)

Nine

ELSEWHERE

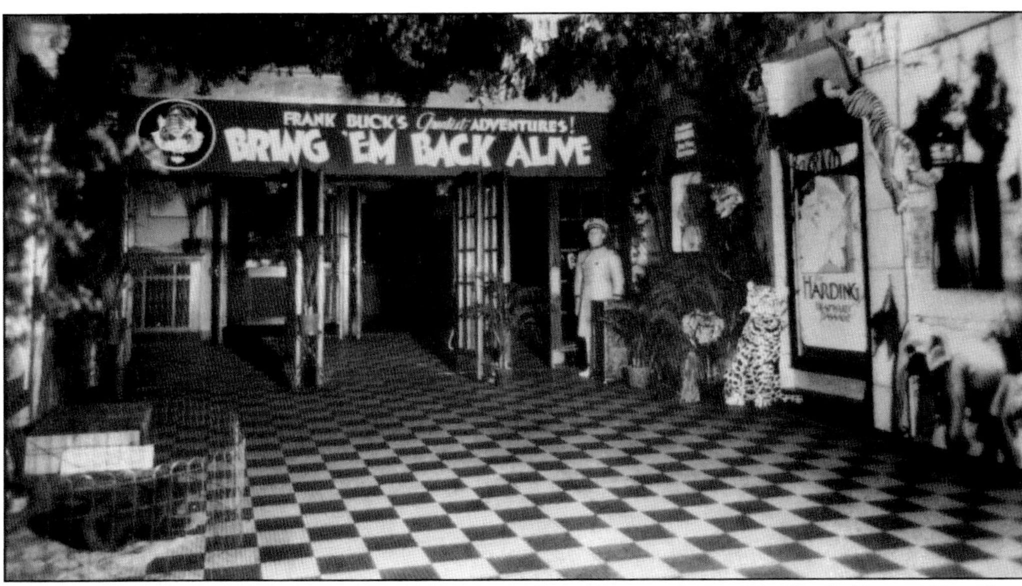

New Brunswick's historic State Theatre in 1933 played host to *Bring 'Em Back Alive*, a film about Frank Buck's greatest adventures. The adventurer's first autobiographical book by the same name appeared in 1930, followed the next year with 125,000 feet of film he shot in the jungle, which became the basis for the film, according to the East Texas Historical Association. He is said to have served as the model for a character in the 1933 film *King Kong*. In later decades, the stage at the State Theatre featured rock and roll shows with the likes of Chubby Checker and the Satins. (Courtesy of the State Theatre.)

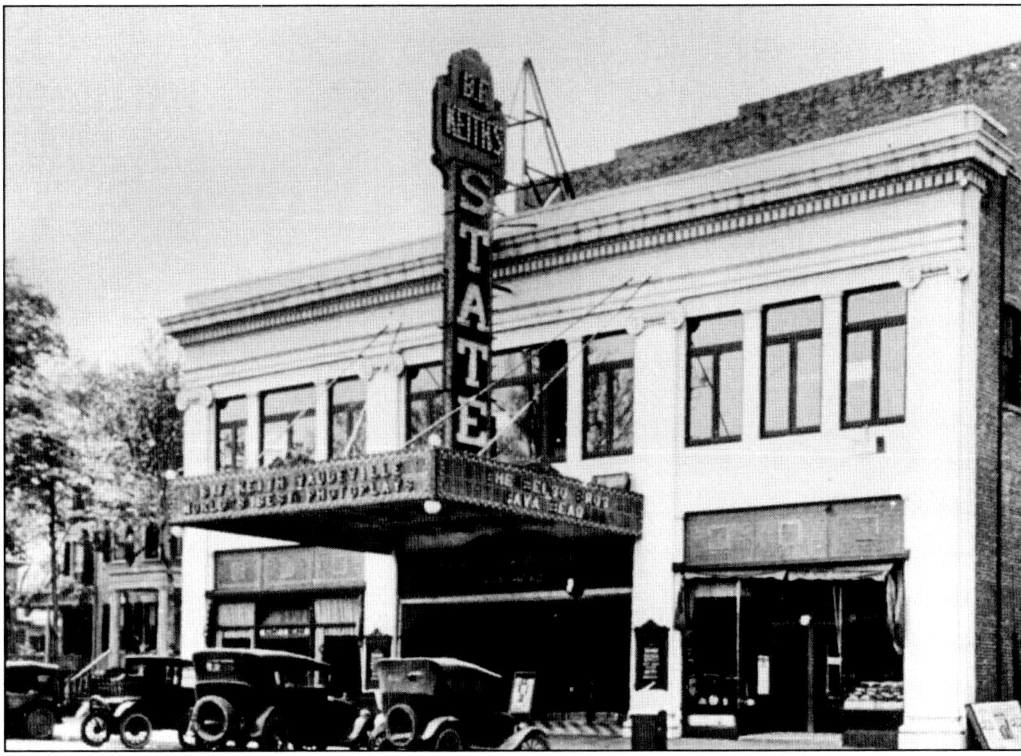

Designed by famed theater architect Thomas W. Lamb, the State Theatre opened as Reade's State Theatre on December 26, 1921. Manager Walter Reade opened the theater with five vaudeville acts and a matinee screening of the silent western *White Oak*, starring William S. Hart. The matinee audience—including the first ticket buyer Victor Levin, nine years of age, of Paterson Street in New Brunswick—paid 20¢ to 30¢ for admission. Later, a crowd of children gathered outside the theater, which in 2011 celebrated its 90th year. (Courtesy of the State Theatre.)

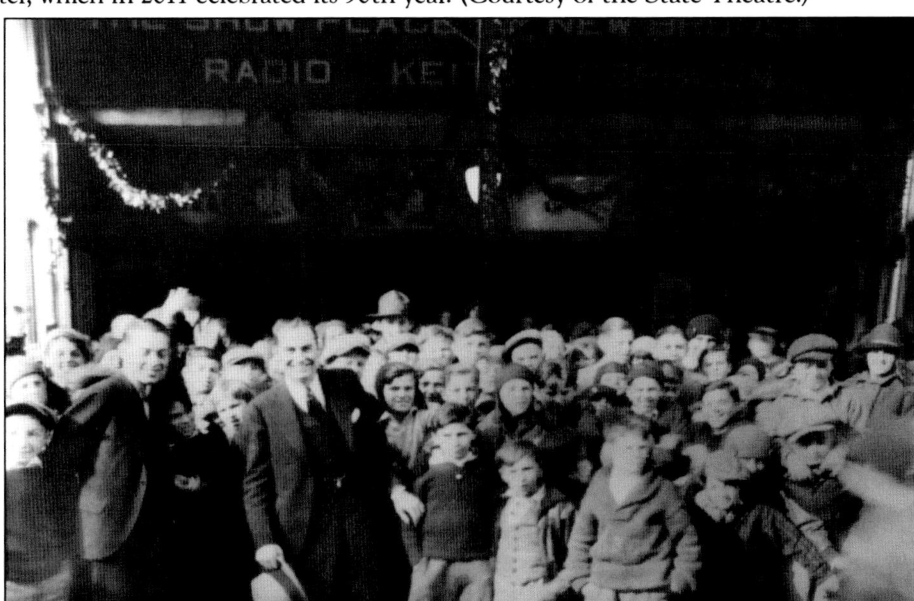

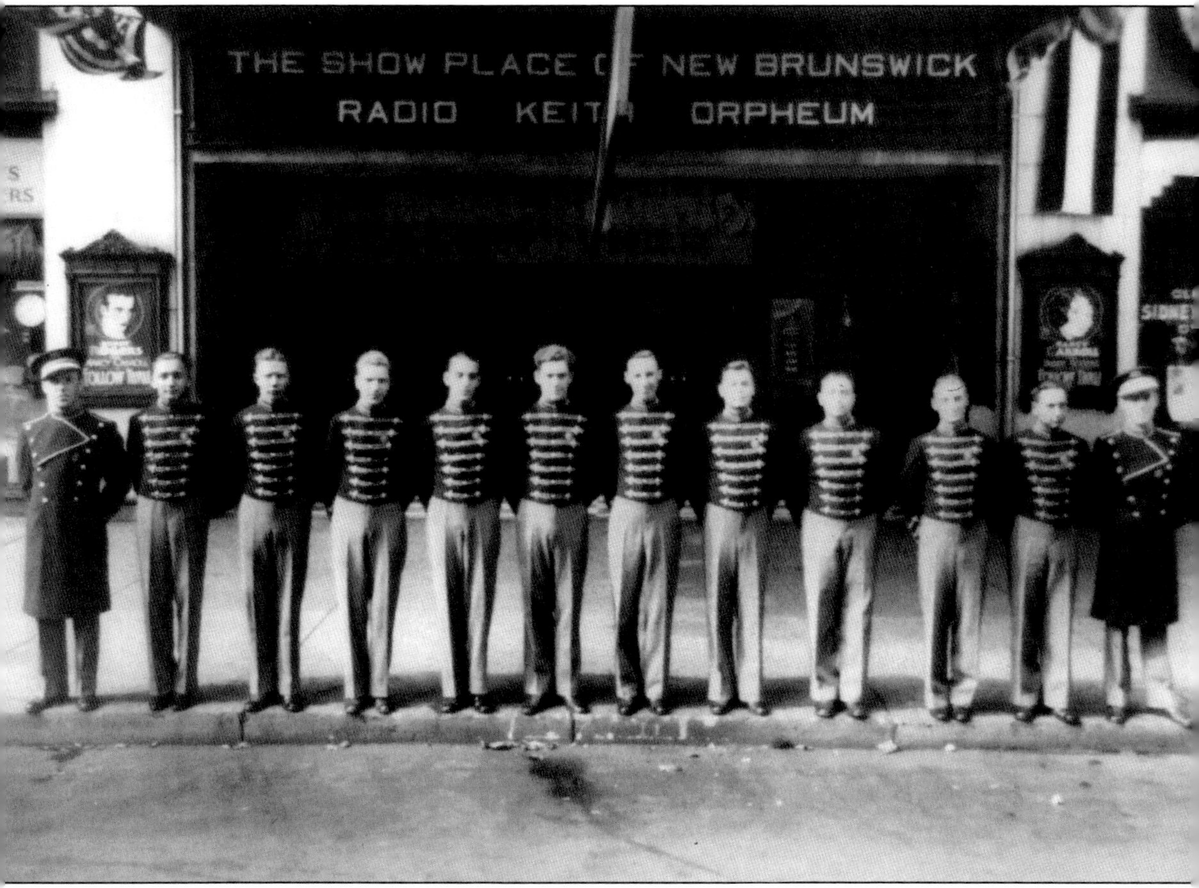

Ushers are seen in 1930 lined up outside "The Showplace of New Brunswick," the Radio Keith Orpheum, then showing the musical comedy *Follow Thru*, an early talkie filmed entirely in Technicolor. It starred Charles "Buddy" Rogers and Nancy Carroll in an adaptation of a 1929 Broadway show. "RKO Always a Good Show" reads the marquee. At the time, Paramount Pictures was talking up the picture in an advertisement in the *Saturday Evening Post*, stating, "Today the world's greatest entertainment is found on the talking screen!" (Courtesy of the State Theatre.)

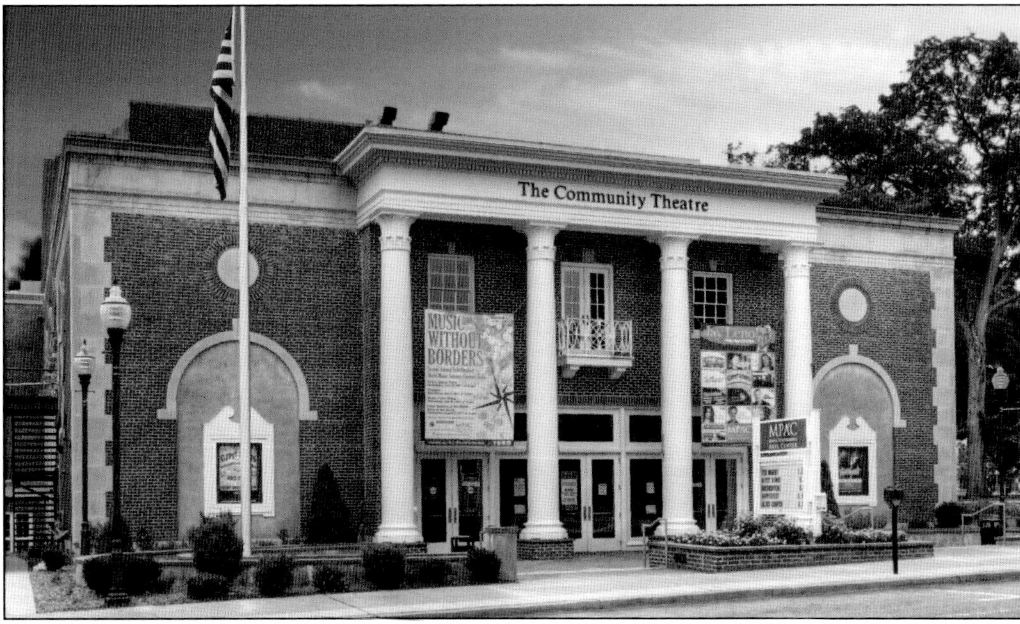

The Community Theatre, built in 1937 on Morristown's South Street, was considered the crown jewel of Walter Reade's chain of New Jersey movie theaters. By the 1980s, however, it fell on hard times and sat vacant for nearly a decade. But, in 1994, a group of volunteers saved the theater, leading to today's Mayo Performing Arts Center. In 2011, it began its 17th season with a sold-out performance by Diana Ross, followed in 2012 with three consecutive sold-out performances by Frankie Valli and the Four Seasons. It is seen here that year. (Courtesy of Mayo Performing Arts Center/David Patino.)

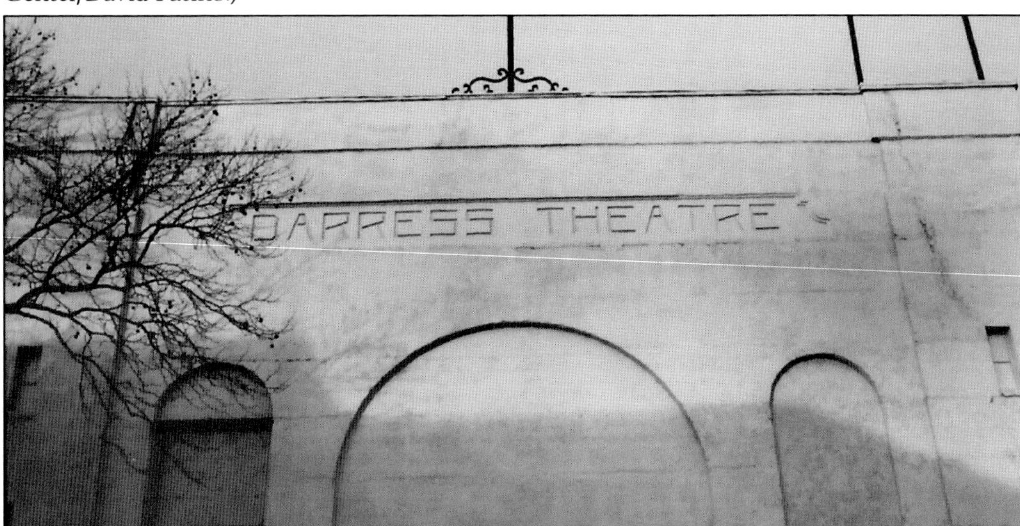

The 700-seat Darress Theatre has an imposing facade along Boonton's Main Street, where it was erected in 1919 and first featured silent films and vaudeville acts. It is said to be "the only reverse theater remaining in America today," according to an article in the *Daily Record* of Morris County. A reverse theater is where the audience entered from the stage side instead in the rear, so everyone noticed if someone came in late. This theater, which for a time was known as the State Theatre, today features plays, stand-up comics, and concerts. (Courtesy of the Hauss/Lewis Collection.)

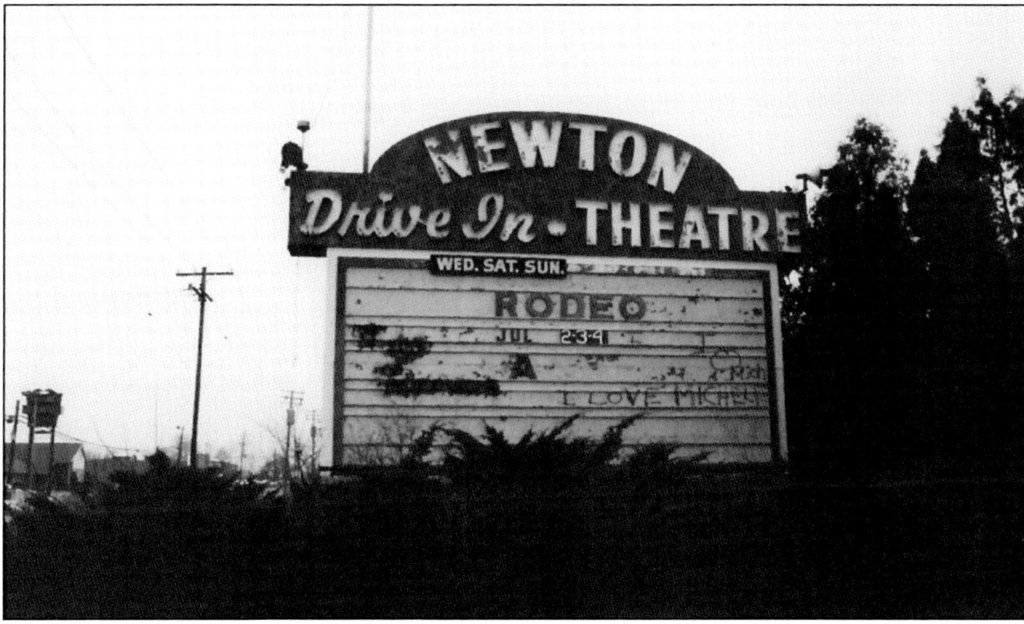

The Newton Drive-in opened in 1957 and was the handiwork of Wilfred "Bill" Paul Smith, who built most of New Jersey's drive-ins. He was a movie buff, too: "Dad could tell you the names of the sound guys, the producers, everyone connected with a film," son Wilfred P. Jr. of Denville said in a 2002 column by Fran Wood in the *Star-Ledger*. The newspaper story's title was "The King of the Drive-In." (Courtesy of the Hauss/Lewis Collection.)

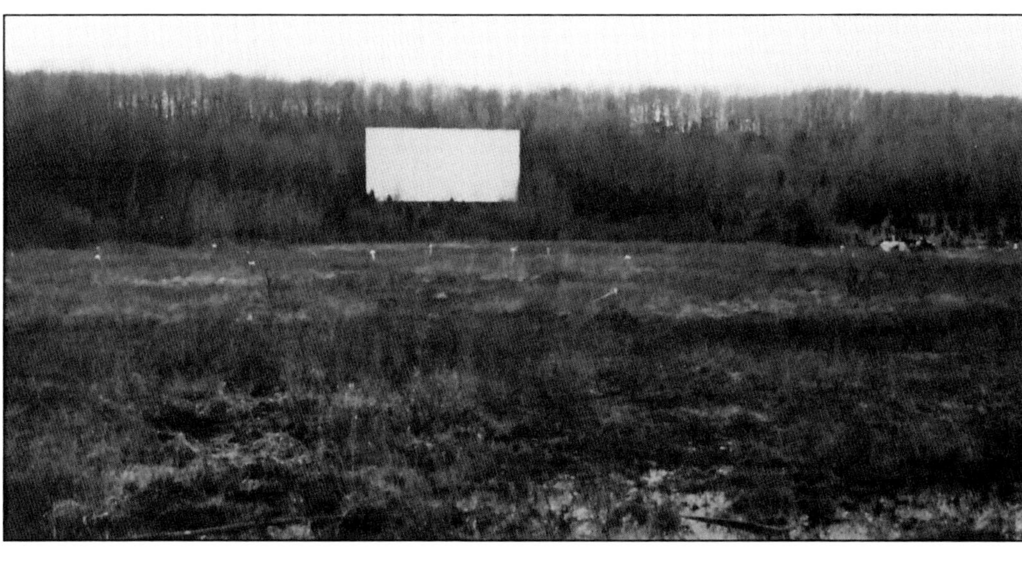

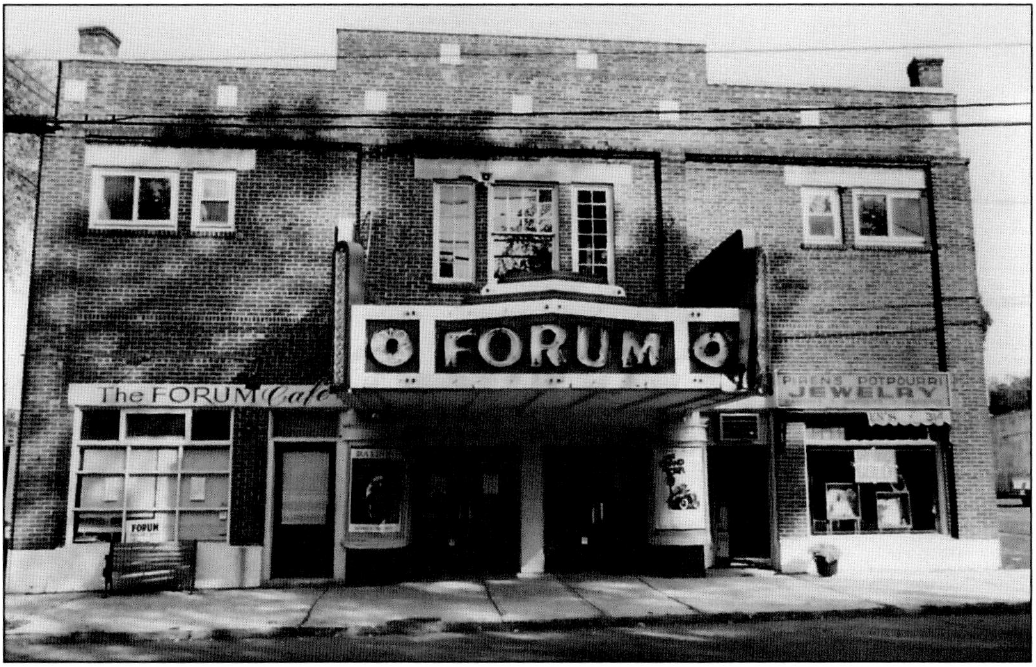

Peter Loewy used to come to the 500-seat Forum Theatre in Metuchen as a kid. And he still does—he owns it. Since 1983, he has overseen what is described as one of the last single-screen downtown theaters. "We show first-run art films, but having only one screen obviously limits your audience," he told *Star-Ledger* columnist Mark Di Ionno in 2012. "We do live theater but can't compete with bigger, regional theaters. And we're not subsidized. But we keep going." (Courtesy of the Hauss/Lewis Collection.)

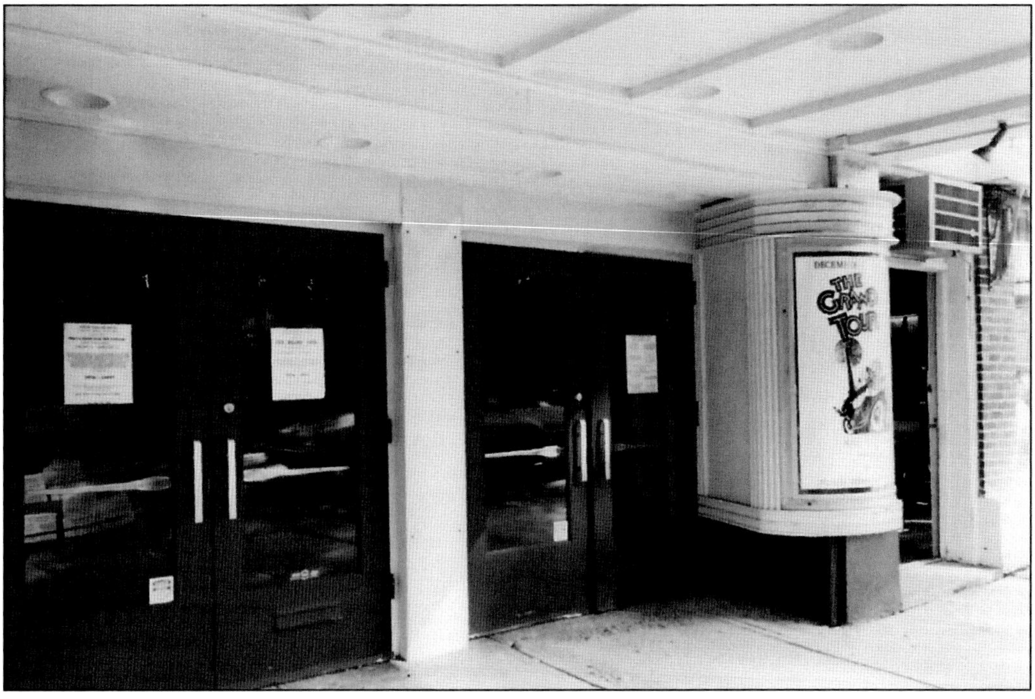

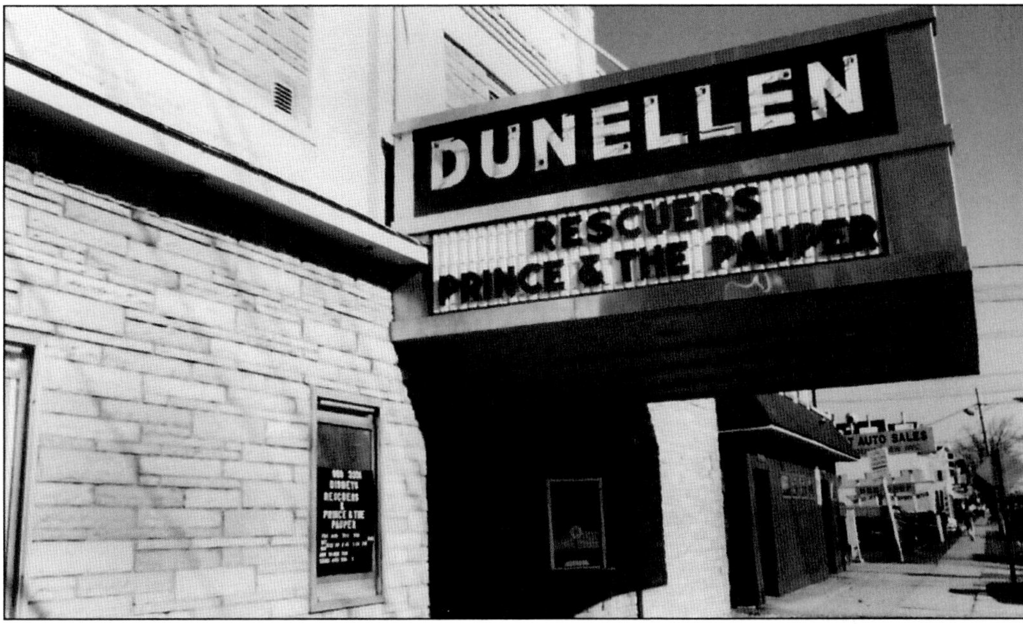

The 500-seat Dunellen, which takes its name from its Middlesex County locale, dates to 1921. In its early years, the theater had several run-ins with the law when it showed films on Sundays, a then violation of the state's "Blue Laws." It shows movies today under the motto "New Jersey's Original Cinema Café." (Courtesy of the Hauss/Lewis Collection.)

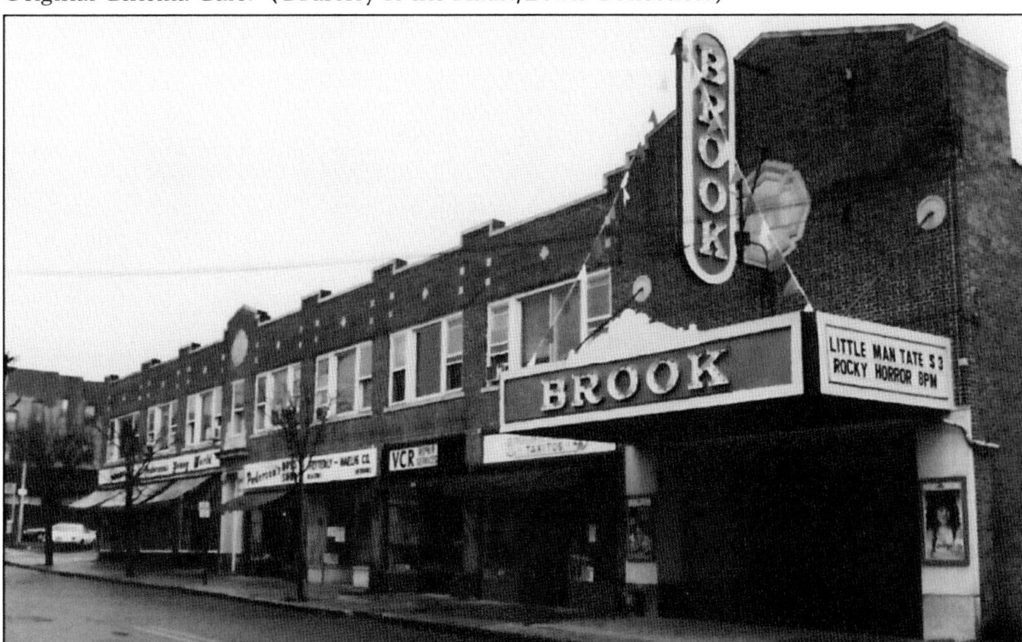

The Brook, in Somerset County's Bound Brook, opened in 1927, the year after R.B. Casey won $25 for his nomination of the theater's name, according to the website of what is now a performing-arts center. Its 1,300 seats were filled on January 27, 1927. In June 1931, the film *Romance and Bound Brook*, shot with thousands of locals as actors, debuted there, but a copy given to the town is believed to have perished in a borough hall fire in 1946. (Courtesy of the Hauss/Lewis Collection.)

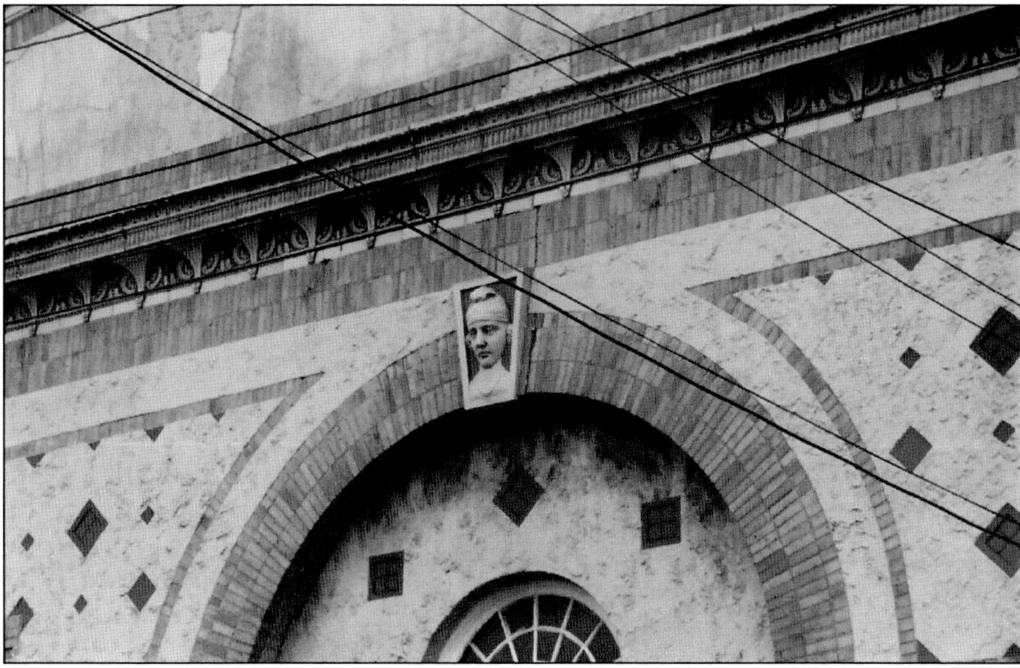

One of the embellishments on the facade of the 800-plus-seat, c. 1930 Colony Theatre in Sayreville is a stone relief of a face staring down on the arriving public. Sayreville once made movie history of its own, with the filming of 1915's *Juggernaut* at a train trestle in the town. In one scene, a train and three passenger cars filled with mannequins plunges off a trestle into the waters below. (Courtesy of the Allan/Hauss Collection.)

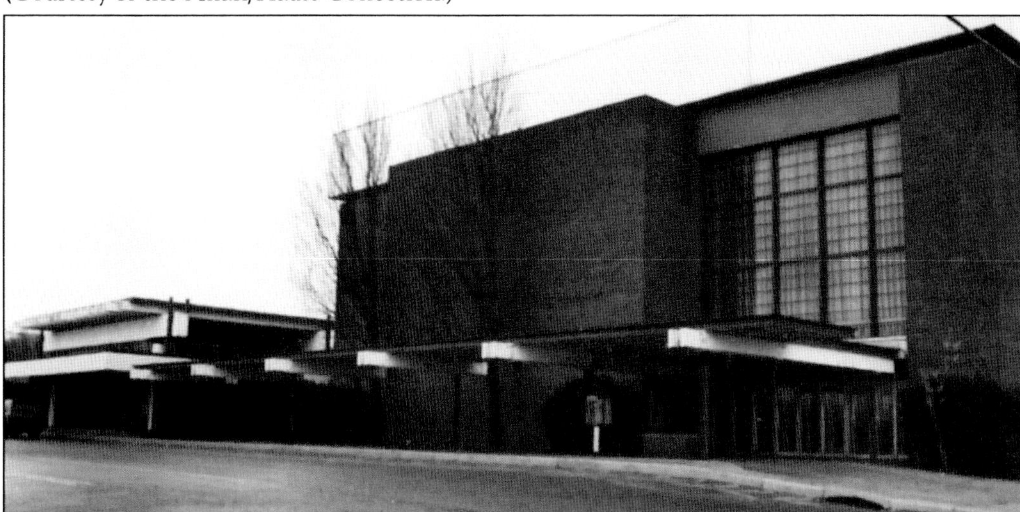

"A Beautiful Showcase for Menlo Park," read the headline in a 1962 edition of *Box Office* magazine shortly after the opening of the Cinema Theatre. One of the vanguard of shopping-center movie houses erected by General Drive-In Corp., it featured 1,200 seats in the orchestra, 400 in the loge, and a massive glass lobby also used as an art gallery. The cinema, attributed to designer Elliott Willensky of New York's Architectural Design Group, featured a 58-foot-wide screen. Later, the movie house was converted into a twin theater and ultimately demolished in 1991 after a 12-plex opened nearby. (Courtesy of the Allan/Hauss Collection.)

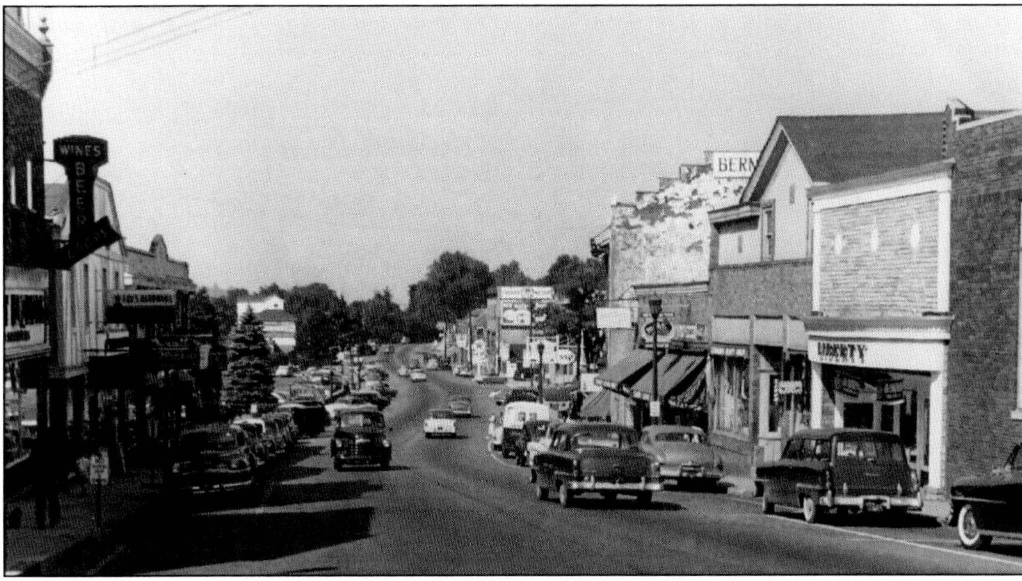

The 400-seat Liberty Theatre (now the Bernardsville Cinema), which is in affluent Somerset County, was said to have had some notable moviegoers, namely some of Bernardsville's more elite homeowners. Among them were boxer Mike Tyson and actress Robin Givens, "regulars" who once took in a showing of the 1988 adventure film *Midnight Run*, and Jackie Onassis, the one-time first lady of the United States. In the ensuing years, the cinema converted to a triplex but retained its large screen in the main theater, with two smaller ones in the back. The lobby of the marquee-less movie house, shown in a 1954 street scene (above) and in 1992 (below), displayed posters of the Marx Brothers, W.C. Fields, and Clark Cable, as well as a model of a wooden ship whose origin no one could remember, according to a late 1980s column by *Daily Record* staffer Jim Reisler. (Courtesy of the Bernardsville Public Library/Homer R. Hill and the Hauss/Lewis Collection.)

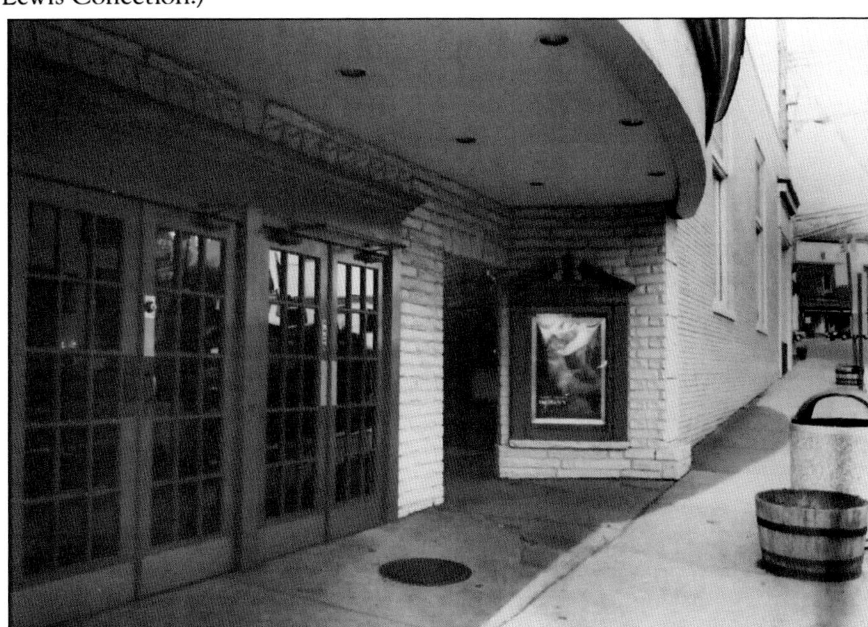

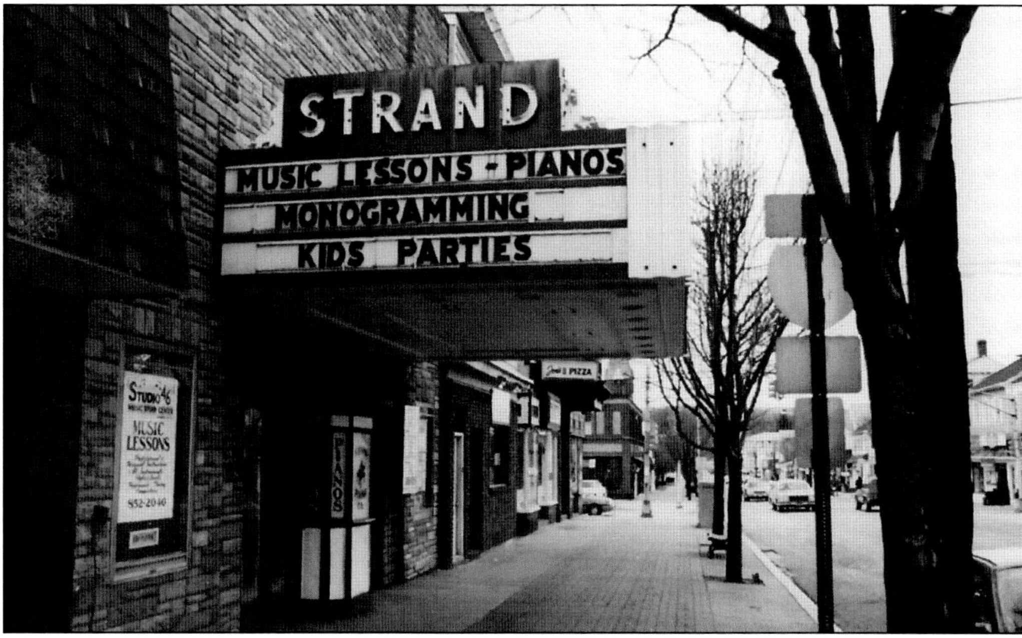

The Strand Theater, on Hackettstown's Main Street, had some 768 seats. In recent years, long after it stopped showing films, the theater has been home to such uses as a piano studio and dance ballroom. (Courtesy of the Allan/Hauss Collection.)

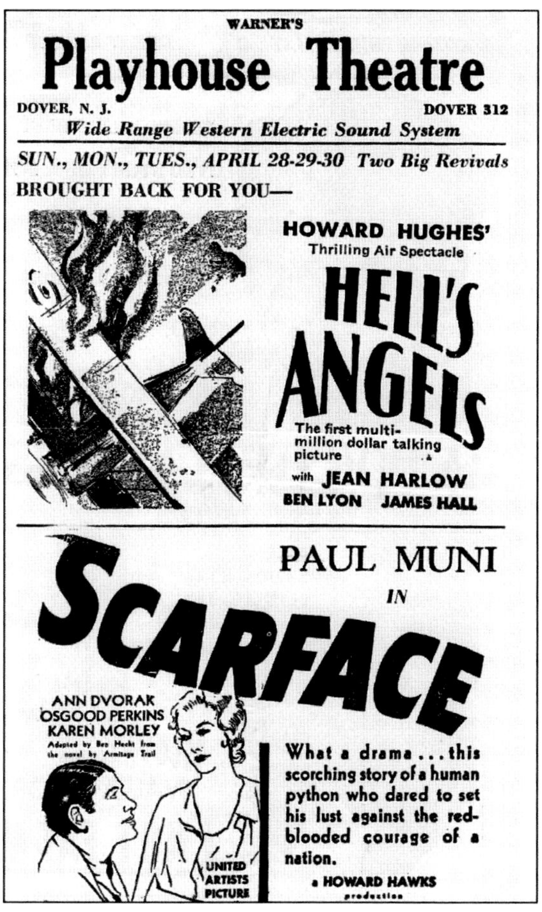

WARNER'S

Playhouse Theatre

DOVER, N. J. DOVER 312

Wide Range Western Electric Sound System

SUN., MON., TUES., APRIL 28-29-30 Two Big Revivals

BROUGHT BACK FOR YOU—

HOWARD HUGHES'
Thrilling Air Spectacle

HELL'S ANGELS

The first multi-million dollar talking picture

with JEAN HARLOW
BEN LYON JAMES HALL

PAUL MUNI
IN
SCARFACE

ANN DVORAK
OSGOOD PERKINS
KAREN MORLEY

What a drama . . . this scorching story of a human python who dared to set his lust against the red-blooded courage of a nation.

a HOWARD HAWKS production

UNITED ARTISTS PICTURE

The 75-seat Playhouse Theatre on Dover's South Morris Street opened on Saturday, October 18, 1913, with a facade bearing a stone figure believed to depict Dionysus, the god of tragic art and protector of theater. In 1930, its guide to moviegoers toted the arrival of Howard Hughes's 1930 war classic *Hell's Angels*. Amid urban renewal of the 1970s, the movie house was demolished, with many of the seats and main curtain donated to the Dover Little Theatre, according to the Dover Area Historical Society. The Masonic Temple received several chairs with "PH" written on the sides. The only remnant of the playhouse is the stone face of Dionysus sitting on the ground at Triangle Park at West Blackwell and Prospect Streets. (Author's collection.)

Ten

AFTER THE MATINEE

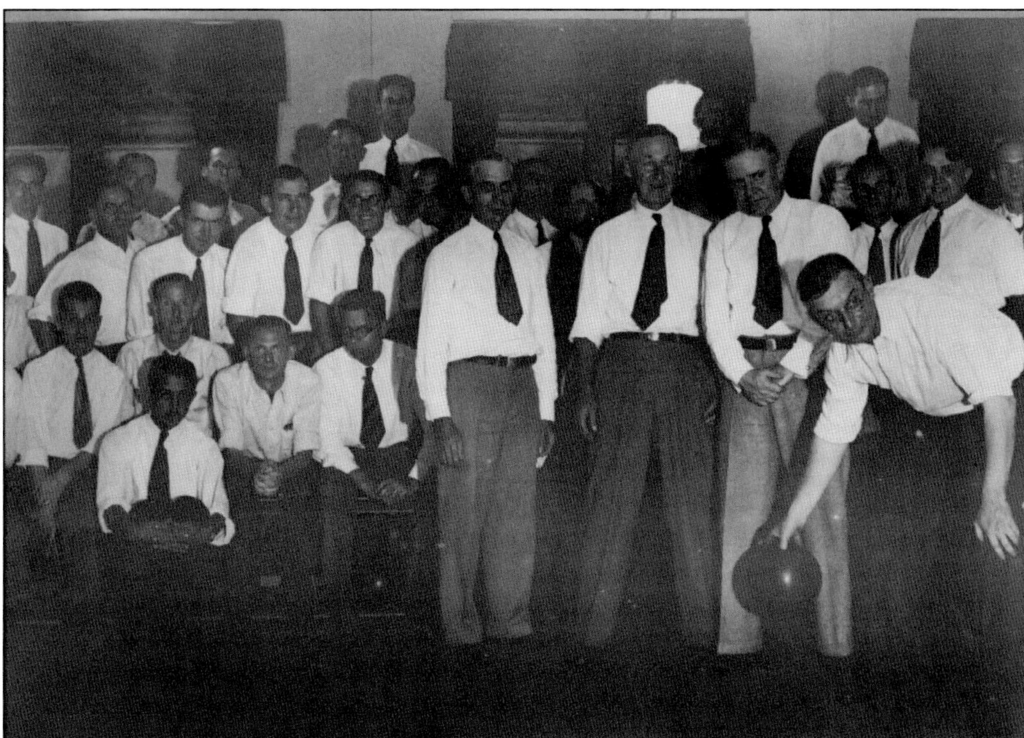

The once preeminent American manufacturer Westinghouse occupied a massive complex near Newark's Broad Street train station. There, for some 100 years until 1983, it made everything from curling irons to speakers for early radios. Its many employees also found time to gather with the company bowling club, shown here in 1932. (Courtesy of the Newark Public Library.)

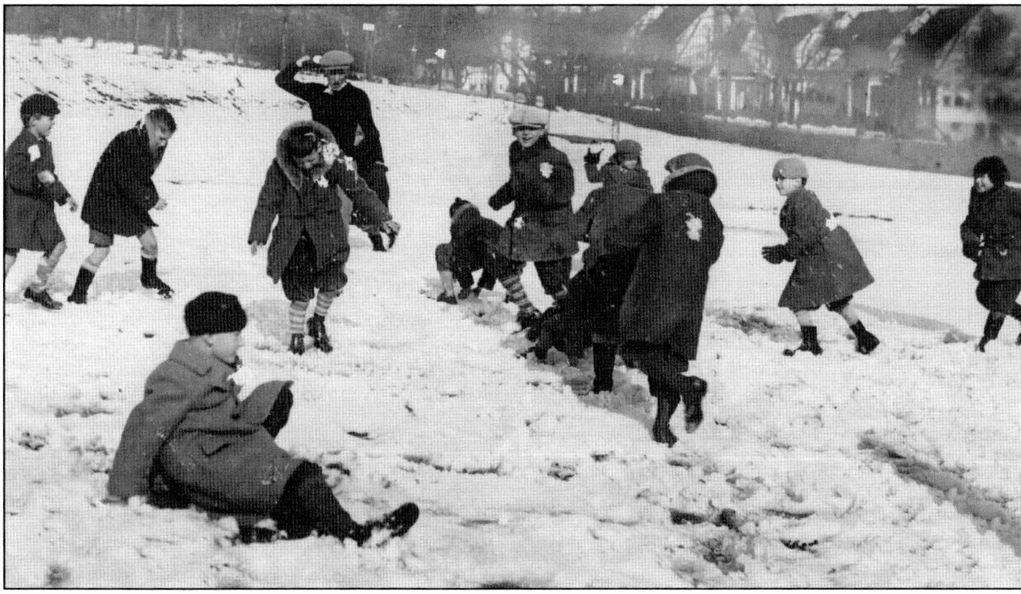

These young Newarkers are in the thick of a favorite pastime, other than the movies, in their neighborhood: snowball fighting. (Courtesy of the Newark Public Library.)

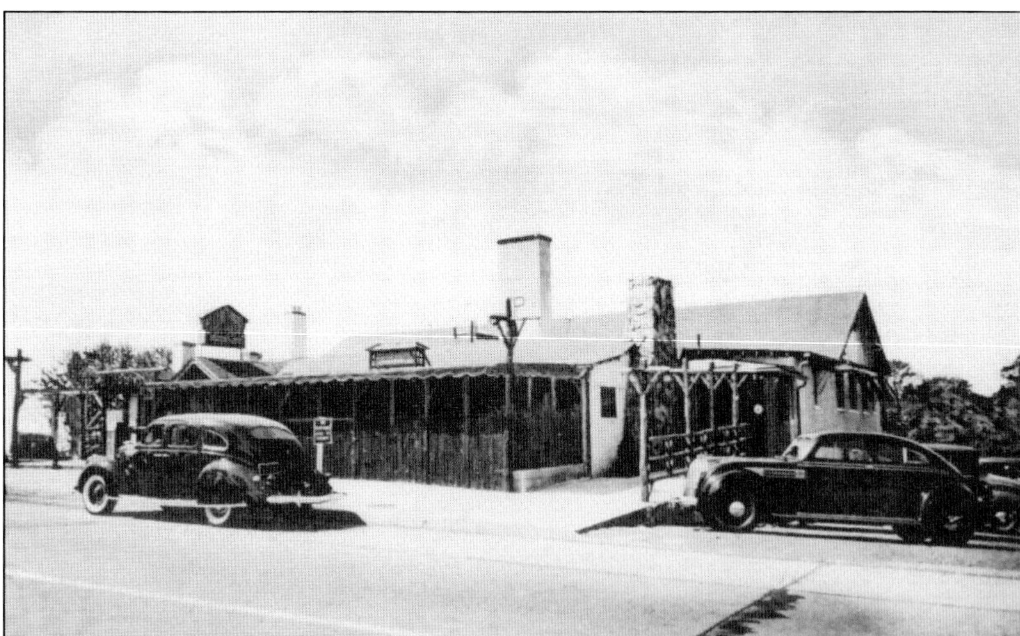

In 1932, Pals Cabin was opened amid the Great Depression by two pals, Martin L. "Marty" Horn and Bion LeRoy "Roy" Sale. "It was better than selling apples on a street corner," Horn said of the decision. It was not until 1935 that the pals began serving charcoal-broiled steaks for 50¢, cementing the future of the West Orange restaurant as an Essex County institution. (Courtesy of the Newark Public Library.)

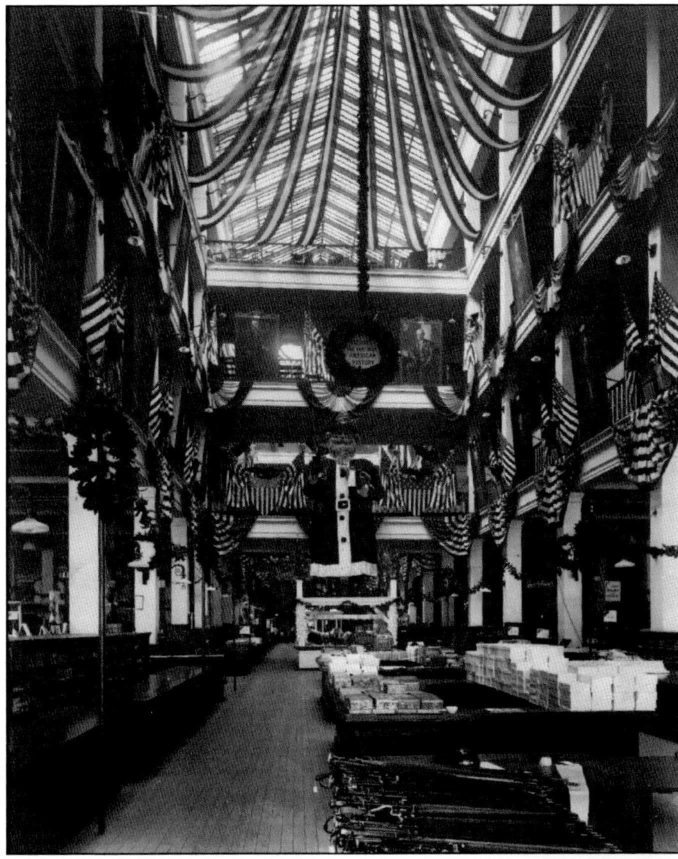

Hahne & Co., a massive downtown department store, provided more diversion for visitors to Newark, many of whom went to movies at the nearby Loew's State on Broad Street. Back in 1918, the era of silent films, its rotunda was a sight to behold along with a soda fountain dubbed the largest in the world. (Courtesy of the Newark Public Library.)

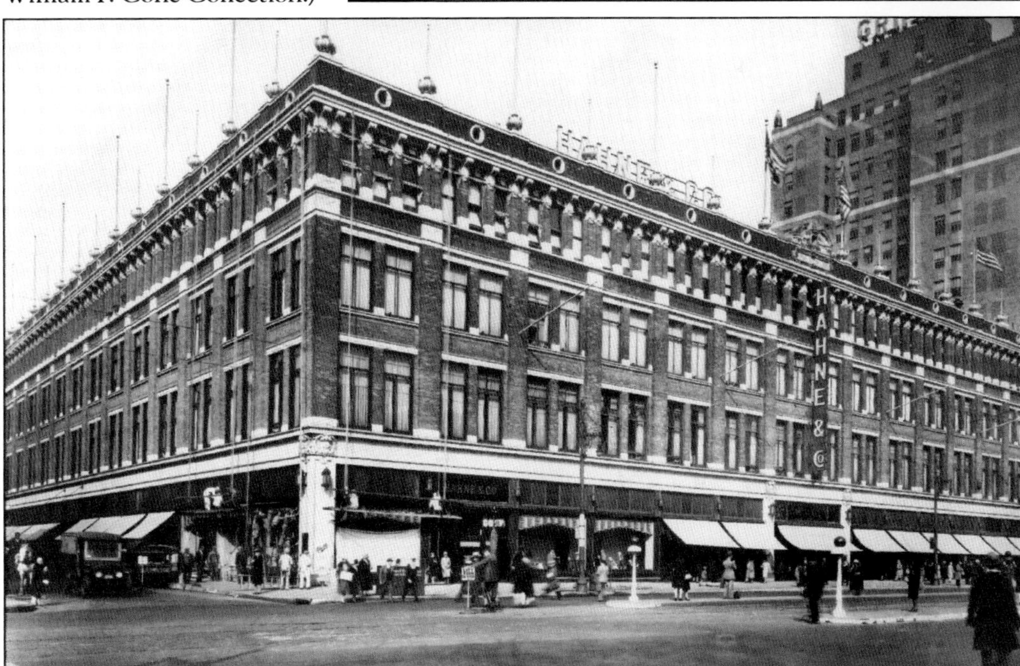

The block-long Hahne & Co.'s was considered among the "Big Three" of downtown retailers, along with L. Bamberger & Co. and Kresge's. It closed in 1987. (Courtesy of the Newark Public Library/ William F. Cone Collection.)

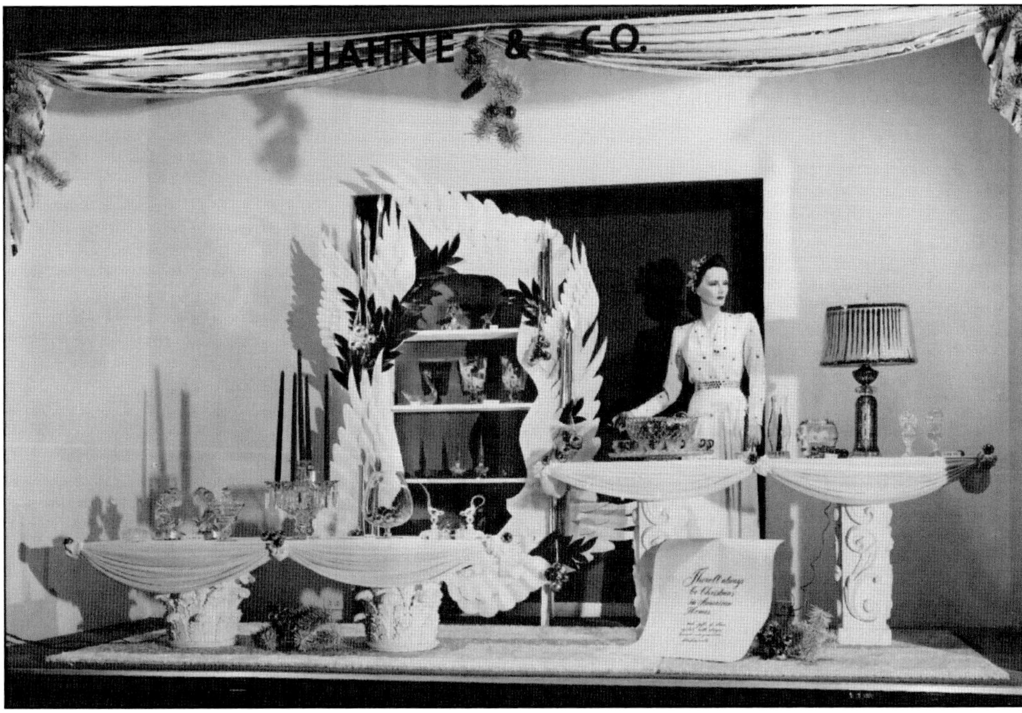

Display windows changed seasonally at Hahne & Co., with this one decked out for the holidays. "There'll always be Christmas in American Homes," read the message alongside a display of punch bowls and the like surrounded by angel wings. (Courtesy of the Newark Public Library.)

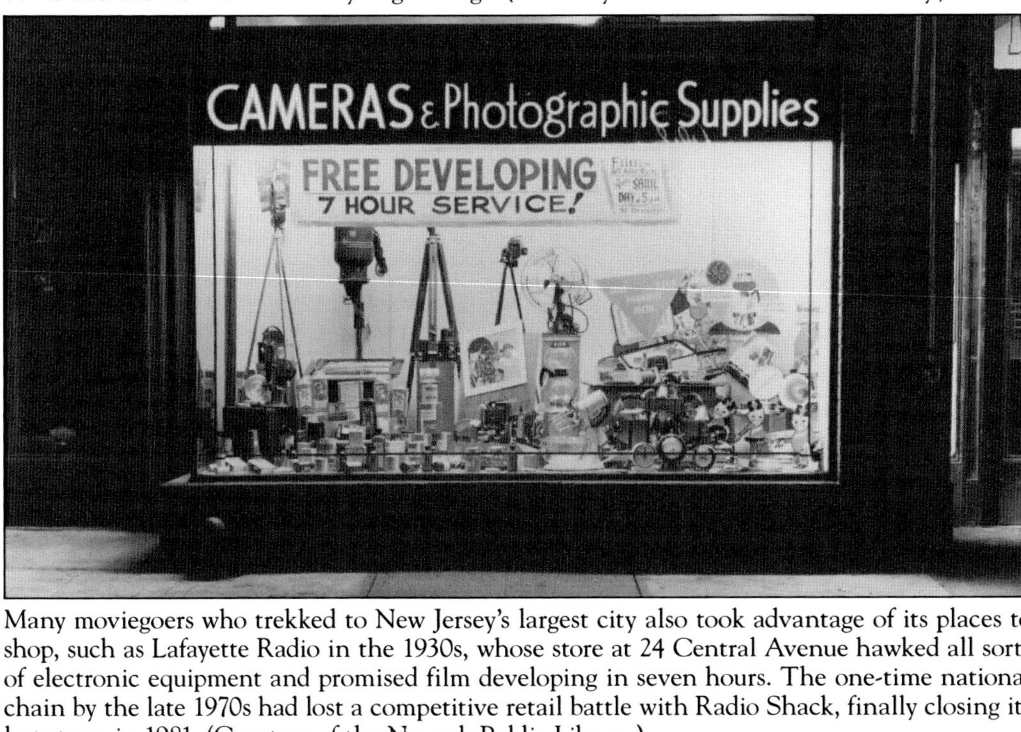

Many moviegoers who trekked to New Jersey's largest city also took advantage of its places to shop, such as Lafayette Radio in the 1930s, whose store at 24 Central Avenue hawked all sorts of electronic equipment and promised film developing in seven hours. The one-time national chain by the late 1970s had lost a competitive retail battle with Radio Shack, finally closing its last stores in 1981. (Courtesy of the Newark Public Library.)

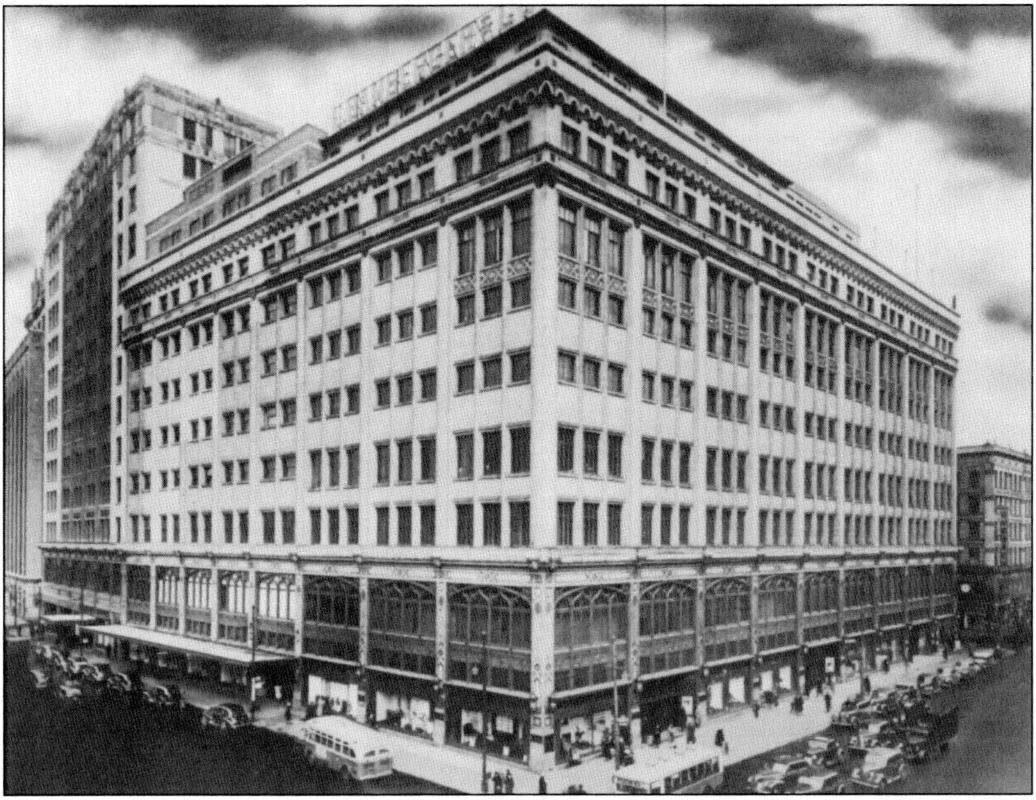

Bamberger's flagship department store could be found on Newark's Market and Halsey Streets, with its 14 floors of merchandise a go-to destination for the public. In its heyday, the department store sponsored the Newark Thanksgiving Day Parade, later embraced in New York by Macy's, which gave the once venerable retailer its name in the late 1980s. The store, known affectionately as "Bams," closed in the early 1990s. (Courtesy of the Newark Public Library.)

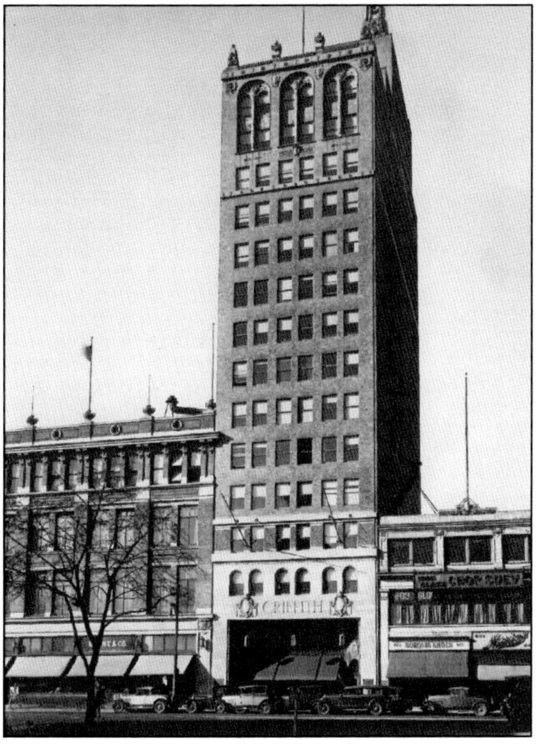

From the late 1920s to the late 1950s, the Griffith high-rise, alongside Hahne & Co., was a high-priced address for professionals and a bustling architectural jewel that was the headquarters for the Griffith family, sellers of pianos, organs, and other musical instruments in a time when no home was complete without one. So were the words used by Guy Sterling, a reporter for the *Star-Ledger*, in a must-read 2008 telling of its influence on Newark. (Courtesy of the Newark Public Library.)

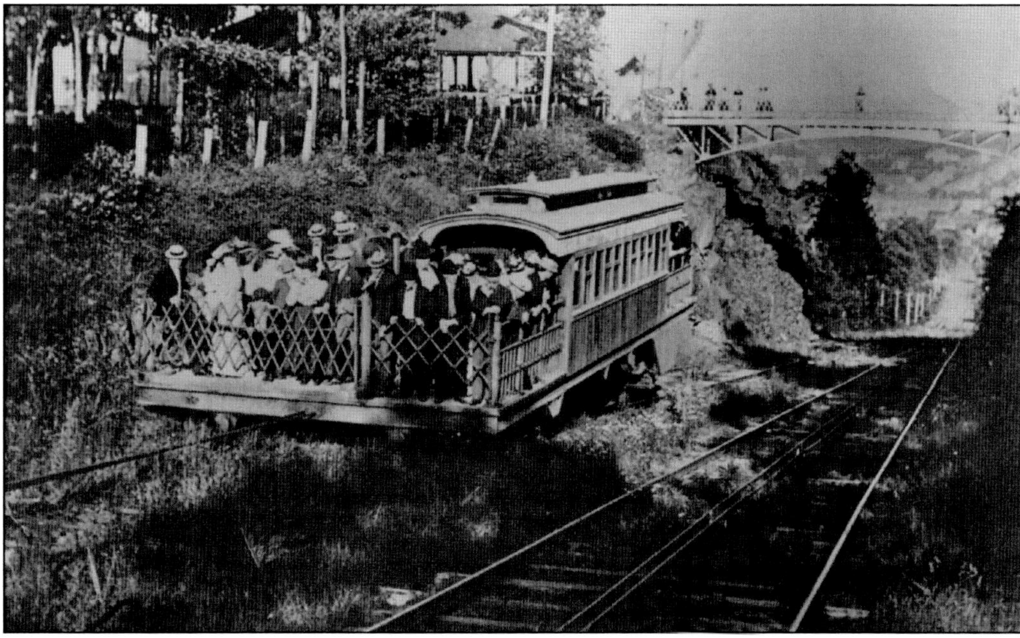

For some spectacular views off the big screen, people would trek to First Mountain at Eagle Rock Reservation in West Orange for a cable-car ride to the summit—600 feet above sea level. (Courtesy of the Newark Public Library.)

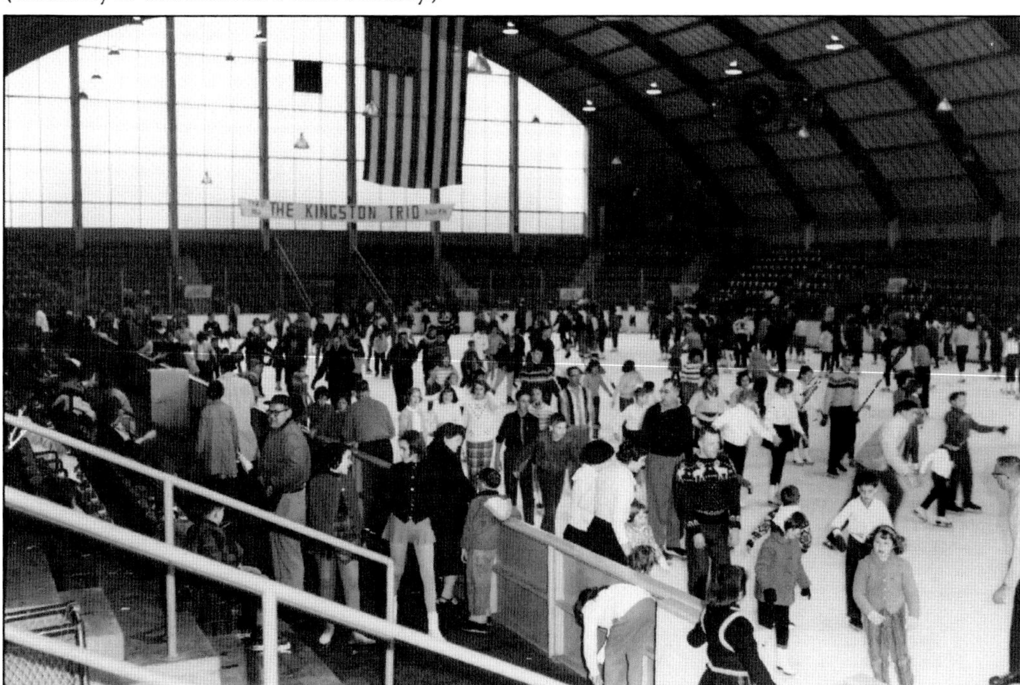

The popularity of ice-skating extended to New Jersey, where skaters in West Orange, not far from Newark, took to the ice under a banner proclaiming a coming concert by the Kingston Trio, which launched a revival of folk music in the late 1950s and 1960s. (Courtesy of the Newark Public Library.)

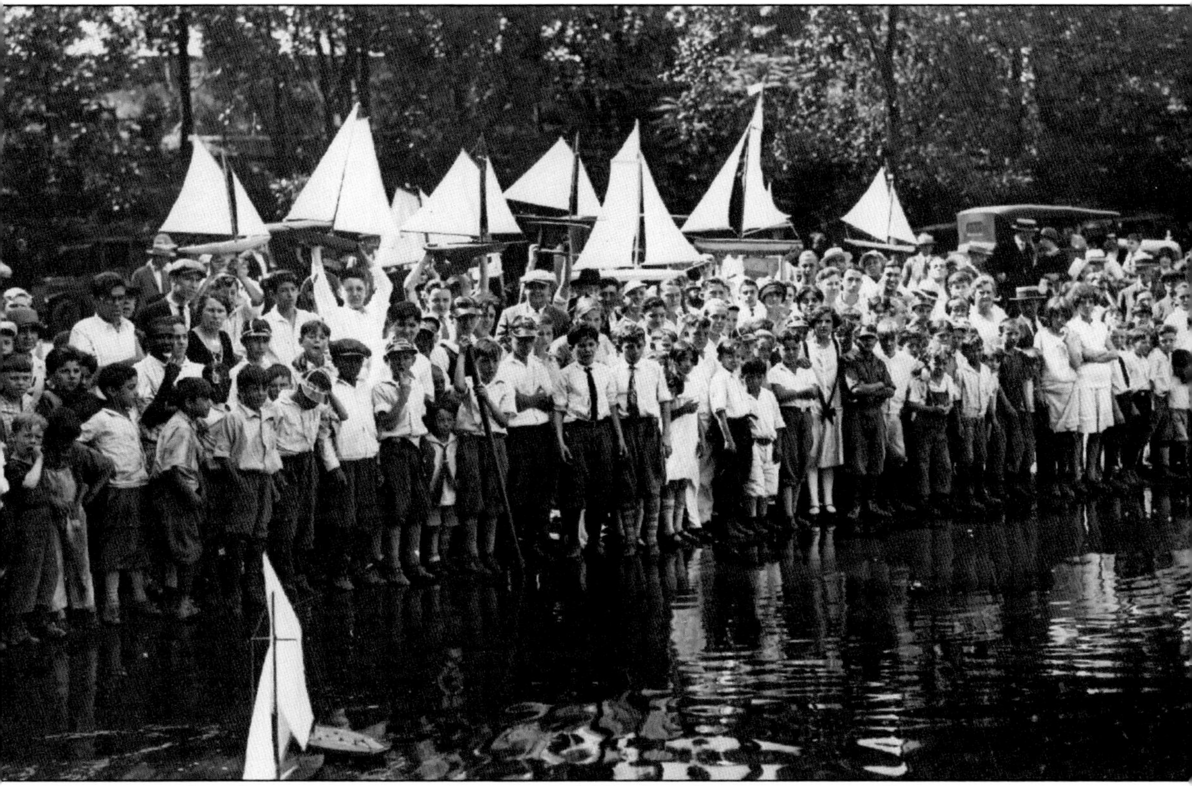

Young people, when not in movie theaters, could be found at miniature sailboat competitions, such as this one in an Essex County park early in the 20th century. (Courtesy of the Newark Public Library.)